Regime Threats and State

The state is a powerful tool for social control because it has the power to help leaders put down popular threats to their rule. But a state does not act; bureaucrats work through the state to carry out a leader's demands. In turn, leaders attempt to use their authority over the state to manage bureaucrats in a way that induces the type of bureaucratic behavior that furthers their policy and political goals. Focusing on Kenya since independence, Mai Hassan weaves together micro-level personnel data, rich archival records, and interview evidence to show how the country's different leaders have strategically managed, and in effect weaponized, the public sector. The analysis shows how even states categorized as weak have proven very capable of helping their leader stay in power.

MAI HASSAN is an assistant professor of political science at the University of Michigan. Her work has been published or is forthcoming in various outlets, including the *American Journal of Political Science, Comparative Political Studies,* and the *Journal of Politics.*

Cambridge Studies in Comparative Politics

General Editors

Kathleen Thelen   *Massachusetts Institute of Technology*
Erik Wibbels   *Duke University*

Associate Editors

Catherine Boone   *London School of Economics*
Thad Dunning   *University of California, Berkeley*
Anna Grzymala-Busse   *Stanford University*
Torben Iversen   *Harvard University*
Stathis Kalyvas   *Yale University*
Margaret Levi   *Stanford University*
Helen Milner   *Princeton University*
Frances Rosenbluth   *Yale University*
Susan Stokes   *Yale University*
Tariq Thachil   *Vanderbilt University*

Series Founder

Peter Lange *Duke University*

Other Books in the Series

Christopher Adolph, *Bankers, Bureaucrats, and Central Bank Politics: The Myth of Neutrality*
Michael Albertus, *Autocracy and Redistribution: The Politics of Land Reform*
Santiago Anria, *When Movements Become Parties: The Bolivian MAS in Comparative Perspective*
Ben W. Ansell, *From the Ballot to the Blackboard: The Redistributive Political Economy of Education*
Ben W. Ansell and David J. Samuels, *Inequality and Democratization: An Elite-Competition Approach*
Adam Michael Auerbach, *Demanding Development: The Politics of Public Goods Provision in India's Urban Slums*
Ana Arjona, *Rebelocracy: Social Order in the Colombian Civil War*
Leonardo R. Arriola, *Multi-Ethnic Coalitions in Africa: Business Financing of Opposition Election Campaigns*
David Austen-Smith, Jeffry A. Frieden, Miriam A. Golden, Karl Ove Moene, and Adam Przeworski, eds., *Selected Works of Michael Wallerstein: The Political Economy of Inequality, Unions, and Social Democracy*
S. Erdem Aytaç and Susan C. Stokes *Why Bother? Rethinking Participation in Elections and Protests*
Andy Baker, *The Market and the Masses in Latin America: Policy Reform and Consumption in Liberalizing Economies*
Laia Balcells, *Rivalry and Revenge: The Politics of Violence during Civil War*
Lisa Baldez, *Why Women Protest? Women's Movements in Chile*
Kate Baldwin, *The Paradox of Traditional Chiefs in Democratic Africa*

Continued after the index

Regime Threats and State Solutions

Bureaucratic Loyalty and Embeddedness in Kenya

MAI HASSAN
University of Michigan

CAMBRIDGE
UNIVERSITY PRESS

CAMBRIDGE
UNIVERSITY PRESS

University Printing House, Cambridge CB2 8BS, United Kingdom

One Liberty Plaza, 20th Floor, New York, NY 10006, USA

477 Williamstown Road, Port Melbourne, VIC 3207, Australia

314-321, 3rd Floor, Plot 3, Splendor Forum, Jasola District Centre, New Delhi - 110025, India

79 Anson Road, #06-04/06, Singapore 079906

Cambridge University Press is part of the University of Cambridge.

It furthers the University's mission by disseminating knowledge in the pursuit of education, learning and research at the highest international levels of excellence.

www.cambridge.org
Information on this title: www.cambridge.org/9781108796491
DOI: 10.1017/9781108858960

© Mai Hassan 2020

First published 2020
First paperback edition 2021

A catalogue record for this publication is available from the British Library

Library of Congress Cataloging in Publication data
NAMES: Hassan, Mai, 1987– author.
TITLE: Regime threats and state solutions : bureaucratic loyalty and embeddedness in Kenya / Mai Hassan.
DESCRIPTION: [New York] : [Cambridge University Press], [2020] | Includes bibliographical references and index.
IDENTIFIERS: LCCN 2019038194 (print) | LCCN 2019038195 (ebook) | ISBN 9781108490856 (hardback) | ISBN 9781108796491 (paperback) | ISBN 9781108858960 (epub)
SUBJECTS: LCSH: Bureaucracy–Kenya. | Civil service–Kenya. | Social control–Kenya. | State, The. | Kenya–Politics and government.
CLASSIFICATION: LCC JQ2947.A67 H37 2020 (print) | LCC JQ2947.A67 (ebook) | DDC 320.96762–dc23
LC record available at https://lccn.loc.gov/2019038194
LC ebook record available at https://lccn.loc.gov/2019038195

ISBN 978-1-108-49085-6 Hardback
ISBN 978-1-108-79649-1 Paperback

For Mama Lulu and Baba Gidu

Contents

Contents

Figures

Tables

List of Tables

Preface

Many people helped me develop the ideas that became part of this book, but one exchange early in the process stands out. I met the late Joel Barkan, an eminent scholar of Kenyan politics, in 2013. I was in the middle of writing my dissertation after having completed a year of field research in Kenya.

At the time, my dissertation focused on Kenya's decentralization reforms that were carried out through waves of administrative unit proliferation. According to official rhetoric, unit proliferation was supposed to bring government closer to the people. To make the state more efficient. But what explained where new districts were created, and thus which areas received this infusion of resources? Why did the government choose to engage in this type of decentralization reform over others? And how, exactly, did unit proliferation lead to development? I told Joel my ideas about what drove Kenya's district proliferation: that presidents created new districts to help them get reelected. To the extent that unit proliferation brought development, it did so among the communities from which a president needed support.

Joel was not as excited about my project as I had hoped he would be. I made a mental note to work on my elevator pitch (it did not initially occur to me that he was bored by the subject matter rather than my pitch). I tried to keep the conversation going by recounting stories from my interviews. I had talked to dozens of bureaucrats who created new districts or were transferred to them. Many of them were not very interested in discussing the new districts themselves; they instead wanted to rant about their experiences in the Provincial Administration, the bureaucracy that staffed administrative units. They described their transfers across units and their inability to put down roots in one part of the country; the nepotism that some of their colleagues used (but never the person I was interviewing) to get their positions; the favoritism in promotions (again, always framed as a complaint about others); the extravagance of their superiors; and their dread (or for others, unbridled optimism) about the upcoming presidential election and what it would mean for potential promotions.

It was at that point that Joel's interest in the conversation returned; he told me a rumor that has served as a guide for this book. When the Kibaki administration came in to State House, the presidential residence and executive office, they found a large map showing the country's (original and newly created) districts. Each district capital had a little note pinned on it, with the name of the District Commissioner. Apparently, former President Moi would personally decide the postings of these officers by walking to the board, unpinning some pins, shuffling others, and having staff make new ones for new appointees. He chose appointments deliberately and with great care, after weighing a particular bureaucrat's abilities and potential liabilities. To the extent that new districts enjoyed more or less development, it was in part because they were managed differently. Understanding decentralization, and ultimately state performance, is not just about where the state is. We also need to know who is running it.

Acknowledgments

This project would not have been possible without the more than 100 formal interviews and informal conversations I had with bureaucrats in Kenya's Provincial Administration. I thank the men and women who generously gave their time to recount their experiences and give me a nuanced understanding of their duties, incentives, and motivations. Though this book is ultimately about the politicization – and weaponization – of bureaucracy, the officials I interviewed spoke with conviction about their duty to public service and devotion to *wananchi* [the people]. I am also indebted to the staff at the different branches of the Kenyan Archives, and especially to Richard Ambani and Philip Omondi for their help in the National Archives in Nairobi.

The ideas in this book were initially nurtured by my dissertation committee at Harvard – Robert Bates, Steven Levitsky, Ryan Sheely, and Daniel Ziblatt. They each pushed me, in their own way, to develop my voice as a scholar. The first wave of field research for this project was supported by a National Science Foundation Doctoral Dissertation Improvement Grant, the Institute for Quantitative Social Science, and Harvard's Center for African Studies. Later waves were supported by the University of Michigan. The final touches of the manuscript were completed while I was at Stanford's Center for Advanced Study in the Behavioral Sciences.

I was also fortunate to get insightful feedback from many graduate students at Harvard's Government Department – Ashley Anderson, Joan Cho, Emily Clough, Shelby Grossman, and Janet Lewis. Working with Brett Carter on our joint paper, which compares the posting and shuffling of bureaucrats in Kenya and the Republic of Congo, was integral to helping me refine my ideas about politicized management. Special thanks go to my roommates, both in the field and in Somerville, for giving me the support network I didn't know I needed – Amanda Johnson, Sparsha Saha, Joelle Siemens, and Kris-Stella Trump. And a sincere thanks to the ladies in the Nairobi Book Club for their company over these past nine years, and for letting me escape into much more compelling, and better written, books on Africa.

I began a post-doc at the University of Michigan after I graduated. It was only in Ann Arbor that I gathered the confidence to pivot the book completely toward the seeds that Joel Barkan had sowed. Conversations with, and feedback from, Yuen Yuen Ang, Christian Davenport, Mary Gallagher, James Morrow, Derek Peterson, Anne Pitcher, Charles Shipan, and Daniel Slater made the book better. I owe a special thanks to Beatriz Magaloni, who graciously offered to hold a book workshop for me at Stanford. I am grateful to the other participants – Aala Abdelgadir, Leonardo Arriola, Lisa Blaydes, Sarah Brierley, Alberto Diaz-Cayeros, Anna Grzymala-Busse, and Noah Nathan – who helped me significantly improve the manuscript.

This book has also benefited from feedback from scholars at the Center for Development & Public Policy (Khartoum), Emory University, Georgetown University, George Washington University, Harvard University, Johns Hopkins SAIS, the University of California – Berkeley, the University of California – Los Angeles, the University of California – Merced, the University of Chicago, the University of Pennsylvania, and Uppsala University. The manuscript was also made better after I received excellent feedback from Michael Albertus, Cameron Ballard-Rosa, Alex Dyzenhaus, Jennifer Gandhi, Denis Galava, Daniel Honig, Charles Hornsby, Kimuli Kasara, Kathleen Klaus, Ahmed Kodouda, Horacio Larreguy, Anne Meng, Susanne Mueller, Jan Pierskalla, Allison Post, Pia Raffler, Rachel Riedl, Amanda Robinson, Rachel Sigman, Chris Sullivan, Jakana Thomas, and Martin Williams.

This project would not have been possible without my family. My parents worked hard to be offered the chance to move our family from Khartoum to the United States. Once here, they worked that much harder to make sure my siblings and I could take advantage of all the opportunities the United States could provide. It is only fitting, then, that I've used these opportunities to return to Africa. I'm grateful to my siblings – Hind, Maha, and Khalid – for keeping me grounded and keeping me laughing. I dedicate this book to my maternal grandparents, Mama Lulu and Baba

Gidu.[1] Though they passed before the book took shape, I credit them with sparking my interest in politics.

I owe the deepest gratitude to my husband and best friend, Noah. He was not only my biggest cheerleader during this entire process, but he helped the project develop at every stage – from serving as a sounding board when I began talking through my initial ideas, to helping me brainstorm different data collection strategies while I was in the field, to commenting on countless drafts during the writing process. And all done with such love and affection.

---

[1] Arabic speakers may wonder about my grandfather's nickname. When we were still in Khartoum, my parents would often drop me off at my maternal grandparents house (free babysitting) while they went to work. People who would visit the house while I was around would call my grandfather either Baba Abdelgadir or Gidu Abdelgadir – in Arabic, one tends to refer to a grandfather by placing an honorific, either "Baba" or "Gidu," in front of the grandfather's first name. But Abdelgadir is a mouthful, so I compromised and began to call him Baba Gidu – "Grandfather, Grandfather." He loved the nickname. So it stuck. Everyone in the family still refers to him as Baba Gidu.

1

Bringing Bureaucrats In

1.1 INTRODUCTION

Esther Kipsang joined Kenya's administrative and security bureaucracy, the Provincial Administration, in 1995. Her first posting was to Busia, a town 450 kilometers by road from Nairobi, near Kenya's border with Uganda.[1] Kipsang's formal responsibilities included maintaining order by locally administering national-level policies and improving local development outcomes by coordinating the provision of local public goods, such as boreholes and health clinics. The country's president at the time, Daniel arap Moi, relied heavily on bureaucrats in the Provincial Administration for an additional purpose, however: to help him hold onto power.

It is therefore unsurprising that residents of Busia complained that their local Provincial Administration officer spent more time beating suspected dissidents than working to improve the area's development.[2] Kipsang effectively corroborated the allegations, explaining "I was deployed with a mission to supervise opposition activity."[3] So did ruling elites, who concurred that local state officials sometimes played a coercive role; one senior official maintained that Moi's co-ethnic Kalenjin officers – including Kipsang – could be "trusted" to prevent the regime's opponents from mobilizing local residents.

---

[1] I have changed the names of the officers and their precise postings in this chapter to preserve anonymity. However, the surnames I use are indicative of the officer's ethnic identity, and the postings have a similar ethnic make-up as the true locations. Though the vast majority of Provincial Administration officers are men, for simplicity I refer to them all as "she" and to the leader as "he."

[2] See DB/1/38, Western Provincial Archives, Kakamega, Kenya.

[3] Interview with former District Officer (DO), November 23, 2011, Nairobi, Kenya.

But Kipsang's behavior changed markedly in her next deployment. After less than 12 months in Busia, Kipsang was rotated, or shuffled, to a town outside Tinderet and its tea estates, about 100 kilometers from her previous post. During her four years there, she constantly met with local community leaders about residents' concerns and demands from the state. This information helped her complete many development projects in the area. For example, she repaired the community's broken irrigation system – a project that she subsidized with her own salary – and secured additional financing from Nairobi for two additional community health workers.

While Kipsang was stationed in Busia, her colleague, Josephine Maina, was working in a small town just outside Mwingi. Maina was unwilling to comply with regime demands to coerce local dissidents. Instead, she used her short time in this post to subtly implement her own agenda, which undermined the regime locally. She granted dissidents permits to hold public rallies, dragged her feet on approving rally permits for the ruling party's local representative, and (justly) jailed fervent pro-regime "youths" who beat residents who spoke out against Moi.[4] Maina's behavior helped augment local support of Moi's political opponent, a co-ethnic of hers. Soon afterwards, she was rotated to a new station.

Another Kikuyu officer named Harriet Gitonga was in charge of governing the entirety of Nyanza Province, an area half the size of Connecticut, during this time. Gitonga was a senior officer in the Provincial Administration, having worked in the Kenyan state for decades. She was also expected to coerce residents. But unlike her co-ethnic Maina, Gitonga complied. For example, she shut down opposition meetings and refused to investigate the deaths of area residents who died at the state's hands.[5] She also prevented opposition parties from campaigning, or even organizing.[6] While Gitonga explained to me that her ethnic group "was very heavy in the opposition," she was considered one of the most loyal officers in the entire Provincial Administration.[7] Nonetheless, just as Gitonga was becoming familiar with local dynamics in Nyanza, she was shuffled away.

The contrasting behavior and posting patterns of Esther Kipsang, Josephine Maina, and Harriet Gitonga bring to the forefront several questions about President Moi's reliance on the state to temper popular

---

4 Interview with former DO, January 8, 2012, Nairobi.
5 "Commissar," *The Weekly Review*, May 9, 1997, pg. 5.
6 For instance, see HT/23/151, Nyanza Provincial Archives, Kisumu, Kenya.
7 Interview with former Provincial Commissioner (PC), July 3, 2017, Nairobi.

challenges to his rule. Why did his government demand that officials coerce residents in Busia, Mwingi, and Nyanza, but co-opt those of Tinderet? What explains why Kipsang and Gitonga complied, but Maina shirked? Indeed, Gitonga's zealous compliance indicates that loyalty to Moi crossed ethnic lines. What explains how these officers were posted and shuffled across the country? Does the way in which an area is governed affect development outcomes? And fundamentally, how do leaders use the state to guard against threats to their rule?

The answers to these questions are important. Much existing research has examined how leaders can use the state to stay in power by focusing on the state's formal institutional design. A state's structure is designed in accordance with local political dynamics (Boone 2003). And in turn, the way in which a state is organized affects the livelihoods of ordinary citizens in a variety of ways, ranging from economic development to the level of coercion they can expect (Greitens 2016).

As the opening paragraphs suggest, however, states and formal institutions do not act: bureaucrats *work through the state* to carry out the leader's demands. Bureaucrats are the link between citizens on the periphery and the government in the center; they "deliver [the] benefits and sanctions [that] structure and delimit people's lives and opportunities" (Lipsky 1980, 2). In turn, leaders have a strong incentive to use their authority to *manage* bureaucrats – a term I use to mean how they are hired, posted, shuffled, and promoted – in a way that induces the type of bureaucratic behavior toward citizens that can further the leaders' policies and political goals.[8] Bringing bureaucrats into our analyses promises to provide insights on regime durability, the state and its effectiveness, and principal-agent dynamics within organizations.

This book explores how bureaucratic management can be used to exert social control. It is premised on the assumption that core tasks of governing – including the distribution of local public goods, administration of the population, and most importantly, the maintenance of law and order – can be carried out in a way that limits popular challenges to the leader in any regime type, from *autocratic* regimes (such as Kenya, roughly from independence until 1991) to *electoral* regimes (such as Kenya since 1992).[9] Either way, the state's ability to govern translates into a leader's

---

[8] I assume that the leader's top advisers carry out these managerial tasks, and that their interests are perfectly aligned with those of the leader.

[9] As I discuss in more detail in Chapter 2, this bifurcation of regime types obscures variation in the presence and strength of regime institutions within each category.

ability to both co-opt societal groups that he needs to support him and coerce the groups most likely to challenge his rule.

A leader cannot carry out his own dirty work, however; he must rely on bureaucrats to carry out the co-optation and coercion he needs. This reliance creates a fundamental principal-agent problem: after the leader (the principal) hires a bureaucrat (agent) to act on his behalf, the bureaucrat might shirk from the leader's demands if her incentives differ from those of the leader. The principal-agent problem is especially salient among bureaucrats whose behavior is hard to monitor.

Conventional wisdom holds that a leader can best ensure the necessary co-optation and coercion from state officials – and thereby prevent popular threats – by hiring and promoting "good types" in the first place. In countries with salient identity cleavages such as Kenya, a bureaucrat's type is affected by her group identity, so leaders are thought to pack the state with their own in-group members. These bureaucrats are presumed to benefit from the leader staying in power, and are thus expected to comply with his orders even when their behavior is not monitored.[10]

But empirically, and despite a widespread assumption that "packing" is the ubiquitous solution to ensure bureaucratic compliance, most state bureaucracies are not actually packed with the leader's in-group members. Elite-led threats have historically been the most dangerous to leaders in both autocratic and electoral regimes.[11] The high risks of elite-led challenges have pushed leaders to use the state to first and foremost stymie elite threats. Leaders use the state to prevent pressing elite-led threats by inviting both "loyal friends" (Magaloni 2008) and rival elites into the regime (Gandhi 2008; Roessler 2017). This incorporation of elites buttresses a leader's rule both by allowing a leader to increase his current coalition of support as well as by sharing state spoils with rivals in an attempt to neutralize the threat that they pose. Importantly, leaders allow

---

But I theorize management of the state across these two regime types because threats from the population differ across these categories and are similar within them: under autocracy, leaders face sporadic collective action such as riots, protests, and strikes, whereas leaders of electoral regimes must worry about their performance at the polls.

10 I provide an overview of why in-group state officials are thought to be the most loyal in Chapter 2. While most of this literature has been developed for the coercive apparatus within autocracies, as opposed to bureaucracies across regime types more generally, the same logic applies.

11 Svolik (2012) finds that more than 60 percent of autocrats from 1945–2008 lost power in an elite-led coup. An elected leader is more likely to lose reelection when the opposition is led by elites who are well financed and coordinated. For evidence of this in sub-Saharan Africa, see Arriola (2012).

**Largest Ethnic Groups,
Representation in Cabinet and Provincial Administration**

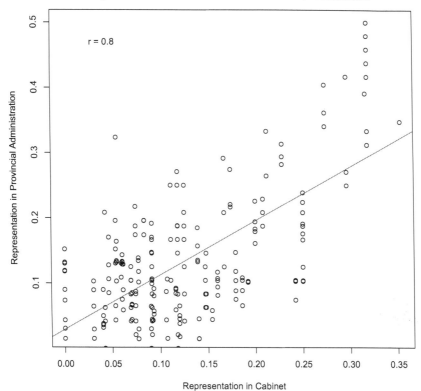

FIGURE I.I The relationship between cabinet representation and representation in the Provincial Administration for Kenya's five largest ethnic groups, 1964–2012.

elites' supporters into state positions – i.e., bad types – in the process of incorporating those elites. Incorporation is expected in electoral regimes as leaders try to build a minimum-winning coalition at the polls. But surprisingly, it is nearly ubiquitous within autocratic regimes too: almost 80 percent of autocrats from 1945–2005 worldwide (Wimmer, Cederman, and Min 2009) and 90 percent from 1960–2010 in sub-Saharan Africa (Roessler 2017) incorporated out-group elites.

Figure I.I illustrates the lack of packing in Kenya. The country's presidents have historically incorporated elites into the cabinet. The *x*-axis thus

plots the percentage of cabinet ministers from the country's five largest
ethnic groups from 1964–2012. These five groups collectively comprise
about 70 percent of the population. The y-axis gives the percentage of
bureaucrats from that ethnic group in the Provincial Administration with
a one-year lag.[12] Figure 1.1 shows that not only did each president's
co-ethnic bureaucrats never comprise a majority in the country's largest
administrative and security agency, but that the ethnic composition of
the bureaucratic corps followed the ethnic breakdown of each president's
cabinet.

At first blush, then, using the state to neutralize both elite and popular
challenges would seem to be at odds. Relying on the state to engage in
social control seems to require a packed state to ensure compliance, especially among bureaucrats who have sustained interaction with citizens in
their jurisdiction. But leaders are reluctant to staff state institutions only
with in-group members, because doing so would preclude their ability to
incorporate other elites and to stave off elite challenges.

I argue that leaders can jointly use the state to prevent *both* elite and
popular threats by strategically managing bureaucrats. My argument proceeds in two steps. First, when elite threats are more pressing, the leader
appeases other elites by reserving spots for bureaucrats who are loyal to
elites other than himself. How a leader manages bureaucrats to ensure
compliance, therefore, must take into account variation in officer type.
Second, the leader uses the current pool of bureaucrats to forestall popular
threats through deliberate choices on their posting and shuffling patterns.
Threats from the population are not equally distributed across all state
posts and sub-national jurisdictions, and thus compliance is not equally
necessary for the leader's political goals across the country. The areas
of the country where compliance is most necessary are governed by the
officials who are most willing – and if possible, best able – to help keep
the leader in office. The ability to strategically post and shuffle bureaucrats allows the leader to recruit potentially disloyal bureaucrats, thereby
tempering elite threats, and still rely on bureaucrats in order to prevent
popular threats where they are most likely to emerge.

This book presents a theory about how governments strategically manage bureaucrats when monitoring is weak. I argue that the leader assigns
officers across jurisdictions by evaluating the interacting preferences of

---

[12] I graph the country's top-ranking Provincial and District Commissioners. These bureaucrats are similar to the type described in the case of Harriet Gitonga earlier in this chapter.
I describe the data used to create the graph in Section 1.4.

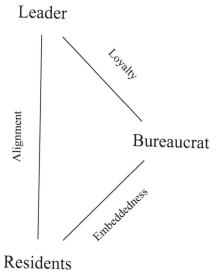

FIGURE I.2 Visual representation of the relationships that affect how a leader decides to govern different areas.

three key actors who decide, execute, or are affected by the resulting governance decisions: 1) his (the leader's) own, 2) an individual bureaucrat's, and 3) residents of the jurisdiction to which a bureaucrat is posted. These relationships are visualized in Figure 1.2 and discussed at length in Chapter 2. The *alignment* between the leader and the local area affects the leader's perceived level of popular threat in the area, which in turn shapes how he intends to have officials govern local residents. Second, the bureaucrat's *loyalty* to the leader influences her expectations of the benefits she may receive from the leader staying in office, and therefore her willingness to comply with his orders. Third, the degree of the bureaucrat's *embeddedness* among area residents affects her willingness and ability to carry out the leader's orders.

The examples described at the beginning of this chapter illustrate the logic of the strategic management of bureaucrats. Beginning with the *alignment* between the leader and an area, Moi felt secure in Tinderet, where the vast majority of residents were from his co-ethnic Kalenjin group. Moi needed to co-opt places like Tinderet: by having bureaucrats favorably implement the policies under their control, bureaucrats could sustain the area's genuine support for the regime. However, popular threats had a strong potential of arising in Busia and Nyanza.

Moi reserved the harshest levels of coercion for these places, for example by demanding that bureaucrats restrict civil liberties and violate the personal integrity of regime dissidents.

Turning to an individual officer's *loyalty* to the leader, Kipsang, as a co-ethnic of President Moi, could expect to benefit from him staying in power and was therefore considered likely to comply with his orders. There was little expectation, however, that Maina would comply with orders as she owed her appointment (and thus much of her loyalty) to a co-ethnic of Moi's most powerful elite rivals. Maina's fortunes were therefore less tied to Moi's; in fact, she could reasonably expect to benefit if her patron or another co-ethnic replaced Moi as president.

Although Gitonga was a co-ethnic of the main opposition candidate like Maina, she was loyal to Moi through patronage. Gitonga was one of the best paid and most revered civil servants in the entire country; Moi personally selected her to serve at the highest possible rank within the Provincial Administration. Perhaps more importantly, her high-ranking position allowed her ample opportunity to predate, or as it is referred to in Kenya, to "eat."[13] Moi's elite rivals were sure to fill Gitonga's coveted spot with their own personal pick if they came into office, and perhaps even investigate her for graft or the misuse of power. Gitonga's continued career in the state and even her personal livelihood were closely tied to Moi's fate, despite her ethnicity.

Regarding a bureaucrat's *embeddedness* in a jurisdiction, Moi hoped to co-opt residents around Tinderet by posting a co-ethnic bureaucrat and lengthening her tenure there – increasing Kipsang's local embeddedness made her better able and personally willing to co-opt residents by delivering on the area's development needs, regardless of Kipsang's presumed loyalty to Moi. However, Moi sought to prevent this local embeddedness elsewhere. Though locally embedded officers know an area best and can theoretically better repress it, they are often unwilling to carry out coercive orders because of their strong social bonds with area residents. Kipsang's local embeddedness was beneficial to Moi in Tinderet, but the regime carefully managed officers in jurisdictions it wanted coerced – Kipsang in Busia, Gitonga in Nyanza – by posting non-co-ethnic bureaucrats and shortening their tenures.

---

[13] There were even reports of Gitonga "grabbing," or signing over the title deed to herself for, the valuable state land where her office was located in the Kenya National Assembly Official Record (Hansard).

Taken together, these relationships between Moi, individual bureaucrats, and the jurisdictions in which they served explain the posting patterns of Kipsang, Maina, and Gitonga, and ultimately how subnational areas are governed. The regime sent Kipsang to Busia and Tinderet, and Gitonga to Nyanza, because they could be trusted to comply where it mattered most. The center also manipulated their degree of embeddedness. Kipsang's local embeddedness in Tinderet helped ensure the co-optation of locals, thereby increasing Moi's support in the area. But her lack of embeddedness in Busia, and Gitonga's lack of embeddedness in Nyanza – due to their non-co-ethnicity and short tenures – precluded them from having or gradually developing an attachment to the area's residents that might weaken their resolve to coerce. Meanwhile, Moi sent Maina to Mwingi because her presumed unwillingness to coerce on his behalf would have less of an impact in an area where popular challenges were less threatening to his ability to remain in office.

This book expands on the posting and shuffling patterns of Kipsang, Maina, and Gitonga to explore how social control is exerted through bureaucratic management. Chapter 2 presents a theory of bureaucratic management that is tested in later empirical chapters through an in-depth account of the politicized management of the Kenyan state for the first five decades after independence. I use micro-level quantitative bureaucratic data on the staffing of the country's primary security and administrative apparatus that cover the careers of some 2,000 bureaucrats and 15,000 individual bureaucratic postings. I flesh out the quantitative data by drawing on archival material from all of Kenya's major archives and dozens of interviews with bureaucrats and regime elites collected during sixteen months of fieldwork. Together, the empirical chapters trace how each of Kenya's first three presidents – spanning both autocratic and electoral regimes, sometimes even within a single presidency – governed different subnational jurisdictions differently based on the perceived challenges to their rule in the area. Moreover, by examining how Kenya has been governed both before and after its formal democratic opening in 1992, I show that vestiges of authoritarianism continue to linger within state institutions and have affected the trajectory of the country's democratization.

The evidence provides strong and consistent support for the strategic management of bureaucrats. The book's empirics begin with the country's first thirty years, under a one-party authoritarian regime. Though many look to this period for evidence of the ruling party's capacity to sustain authoritarianism (e.g., Widner 1992), I find that the durability of Kenya's autocratic regime was actually rooted in the state, which in effect bolstered a weak ruling party. The empirics track the management of high-ranking officers like Gitonga, whose loyalty to their respective president was sustained through patronage. The country's first autocrat, Jomo Kenyatta, sought to forestall popular challenges to his rule by consolidating the support of his base and coercing parts of the country where popular challenges had arisen early in his presidency. In response, I find that his strongholds were managed by locally embedded officers – some of whom were co-ethnics, and some of whom had served long tenures at their stations – in an attempt to co-opt, and sustain support in, these aligned areas. Elsewhere, and especially in areas where popular threats had previously emerged, officers showed lower levels of embeddedness. During the one-party reign (1978–1991) of Kenyatta's successor, Daniel arap Moi, bureaucrats were posted and shuffled following a similar pattern when we consider the alignments of different parts of the country to Moi. Moi increased embeddedness to co-opt his co-ethnic base and lowered it elsewhere, especially in areas inhabited by the ethnic groups considered most likely to launch a popular challenge against him. In other words, when ethnic coalitions switched, so did the management of bureaucrats in response. Further, I find that management patterns mattered for important livelihood outcomes – jurisdictions governed by embedded bureaucrats saw higher levels of resource distribution.

Evidence from the country's next twenty years, after Kenya's transition to an electoral regime in 1991, also supports the theory. As in the first part of the book, I follow high-ranking officials like Gitonga as well as lower-level officers like Kipsang and Maina. These bureaucrats earned, and "ate," much less than their senior colleagues. Their loyalty toward their respective president was based on their perceived ability to advance through the ranks to a lucrative high-ranking position, which in turn was affected by co-ethnicity with the president. As this chapter's opening suggests, Moi continued to increase officers' local embeddedness in co-ethnic areas while lowering it elsewhere. Moreover, Moi sent loyal officers such as Kipsang and Gitonga to electorally valuable unaligned, or swing, areas, while keeping potentially disloyal officers like Maina away from these strategically valuable places. Moi's successor, Mwai Kibaki, continued many of the same management practices. Kibaki increased bureaucrats' local embeddedness among his co-ethnic base and lowered it elsewhere. And in patterns that mirror Moi's, he kept disloyal officers away from his strategically valuable swing areas during his 2007 reelection campaign.

In the rest of this chapter I discuss the broader implications of the book, motivate the Kenyan case, introduce the data, and outline the subsequent chapters.

1.2 IMPLICATIONS OF THE ARGUMENT

This book contributes to ongoing debates on authoritarian regimes and regime change, the state, and principal-agent dynamics in organizations.

1.2.1 Regimes and Regime Change

This book adds to the intertwined literatures on authoritarian regimes and regime change. I seek to update the literature on authoritarian regimes from an elite-centric view to a more comprehensive one. Elite threats have empirically proved the most dangerous to autocrats (Svolik 2012). As such, much recent work on autocracy has examined why some autocrats create ruling parties, why others allow meaningful debate in legislatures or use courts, and still others hold elections. Such studies largely conclude that these nominally democratic institutions are useful because they co-opt elites and stave off elite threats.[14] This book follows in this tradition, examining how autocrats rely on the state to incorporate rival elites. Unlike much work on autocracy, however, I consider the downstream effects of incorporation on popular threats. The literature has paid less attention to the potential for popular threats to unseat an autocrat, or how elite and popular threats interact, because popular challenges are assumed to be less threatening.[15] Instead, I recognize that leaders face multiple threats simultaneously and sequence their strategies based on their perception of which threat is most dangerous (Wilson 2015;

---

[14] For work on ruling parties, see Zolberg (1966), Huntington (1968), Geddes (1999), Grzymała-Busse (2002), Nathan (2003), Lazarev (2005), Smith (2006), Brownlee (2007), Greene (2009), Slater (2010), Magaloni and Kricheli (2010), Svolik (2012), Boix and Svolik (2013), Meng (2019), and Reuter (2017). For research on legislatures, see Boix (2003), Gandhi (2008), Gandhi and Przeworski (2007), Wright (2008), Malesky and Schuler (2010), Truex (2016), and Opalo (2019). For studies on elections in authoritarian regimes, see Lust-Okar (2006), Magaloni (2006), Gandhi and Lust-Okar (2009), Blaydes (2011), Manion (2015), and Gehlbach, Sonin, and Svolik (2016). For research on courts in authoritarian regimes, see Ginsburg and Moustafa (2008), Helmke and Rosenbluth (2009), Popova (2010), Hanson (2018), and Shen-Bayh (2018).

[15] Some notable recent exceptions are Slater (2010), King, Pan, and Roberts (2013), Wallace (2014), and Thomson (2018).

Greitens 2016). And strategies used to prevent one type of threat may aggravate the other (Frantz and Kendall-Taylor 2014; Woo and Conrad 2019), making it problematic to study any threat on its own.

In addition, this book contributes to debates on regime change. After the end of the Cold War, many countries transitioned away from autocracy. Yet, despite the formal introduction of multiparty elections, many of these electoral regimes have not seen the consolidation of their democracy – though these countries hold regular, competitive multiparty elections, incumbents are systematically tilting the playing field to their advantage (Levitsky and Way 2010). Recent research has suggested that these "stalled" transitions may be a function of the formal institutional remnants of the authoritarian era. For instance, outgoing autocrats can design constitutions that protect their interests and hinder impartial competition (Albertus and Menaldo 2018). This book, however, suggests that the subpar quality of these democracies may be a result of *informal* practices that have been held over from the autocratic era. Through their control over the bureaucracy, leaders can politicize the public sector and tilt the playing filed by relying on bureaucrats to co-opt their supporters and coerce opponents.

Relatedly, and through an empirical focus on Kenya's largest security apparatus, this book suggests that full democratization cannot occur without changes to domestic security organs (Weitzer 1990). Security organs maintain significant clout during authoritarian periods because of their symbiotic relationship with the leader: they are the main executers of the coercion that keeps the autocrat in office and, in return, are given a central place within the regime. A transition to mutiparty elections, therefore, threatens to disrupt this relationship and disrupt the identity of security organs that are wedded to the regime (Bellin 2004). Thus, whereas distributive state bureaucracies – e.g., education or health ministries – are managed in such a way as to sustain neopatrimonial relationships and ensure compliance during autocracy, a transition to democracy does not challenge their core mission in the same way that it does for the security apparatus. Transitions to democracy risk a decrease in the status, budgets, and personnel of the security apparatus that is opposed by elites in the organization. As such, many elites within these agencies see the benefit of continuing their neopatrimonial relationship with the president after the formal introduction of multiparty elections: by perpetuating many of the same tactics used before the transition, the coercive apparatus maintains its clout and undermines full democratic consolidation.

1.2.2 The State and Its Capacity

This book helps us reconceptualize state capacity or "infrastructural power" (Mann 1984), which refers to the state's ability to efficiently redirect resources to achieve its goals (Skocpol 1985). Though clearly important, this definition has proven difficult to operationalize in practice. Some scholars treat state capacity as a fixed (or at least slow-moving), uniform characteristic of a state, such as work that measures capacity using national-level GDP (e.g., Fearon and Laitin 2003). Many scholars have moved beyond this simplification and recognize that a state's capacity to carry out its functions depends on the capabilities, resources, and training of its bureaucrats (e.g., Evans and Rauch 1999). Indeed, many databases today incorporate measures of a country's bureaucracy.[16] Yet these measures still assume that capacity is constant across bureaucrats and across subnational areas. Such measures of capacity may be a "convenient shorthand" for the numerous, and often unmeasurable, factors that affect policy implementation, but they cannot capture "the mechanisms that are critical for understanding and improving bureaucratic performance and policy implementation" (Williams 2019).

This book demonstrates that state capacity is neither uniform across a country, nor fixed even in the short run. Instead, the capacity of the state to carry out the executive's demands is highly context-specific. A bureaucrat's abilities vary depending on the nature of the task and her local embeddedness in a post. And since the executive strategically manages the bureaucracy, we should expect purposeful, subnational and over-time variation in a state's capacity.

This critique of state capacity helps broaden existing work on its origins. Many scholars look to medium- or long-run factors to explain capacity.[17] These factors are important for determining the level of effectiveness that a state can theoretically achieve. But a more complete understanding of why some subnational bureaucracies are more capable than others within the same state, and why some bureaucrats

---

[16] For instance, Political Risk Services includes a measure of bureaucracy quality. The Business Environmental Risk Intelligence has a measure for bureaucratic delays. The Global Competitiveness Report includes a measure of civil service independence. Looking at coercive institutions in particular, the National Material Capabilities dataset by the Correlates of War Project considers military personnel and expenditure.

[17] Some examples of long-run factors are geography (Diamond 1998; Herbst 2000) and conflict (Tilly 1985; Besley and Persson 2009; Slater 2010; Pierskalla, De Juan, and Montgomery 2017). An example of a medium-run political factor is party competition (Grzymała-Busse 2007).

perform better at some activities than others, requires us to examine the state's formal and informal management practices. A more in-depth understanding of state capacity will contribute to work that uses this concept as an independent variable. Much work has examined the causal effect of state capacity on important outcomes such as regime durability (Levitsky and Way 2010; Slater 2010; Albertus and Menaldo 2012) and, more generally, the center's ability to penetrate society and engage in social control (Migdal 1988). This research has largely been carried out at the nation-state level, with higher capacity seen as more useful for a leader. But recent work has begun to question whether the deployment of a state's full ability is actually in politicians' best interests. Indeed, forbearance can help politicians at the polls (Holland 2017), as well as spur bureaucratic innovation and economic growth (Ang 2016) and prevent violence from armed groups (Lessing 2017).

I find that the variability of capacity – over space, across agencies, and within bureaucracies – is a strategic choice. This logic helps us reconcile the fact that many states categorized as "weak" – such as Kenya – have proven very capable of helping their leaders meet critical policy and political goals. Though the Kenyan state as a whole is considered inefficient at carrying out its functions, its leaders have consistently deployed the state selectively to the problems and places that are the most important for their political survival.

This strategic variation of capacity thus provides a new mechanism to help understand leaders' in-group favoritism. Much work has empirically established that leaders' in-group areas see better development outcomes.[18] These outcomes are said to be simply the result of a leader's decision about where to channel state resources. However, the results of this book show that in-group areas may experience better development outcomes because the leader decides to *manage* these areas differently: though in-group areas may see higher taxes (Kasara 2007) – perhaps because embedded bureaucrats can more efficiently extract resources – central resources distributed to aligned areas will go substantially further than resources sent elsewhere.

1.2.3 Principal-Agent Dynamics

This study also contributes to our understanding of principal-agent dynamics within organizations. To begin, I show that a principal does

---

[18] For instance, see Bates (1989), Cammett and Issar (2010), Franck and Rainer (2012), Briggs (2014), Hodler and Raschky (2014), Jablonski (2014), Burgess et al. (2015), and

not always hire "good types." Standard literature on organizations has long assumed that principals always avert the adverse selection problem if they can easily identify agent type in advance of hiring. According to these studies, we should only see bad types hired into an organization, and thus the possibility of a principal-agent problem arising at all, because good types find it difficult to preemptively signal their type and the principal finds it too costly to screen during the hiring process. But I theorize the conditions under which a principal can benefit from doing the opposite – deliberately hiring bad types who are likely, and even expected, to shirk. This decision to forgo solving the adverse selection problem is rational once we recognize that a principal faces different threats at the same time, and can use his organization in different ways to address each distinct threat. But preempting each type of threat suggests a different management strategy for the organization, and ultimately the principal cannot implement different strategies simultaneously. In the context studied here, leaders will forgo a packed state and introduce a moral hazard problem in an attempt to preempt dangerous elite threats at the expense of popular ones.

The theory and empirics also contribute to the literature on the role of identity in principal-agent dynamics. Agents are not blank slates who operate on command; they weigh the social bonds they have with those over whom they govern. The emotional toll that violence takes on bureaucrats is especially strong when they are expected to coerce their in-group members (Tajfel and Turner 1979). At the same time, the embeddedness that makes shirking from orders to coerce more likely is sometimes purposefully developed. The leader is willing to post a bureaucrat among the bureaucrat's in-group when the leader wants the area to be co-opted. In these situations, the agent is complying with central directives due less to a desire to secure the leader's continued tenure and more because of social obligations to the area's residents; an embedded bureaucrat improves local outcomes because she is an agent of the local area, not an agent of the leader. But the leader has leveraged this social relationship to achieve his desired governance outcome in the locality.

The book's focus on embeddedness informs debates about delegation. Existing work on delegation tends to examine the conditions under which principals change the level of *de jure* power delegated to an agent (Epstein and O'Halloran 1994; Huber and Shipan 2002; Gailmard and Patty 2012). My study contributes to this argument, showing that delegation via increased embeddedness is most likely in areas where popular threats are unlikely and regime stability is secure. But in addition, I further the literature by suggesting that a bureaucrat's ability to implement policies does not only depend on her formal authority. Instead, the bureaucrat's level of embeddedness in the jurisdiction determines the limits of her authority – the greater the extent of her embeddedness, the greater her ability to exercise her full authority. Research must recognize that delegation is not only about the level of formal authority conferred onto an agent, but her real authority to produce change (Aghion and Tirole 1997).

Relatedly, the book also has implications for the relationship between bureaucratic embeddedness and the improvement of service delivery.[19] Embeddedness can be detrimental because it creates centrifugal forces whereby agents unevenly apply their mandate (e.g., Kaufman 1960; Epstein and O'Halloran 1994) or engage in higher levels of corruption (e.g., Landry 2008; Xu, Bertrand, and Burgess 2018). Similarly, embeddedness can increase bureaucratic drift: when bureaucrats implement policy that differs from the principal's original mandate, this undermines the integrity of the delegation relationship. But allowing a bureaucrat discretion to shape policy responses based on the area's conditions can result in better outcomes (Honig 2018). I recognize this duality and show that leaders allow embeddedness in places where they benefit from its positive externalities, and prevent it where they fear the negative consequences.

More broadly, this book hopes to expand the empirical focus of bureaucratic politics past developed democracies, and especially the United States, to developing and nondemocratic contexts. My empirical focus on Kenya builds on accumulated knowledge of bureaucratic politics. But by focusing on a new case, I show how assumptions in existing research on developed democracies – such as the space between *de jure* laws and *de facto* procedures, or rational-legal norms of advancement – have limited our ability to develop a more complete understanding of bureaucracies. And the large role of the state in developing countries, from overseeing economic development programs to securing regime survival, heightens the importance of understanding bureaucratic management.

---

[19] See Pepinsky, Pierskalla, and Sacks (2017) for a review of the literature on bureaucratic embeddedness in comparative politics.

1.3 THE CASE

I explore the argument using an in-depth examination of the Kenyan state for the first five decades after independence in 1963.[20] Kenya is an ideal setting for this book because of the variation in regime type and ethnic coalitions. President Jomo Kenyatta started his reign under an electoral regime before he consolidated power under a one-party authoritarian regime. One-party authoritarianism continued under President Daniel arap Moi, until he was forced to hold multiparty elections in 1992. Kenya has remained an electoral regime since then, including a decade each under Presidents Moi and Mwai Kibaki. Ethnicity was (and remains) a salient political cleavage in Kenya (Elischer 2013; Horowitz 2016), and there is variation in ethnic identity – and thus the alignment of different ethnic groups toward each president – across regime type. Presidents Kenyatta and Kibaki hail from the country's pluarlity Kikuyu ethnic group, while President Moi is a member of the Kalenjin ethnic group. Examining the theory since independence allows me to leverage multiple regime types with different ethnic coalitions, and to observe geographic variation in where each leader's threats emerged.

I focus on Kenya's largest administrative and security apparatus, the Provincial Administration.[21] This bureaucracy is unequivocally the most important within the Kenyan state. Its bureaucrats are responsible for overseeing the maintenance of law and order, land administration in this agrarian nation, and the distribution of resources. Its centrality in the country's political development is partly demonstrated by the sheer volume of studies devoted to it.[22]

The Kenyan state is also similar to others across the world. Kenya was a unitary state for much of the study period and the president exerted strong executive control over all state bureaucracies. This setup is akin to the majority of countries across the world. Moreover, even executives

---

[20] Kenya was a centralized, unitary state for the majority of the study period. It gained independence with a devolved, federal state structure, but its first president quickly dismantled that state structure in favor of a centralized, unitary state. The country's new constitution, only fully adopted in 2013, devolves significant authority to sub-national counties.

[21] Although the Provincial Administration has since been renamed the National Administration, I refer to this agency by its original name throughout.

[22] For instance, see Gertzel (1970), Mboya (1970), Tamarkin (1978), Hyden (1984), Mueller (1984), Berman (1992), Oyugi (1994), Throup and Hornsby (1998), Kanyinga (2000b), Adar and Munyae (2001), Klopp (2001), Anderson (2005b), Branch and Cheeseman (2006), Branch (2011), Hornsby (2011), Lynch (2011a), Opalo (2014), and Hassan (2017).

of federal countries maintain control over centralized bureaucracies, as I show in the conclusion. In addition, to the extent that bureaucracies are run by governors of federal units, my theory can be adapted to consider the governor's elite threats, the governor's relationship with bureaucrats under his control, and his alignment with different subunit areas. And like many sub-Saharan countries, Kenya has strong ethnic cleavages, but no group comprises a majority (Ferree 2010). Most presidents have found it necessary to incorporate elites from other ethnic groups (Roessler 2017).

Further, Kenya's Provincial Administration is similar to prefectural administrations and executive bureaucracies in other countries. An executive bureaucracy tends to be in charge of both administrative and security functions across the country. Their duties include tax collection, the protection of property, overseeing local development, and maintaining law and order – by force if necessary.[23] Taken together, this means that executive bureaucracies have the authority to either co-opt or coerce. Moreover, these agencies have a direct line of command to the leader or indirectly through the Interior Ministry. Indeed, even though presidents often hand over control of service ministries to other elites in an attempt to incorporate them, the Interior Ministry and the executive bureaucracy tend to stay squarely in the hands of the leader or a most-trusted adviser: a leader would not outsource security to a rival. As such, state officials across executive bureaucracies serve as the leader's "hands on the ground" within their jurisdiction. Bureaucrats in these organs have various names, such as regional executives, local prefects, (appointed) governors, or county commissioners.

Executive bureaucracies are common for two reasons. First, they were initially adopted in countries across Europe, including among some of sub-Saharan Africa's colonizers, which later replicated this structure in their colonies (Fesler 1965; Berman 1992). Kenya's colonial Provincial Administration – of which the post-independence Provincial Administration is an almost identical replica – was remarkably similar to those used in other British colonies. In fact, British colonial officers were sometimes rotated between colonies, not only between posts within a colony.[24] Second, this type of bureaucracy allows for governing on the cheap. Instead

---

23 Executive bureaucracies tend to oversee other service bureaucracies in the field.
24 This concentration of authority, with little means of horizontal accountability, is the main normative drawback of an executive bureaucracy in democracies. However, this drawback was less of a concern for imperial powers.

of investing resources into multiple bureaucracies, the center only needs to rely on one agency.[25]

Parallel institutions can be found in other colonies and countries. For example, the legal-administrative *kadi* officers in the Ottoman Empire were "asked to facilitate the performance of their various tasks, from tax collection to special investigations" (Kunt 1968, 12) given their role overseeing administration, the courts, security, and the coordination of other bureaucracies in their jurisdiction. The functions of the *Landespolizei* of colonial Namibia were also similar to Kenya's Provincial Administration. These bureaucrats "handled anything from health and veterinary inspections, the enforcement of mining and labor legislation, to post and customs duties. One leading former officer took pride in the fact that police had acted as 'girl Fridays' of the colony" (De Juan, Krautwald, and Pierskalla 2017). The *Landespolizei* seemed to have been modeled on Prussian *landrats*, who were considered "the linchpin" of the Prussian state.[26] According to Daniel Ziblatt (2009), *landrats* served as the "central government's bureaucratic 'field officer' on the ground, overseeing tax assessment, schools, the military draft, police, and the management of elections."

Many executive bureaucracies in former colonies have persisted past independence, as indicated by the research that cites their importance in, among other countries, Egypt (Blaydes 2011), Ghana (Brierley Forthcoming), India (Bhavnani and Lee 2018; Xu, Bertrand, and Burgess 2018), Iraq (Sassoon 2011; Blaydes 2018), Republic of the Congo (Carter, Building a Dictatorship), Sudan (El-Battahani and Gadkarim 2017), and Zaire (now Democratic Republic of the Congo) (Young and Turner 1985; Schatzberg 1988). Further, executive bureaucracies are exceedingly common in large, populous, and diverse federations including China (Landry 2008), Ethiopia (Woldense 2018), and Russia (Reuter and Robertson 2012; Reuter 2017) precisely because of their ability to help the center control the population. Thus, while I look at one case, management of similar state institutions is a constant concern of leaders around the world.

1.4 THE DATA

Studying governance requires micro-level data about how local bureaucrats are managed, but it is hard to obtain systematic data on the inner

---

[25] Interview with colonial DO, July 13, 2017, Nairobi.
[26] Jacob (1963) as seen in Ziblatt (2009).

workings of any state – especially authoritarian ones. This lack of data has led to theories about states that are empirically unvalidated at best, and inaccurate and misleading – such as an unwavering belief that all leaders pack their states – for theory building at worst. This book attempts to overcome these issues by pairing rich qualitative data that helps us grasp the motivations of individual officers with systematic, micro-level data on how the Kenyan state was run. Together, the data give us an unparalleled look "inside the state."

1.4.1 Qualitative Data

This book draws on interviews and archival data to trace the incentives, motivations, and actions of Provincial Administration bureaucrats under different leaders. Over a period of seven years, I conducted more than 100 interviews with administrators of various ranks and ethnicities who served under all of Kenya's presidents and in the colonial period, political elites under the Moi and Kibaki presidencies, and ordinary citizens.

Given the sensitive nature of the material, all interviews were semi-structured conversations chosen through a snowball sampling method. I was cognizant of interviewees who hesitated to answer questions directly and tailored the interview accordingly. Many subjects asked for the interview to be off the record. Information from these sources is described abstractly so as to avoid identifying information.

This book also makes use of two types of archival data. First, the Kenya National Archives contains official correspondence about the Provincial Administration from the Kenyatta and Moi presidencies.[27] These documents are located in the Kenya National Archives in Nairobi, or provincial branches in Kakamega, Kisumu, Mombasa, or Nakuru. Second, I examined unsorted archival material and community complaint letters about Provincial Administration officers. These files are stored in the headquarters of each of Kenya's provinces and were made available after I received approval from the Permanent Secretary of the Provincial Administration as well as the head administrator of the respective province.[28] These folios are largely from the Moi and Kibaki presidencies.

---

[27] Government folios are not open to researchers until thirty years after they close.
[28] I was only granted access to these folios in two provinces: Coast and Rift Valley. While the files from these provinces cannot provide a representative sample of all communications with the state, they are the two provinces in which the Provincial Administration had

My qualitative data provides a rich description of the management of the Provincial Administration, but each source suffers from bias. Both types of archival folios suffer from potential selection bias: each regime clearly has an incentive to destroy or hide correspondence that incriminates its elites (Balcells and Sullivan 2018). For instance, these folios only contain vague references to the organization's involvement in election violence during the multiparty era, even though the Provincial Administration allegedly played a leading role. Or consider the only archival folio on Kenyatta's main opposition party in the provincial branch of the archives where the party was most active. The folio contains seventeen documents covering a span of over five years. Most folios contain upwards of 150 documents for 1–3 years. This bias of omission, however, runs against me. Documents with the most explicit references to the Provincial Administration's involvement in suppressing popular threats are likely to suffer from "victor's justice" and to be systematically destroyed.

The interviews also suffer from bias. My interviewees were not sampled at random. And my convenience sample is not representative of the ethnic makeup of the Provincial Administration during all presidencies. Moreover, the interviews may suffer from social desirability bias. Many individuals are unwilling to discuss their coercion of fellow citizens, or any predation they may have committed, or they may exaggerate their positive actions. For instance, even though these bureaucrats are widely considered to be "land grabbers," officers steered clear of implicating themselves outright. Bureaucrats instead discussed, for example, how their position gave them advance knowledge of which tracts of land within their jurisdiction would be available for purchase. Others discussed how their knowledge of land titling procedures or their contacts with land officers made it easy to finalize a transaction. For these reasons, I use the qualitative data to trace the logic and mechanisms of the theory, while the quantitative data, discussed in Section 1.4.2, allows me to test empirical implications of the theory with more systematic evidence.

1.4.2 Quantitative Data

Officer Postings Datasets

This book examines the observable implications of the theory on officer management by creating datasets on Kenya's administrative units and the

---

the most contentious role in the distributive outcome I focus on most – land (Kanyinga 2000b; Boone 2014; Klaus 2020).

officers who ran them from 1964–2012. I create three separate datasets on Provincial Administration officers: (1) high-ranking officers (like Gitonga) from 1964–2007, (2) lower-level officers (like Kipsang and Maina) from 1992–2007, and (3) all bureaucrats from 2005–2012. I use fine-grained data on *who* ran the state to rigorously analyze *what* each president was trying to achieve, and *where*.

The first dataset allows me to examine postings of senior administrators who were all considered loyal to their respective president. These presidential appointees are all remunerated exceedingly well, regardless of their ethnicity. And many advanced to their position after displaying loyalty to their respective president. This dataset includes the officer's name and length of tenure in each post. This information was collected from each unit; each office for high-ranking bureaucrats has a large plaque that lists the unit's current and previous administrators, as seen on the left-hand side of Figure 1.3. I collected the management history of more than a dozen jurisdictions myself. I received permission from the Ministry of Provincial Administration to request the information for the remaining units.[29] This dataset contains 576 officer-years under Kenyatta, 1,197 under Moi's entire reign, and 335 under Kibaki. I use this dataset in Chapters 4–8.

The second dataset contains information on lower-level bureaucrats, whose loyalty to the president varied. It was created by collecting and digitizing "administrative officer returns," which are internal documents that the Ministry of Provincial Administration maintains about high- and lower-level bureaucrats at the time of publication. See the right-hand side of Figure 1.3 for an example. These returns are supposed to be updated every month, but this directive is not always complied with. For those periods in which it was, I sampled returns from June and December. For years when records are spotty, I attempted to gather one set of returns from the first six months of the year and a second from the next six months, making sure to collect returns in the run-up to elections to prevent post-treatment bias.[30] Unfortunately, and unlike the dataset on high-ranking bureaucrats, the administrative officer returns

---

29 I excluded officers who were explicitly labeled as "acting" or "temporary." I also removed officers who were in a post for less than six months from the dataset, as they were likely temporary replacements.
30 Some data is still missing. I could not find returns from late 1993–early 1994, or for 1998 for seven of Kenya's eight provinces, and from 1993–1995 for one province. The bureaucrats who maintain these records claim that records were lost at random.

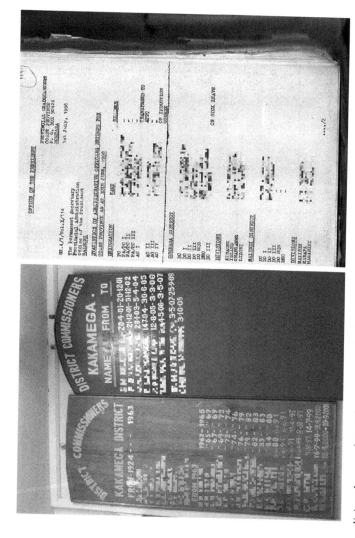

FIGURE 1.3 Visualizing the raw data. The image on the left is of a plaque from a District Commissioner's office (Kakamega district in Western Province). The image on the right is a page from the administrative officer returns data (Coast Province). I have blurred the officers' names for privacy.

are not precise enough to track individual officers or to make inferences
about each lower-level bureaucrat's tenure in a station.[31] I use this second
dataset in Chapters 7–8.

Third, I obtained annual spreadsheets of all officers working in the
Provincial Administration from 2005–2012. I combine these sheets to
track individual officers over time. The spreadsheets also contain information on officers' rank each year. I use this dataset in Chapter 8 to analyze
promotions during the Kibaki era.

1.4.3 Ethnicity

Classifying area alignment, bureaucratic loyalty, and bureaucratic embeddedness for the Kenyan case depends, in part, on the ethnicity of bureaucrats and residents. Neither officer dataset lists officers' ethnicity, however.
Instead, I identified officer ethnicity by leveraging the distinctiveness of
Kenyan surnames to specific ethnic groups.[32] I created a dictionary of
unique surnames associated with each ethnic group using administrative
officer returns of local stationary bureaucrats from 2007–2012 for seven
of Kenya's eight provinces.[33] Whereas the officers that this book follows
were rotated across stations, the stationary bureaucrats I used to create
the surname dictionaries must be from the unit's majority ethnic group
and the local administrative unit in which they serve. I merge the surnames
of stationary bureaucrats with local-level ethnicity data from the 1989
census, the most recent census with sub-national ethnicity data. I collect the surnames of stationary bureaucrats whose administrative units
were at least 90 percent homogeneous to create a dictionary of common
surnames for each ethnic group that I use to determine the ethnicity of
other bureaucrats. I employed nine Kenyan research assistants to code
each officer's ethnicity based on their local knowledge of surnames for
names not found in the dictionary. In cases of discrepancies, the modal
estimate was taken.

---

[31] The returns only reliably contain the officer's last name and first initial. Since many
officers share last names and first initials, I am hesitant to make inferences about the
stay of any particular officer. Moreover, new administrative units were constantly being
created or renamed, such that it is difficult to track the same bureaucrat within a district.

[32] I also recorded the ethnicity of officers I interviewed personally, though this is only a
minority of officers.

[33] The population of these jurisdictions in 2009 was 6,500 on average.

I estimate an area's alignment with the president and the innate embeddedness of the bureaucrat posted there based partly on shared ethnicity. I use official census data to determine the ethnic makeup of each jurisdiction.[34] The analyses that examine management before 1992 rely on the 1962, 1969, 1979, and 1989 censuses.[35] Those that assess management after 1992 rely on a 2.5-percent sample of the 1989 census at the lowest level for which I examine officer management.[36]

1.4.4 Organization of the Book

This book builds a theory of how leaders manage the state to prevent elite and popular threats to their rule, and then empirically evaluates it using the case of Kenya.

Chapter 2 first examines the range of threats that leaders face and investigates why the state is a powerful tool of social control. This discussion highlights the need to understand the actions of the bureaucrats who actually carry out the orders that temper popular threats. Chapter 2 then explores the leader's principal-agent problem that emerges from relying on bureaucrats whose actions are difficult to monitor. I outline existing strategies thought to prevent shirking, but argue that each – when applied in full – has negative costs that inhibit a leader's stability in a manner separate from ensuring compliance. I then describe the book's theory of the management of state officials. I argue that the hiring of bureaucrats is partly motivated by the need to temper elite threats. Though this initially aggravates the leader's principal-agent problem and increases the likelihood of shirking, the leader strategically posts and shuffles bureaucrats to ensure that areas in which a popular threat is most likely to arise are overseen by bureaucrats who are the most willing – and, if possible, the most able – to comply. Bureaucrats' promotions are based on a desire to neutralize elite threats, and also serve as a mechanism to reward bureaucratic compliance.

---

[34] Census information is also used to determine a jurisdiction's population.

[35] The 1999 Kenyan census did not collect ethnicity information.

[36] Kenya saw bouts of administrative unit proliferation from 1992–2010, thereby changing the jurisdictions of the bureaucrats I examine. These boundary changes have implications for the quantitative analyses. I cannot assume that the ethnic makeup of new "split" units matches that of their "parent" unit, as new units were created for local ethnic minorities within parent units (Kasara 2006; Hassan 2016). Instead, I use data from previous work that documented the creation date and boundaries of new districts to determine the ethnic composition of parent and split units (Hassan 2016).

Chapter 3 introduces the Kenyan case and the Provincial Administration. I discuss the origins and growth of the Provincial Administration under colonialism. I next lay out Kenya's postindependence administrative and political landscape, including the *de jure* management of the Provincial Administration.

Chapter 4 chronicles the elite threats faced by Kenya's first three presidents. I show how elite incorporation into the state was useful in preempting some elite threats. I then illustrate the downstream consequences of partial elite incorporation by quantitatively evaluating the makeup of the Provincial Administration. I find that this agency was never packed with any president's co-ethnics. Instead, its ethnic makeup reflected patterns of elite incorporation into the cabinet alongside the country's general ethnic heterogeneity.

Chapters 5 and 6 examine Kenya's one-party authoritarian era under Presidents Kenyatta (1963–1978) and Moi (1978–1991). In each chapter, I determine the alignment of different parts of the country after discussing the popular threats to each president, many of which emanated from unsuccessful attempts at elite incorporation. I then systematically assess the management of the senior ranks of the Provincial Administration. These officers, similar to Gitonga in the opening example in this chapter, had a neopatrimonial relationship with their respective president through patronage. I find that these officers were managed with the intent to increase local embeddedness in each president's aligned areas and decrease it elsewhere. I also find evidence that local embeddedness was especially low in the misaligned areas where popular threats had previously emerged under each president. This strategy increased the willingness of officers posted there to coerce.

Chapters 7 and 8 examine how Presidents Moi (1992–2002) and Kibaki (2002–2013) managed the senior ranks of the Provincial Administration after the reintroduction of multiparty elections. These officers were managed in much the same way under multiparty elections as they were under autocracy, despite the fact that popular threats took different forms between these periods. Officers' local embeddedness increased in each president's aligned areas and decreased elsewhere. Both chapters also study the lower ranks of the Provincial Administration, officers such as Kipsang and Maina. Presidents could not rely on money to create a neopatrimonial bond with these officers. Instead, officer loyalty varied, with the president's (opposition's) co-ethnic officers seen as the most (least) willing to act on behalf of the president. I find that lower-level co-ethnics of the president were sent to electorally valuable areas.

Lower-level co-ethnics of the opposition were sent to places where their shirking behavior would least affect the president's reelection chances.

Chapter 8 also examines promotion patterns in two ways. First, I show that Kikuyu officers, co-ethnics of Kibaki, could expect more promotions than other officers. Second, I leverage the 2007–2008 postelection violence to examine the promotion of lower-level officers after a bout of highly visible violence. Though the center cannot monitor the behavior of officers in the execution of routine and everyday bureaucratic tasks, it can observe how they acted during large-scale violence (Policzer 2009; Hassan and O'Mealia 2018). Administrators whose jurisdictions experienced violence initiated by Kibaki's supporters were promoted at higher rates, despite their ethnicity.

Chapter 9 concludes. After reviewing the argument and empirics, I apply the theory to cases outside the scope conditions, map out areas for future research, and discuss some of the book's policy implications.

2

Managing the State

2.1 INTRODUCTION

The state can serve as a powerful tool to keep a leader in power. Core tasks of governing can be repurposed to co-opt those that the leader needs to support him and coerce those likely to challenge his rule. A leader cannot carry out his own dirty work, however. This chapter presents a theory of how a leader manages bureaucrats – who is recruited into the state, where these bureaucrats are posted, how frequently they are shuffled between posts, and which ones are promoted – in his attempt to meet his most important political goals.

Reliance on bureaucrats often begets a principal-agent problem. A leader expects a bureaucrat to use her state-endowed authority as directed, but she can shirk from his demands and instead use that authority in line with her own preferences. Previous studies have suggested three broad classes of strategies to alleviate shirking, but fully implementing any of the three would threaten a leader's stability in a manner separate from ensuring bureaucrats' compliance. Indeed, the most prominent solution proposed by existing literature – packing the state with the leader's in-group bureaucrats – inhibits a leader from incorporating elites who demand valuable state jobs for *their* in-group members. Many leaders thus avoid packing the state so as not to preclude the ability to solve pressing elite threats.

In this chapter I argue that the leader can ensure compliance with the state actions that keep him in office by strategically managing bureaucrats. The leader makes these management decisions by weighing the political *alignment* of each jurisdiction to him, each bureaucrat's *loyalty* to him, and the bureaucrat's *local embeddedness* in a given jurisdiction.

After considering these factors individually, the theory makes two broad predictions. First, leaders post loyal bureaucrats to parts of the country where compliance is most necessary, and assign other – especially disloyal – bureaucrats away from these vital areas. Second, bureaucrats' local embeddedness is increased in areas that the leader wants co-opted and lowered in places he wants coerced.

My theory makes several contributions. First, it demonstrates that leaders are willing to vary how they solve the principal-agent problem sub-nationally. Previous work on the topic assumes that a leader's management solutions are implemented uniformly across the country; these studies share an implicit assumption that other strategies to solve the principal-agent problem are ineffective. This chapter instead argues that the strategies suggested by past work are useful in moderation but less useful at the limit.

Perhaps more importantly, the theory helps us understand the state and variation within it. The way in which the state interacts with its citizens is a deliberate choice (Boone 2003), and management of the state is an important mechanism to explain variation in resource provision. Indeed, later chapters show that outcomes ranging from land allocation to local budgetary decisions are affected by the embeddedness of the bureaucrat posted in the jurisdiction. In areas where a leader does not fear a popular threat, he allows bureaucrats to govern in a manner that improves locals' livelihoods. Elsewhere, bureaucrats are managed to privilege social control over development. In this way, the decisions that leaders make in pursuit of political stability affect, and in many cases reproduce, an area's underlying political alignment toward the leader (Carter and Hassan Forthcoming).

In the rest of this chapter, I first examine the range of elite and popular challenges that leaders may face. Next, I discuss why the state is a useful tool for addressing these threats. I then describe the principal-agent problem that reliance on state bureaucrats introduces. I give an overview of existing solutions to solve this problem and why they are insufficient. I then present my theory about the strategic management of bureaucrats and its empirical implications. The chapter next lays out several extensions of the theory before concluding.

2.2 A LEADER'S ELITE AND POPULAR THREATS

All leaders face elite and popular threats. This section describes what these threats look like in autocratic versus electoral regimes.

2.2.1 Elite and Popular Challenges

The theory and empirics of this book differentiate between two regime types: *electoral* regimes that hold multi-party elections to choose a leader and *autocratic* regimes that do not. This bifurcation overlooks the vast variation in regime type within both categories: much work on autocracy tends to classify regimes based on the institutions that structure elite inter-action (Geddes 1999). My focus on the presence of elections, as opposed to their quality, means that I lump together consolidated democracies with competitive authoritarian regimes in which elections are neither free nor fair (Levitsky and Way 2010).[1] And variation within these two broad regime types has been shown to have downstream effects on important outcomes.[2]

Yet I stick with the coarse distinction because of this book's main outcome of interest: how leaders manage bureaucrats in an attempt to prevent challenges to their rule.[3] The very presence of multiparty elections changes the nature of political threats. Even when a ruling party domi-nates multiparty elections, the country's leader must take into account the possibility that a viable opposition challenger may emerge and unseat him (Magaloni 2006; Blaydes 2011). And as I describe in greater detail in this chapter, the presence of elections means that a leader needs sufficient support at the polls to win.

---

[1] Other classification systems for authoritarian regimes also focus on the presence and/or strength of institutions. See Cheibub, Gandhi, and Vreeland (2010), Svolik (2012), and Boix, Miller, and Rosato (2013), or see Bratton and van de Walle (1994) for a typology specific to sub-Saharan Africa. For other criteria and/or nomenclature to differentiate between democracies and other regimes that hold multi-party elections, see Schmitter and Karl (1990), Zakaria (1997), Schedler (2002), Munck (2006), Bogaards (2009), and Morse (2012).

[2] For instance, Geddes (1999) and Bratton and van de Walle (1997) find differences in democratization outcomes based on authoritarian regime type; Davenport (2007) finds differences in the level and type of repression that citizens encounter based on authoritarian regime type; and Weeks (2012) finds differences in international conflict based on authoritarian regime type. Much research also finds variation in outcomes based on the quality of electoral competition. For instance, Davenport and Armstrong (2004) find variation in human rights violations based on the openness of electoral regimes.

[3] One benefit of looking at electoral regimes in the Kenyan case is that this coarse bifurcation sidesteps the debate about how to classify Mwai Kibaki's (2002–2013) regime. The 2002 election in which Kibaki won was free and fair, and has led many scholars to classify his reign as democratic (e.g., Howard and Roessler 2006). After he took office, however, Kibaki maintained strong executive power and his administration oversaw many "irregularities" and illegal administrative activities during both his 2007 reelection and the 2013 election of his co-ethnic successor (see Weis (2008), Gibson and Long (2009), and Ferree, Gibson, and Long (2014)).

Leaders face two broad classes of domestic challenges, or threats, across these two regime types: those from elites and those from the population. An *elite* is a politician with popular mobilization capacity in a particular geographic area, whose initial mobilization capacity is at least somewhat separate from bureaucratic postings in the area.[4] I define elites broadly to include those who could credibly challenge the leader for his position (e.g., Gandhi 2008; Roessler 2017) as well as those who support the leader and help him consolidate his rule (e.g., Magaloi 2006; Svolik 2012). Most elite challenges take the form of a coup d'ètat, the introduction of executive constraints, or the elite leading a segment of the population in collective action against the leader.[5]

Leaders also face popular challenges – widespread collective action that aims to weaken, destabilize, or remove them. In authoritarian regimes, popular challenges often take the form of episodic protests, strikes, rallies, riots, or marches. This type of collective action may be even more frequent in countries with multiparty elections,[6] but the larger popular threat that leaders in electoral regimes face is from the ballot box: voters may elect an opponent.

Elite and popular threats are often intertwined. Popular threats are difficult to launch and spread because of the collective action problem. It is hard to organize a large number of civilians for popular action when each individual faces high participation costs – including possible injury or death in autocracies. But even in electoral regimes, the government may constrain protesters' civil liberties (Davenport 2000; Carey 2006) or channel fewer state resources to opposition strongholds (Magaloni 2006; Blaydes 2011). Sometimes, popular discontent is sufficiently high that mobilization happens organically: if conditions are so bad and the leader is clearly to blame, elite involvement may not be necessary to organize a popular threat (Thomson 2018). But many attempts at mobilization only

---

[4] While bureaucrats can gain the ability to mobilize residents in the area to which they are posted, their power there is endogenous to their posting.

[5] While coups are possible in either autocratic or electoral regimes, they are more common in the former. When a leader is chosen through multiparty elections, attaining office through the ballot box is viewed as the only legitimate way to power, so elections are often quickly reintroduced after a successful coup attempt (Marinov and Goemans 2014). Similarly, constraints on executive power are possible across regime type, but are more common in electoral regimes where elites begin with more power relative to the leader than in autocracies.

[6] For instance, Salehyan et al. (2012) document an increase in social conflict in sub-Saharan Africa, including protests, riots, strikes, and other forms of unrest, since the region's political opening after the end of the Cold War.

succeed when an elite with sufficient clout *and* ill will toward the leader coordinates the actions of her followers, as I discuss later in this chapter.[7]

A leader must prepare himself to counter an emerging popular threat regardless of his degree of support among elites. In the leader's best-case scenario, in which he only faces a popular threat if an elite organizes her followers, the leader deems it prudent to prepare for this possibility. But in the leader's worst-case scenario, popular discontent against him is so high that popular collective action may emerge even absent elite organization.

2.3 USING THE STATE TO PREVENT POPULAR THREATS: OPPORTUNITIES AND RISKS

The executive can repurpose the state's core mandate of maintaining control over a given territory to instead prevent popular threats to his rule. However, to understand how leaders use the state to stay in power and more broadly meet their political goals, we must theorize the preferences and behavior of the individuals who carry out the leader's orders – bureaucrats. Focusing on bureaucrats prompts us to consider a leader's principal-agent problem: after bureaucrats are endowed with state authority, they may refuse to comply with the leader's demands.

This section first introduces the initial scope conditions of the argument. It then explains how the state proves useful in co-opting or coercing popular threats. Next, I discuss the "field" bureaucrats who carry out the leader's demands in the periphery and the principal-agent problem that relying on these bureaucrats introduces.

2.3.1 Focus on Countries with Salient Identity Cleavages

I focus on countries with salient identity cleavages for two related reasons. First, the existence of a salient identity cleavage means that all three actors in the theory – the leader, each bureaucrat, and each local area – have a signal about the preferences of other actors. Second, in-group members of the same identity cleavage tend to cluster geographically. Thus the state can target a group by targeting the areas its members inhabit. As such, the theory speaks to the political alignment of an area and a group interchangeably.

---

7 See, for instance, McCarthy and Zald (1977), Popkin (1979), Bates (1981), Lichbach (1998), Robertson (2010), and Tarrow (2011).

This scope condition holds across much of the world. For instance, more than 80 percent of countries in the Ethnic Power Relations dataset, and more than 85 percent in the sub-Saharan Africa sample, have at least two politically relevant ethnic groups (Wimmer, Cederman, and Min 2009). This condition has even broader reach if we consider a more fluid definition of identity cleavages. Though I speak specifically about ethnicity given the Kenyan context, this theory is directly applicable to countries where the salient identity cleavage is religion (e.g., India, Myanmar), sect (e.g., Iraq, Lebanon, Syria), or language (e.g., Zambia). Indeed, in joint work with Brett Carter, we examine bureaucratic embeddedness in the Republic of Congo where the salient identity cleavage is region (Carter and Hassan Forthcoming). To extend the theory beyond ethnic politics, one needs simply to replace the word "ethnic" with another salient cleavage.

Further, and as I discuss in the conclusion, many of the theory's insights also travel to contexts where society's dominant political cleavages are acquired, such as partisanship (e.g., Russia, United States) or political faction (e.g., China), for two reasons. First, while acquired traits such as partisanship and faction are often theorized as mutable, they are fixed identities, at least in the short run. The leader of a country without salient identity cleavages is likely to apply the tenets of the theory, so long as he is aware of the distribution of the acquired trait across bureaucrats and the population. Second, the theory emphasizes that nonidentity factors – including patronage between the bureaucrat and leader and embeddedness through long tenure in a post – play an important role in incentivizing bureaucratic compliance. One could easily apply the theory to countries with acquired identities by focusing on the nonidentity factors that help the leader alleviate the principal-agent problem.

2.3.2 Focus on Countries with Weak Parties

My theory is applicable to countries with weak parties. This scope condition is important for three reasons. First, strong parties often provide bureaucrats with ample progression opportunities (Geddes 1999; Grzymała-Busse 2002). Bureaucrats' incentives in these contexts may thus align with the leader's regardless of their in-group status. Second, monitoring of bureaucrats is plausible in strong party contexts: a strong party has dense ties to grassroots offices that can provide a parallel system with which to monitor bureaucrats. If a bureaucrat shirks from her duties, this is more likely to be relayed to the center, giving officials strong incentives to comply with orders regardless of their preferences. Third, a leader at the helm of a weak party has fewer strategies available to him to prevent popular threats. He finds it difficult to make credible promises about future streams of benefits outside of groups that already support him. And groups that do not currently support him find it difficult to make credible promises to support the leader in the future.

It is difficult to assess the breadth of this scope condition globally, but work on sub-Saharan Africa suggests that it largely holds in the region. Riedl (2014) measures the extent to which parties have stable roots in society on a scale of 1 to 3.[8] The regional average is 2.2, suggesting moderate levels of roots in society in the region as a whole. But the average hides the extent of this variation: more than one-third of the sample (nine of the twenty-three countries) scored less than 2, suggesting the weakness of political parties in a large subset of African countries.

2.3.3 Focus on Countries with Executive Control over Bureaucracy

The book's third scope condition is that the leader is able to manage the bureaucratic corps. This condition runs on a continuum. The more formal and informal control the leader has, the greater his ability to manage the state to meet his political goals. I add two caveats to this condition. First, it holds even if management of the bureaucracy is delegated to top advisers or elites as long as their interests are aligned with those of the leader. In the extensions of the theory in Section 2.7, I briefly consider cases when their interests do *not* align. Second, I recognize that an agency's relative size matters as well. Indeed, managing a bureaucratic corps of 1,000 is different than a corps of 100,000. It is unclear how the size of a bureaucracy will affect the theory, however. The increased cognitive bandwidth necessary to oversee a larger bureaucracy may mean that managers are unable to strategically shuffle bureaucrats, or instead, managers may rely more on identity markers or performance indicators to optimize compliance.

2.3.4 The State Is a Powerful Tool to Coerce or Co-opt Popular Threats

The leader is expected to use the state to govern and meet policy goals, but it can be repurposed to help the leader rule and meet his political goals.

---

[8] I thank Rachel Riedl for sharing this data.

The state is especially useful for putting down popular threats because it interfaces with the population.

The state can *coerce* individuals or areas in an attempt to stop popular threats. At the most basic level, the state is the entity that claims a monopoly over the legitimate use of violence within a territory (Weber 1958). This definition of statehood underscores the necessity of violence: the state needs the threat of force behind it to maintain control. But this authority can also be directed to violate the civil liberties or personal integrity of its citizens. State coercion can take one of two forms. First, the leader can demand outright violence through acts of "high-intensity coercion" – coercive actions that target large numbers of people, well-known individuals, or major institutions. Second, leaders can demand "low-intensity coercion" that tends to be less visible, though often still systematic, to suppress the opposition (Levitsky and Way 2010). Examples of such coercion include surveillance, low-scale harassment of regime opponents, the use of bureaucratic procedures to administratively hinder rival elites, and low levels of ballot stuffing.

The state can also be used to *co-opt* the citizens of some sub-national jurisdictions. In addition to maintaining law and order, states are expected to organize society through the administration of citizens, the regulation of social relationships, the extraction of resources, and the subsequent distribution of those resources as public goods and services. A leader can thus also use the state to, for example, deliver state resources beyond what the area requires or what bureaucratic formulas dictate, or incorporate local leaders into decision-making processes. Co-optation requires more than erratic or one-time preferential treatment, however. It necessitates a long-term relationship between the leader and the group such that the group expects a steady stream of state resources now and in the future (Diaz-Cayeros, Estévez, and Magaloni 2016).[9]

Given my focus on bureaucracy, I define co-optation and coercion broadly so as to incorporate the ways in which local bureaucrats carry out their duties and interpret national laws. For instance, bureaucrats may co-opt by being lenient in the enforcement of legal statues, going "above and beyond" to address community problems, or relying on conciliatory dispute mechanisms to maintain law and order. My definitions of these

---

[9] Co-optation through the distribution of state resources may sometimes enmesh citizens into webs of coercive dependence (Albertus, Fenner, and Slater 2018). This is especially the case for land (Boone 2014; Albertus 2015; Klaus 2020), an empirical focus of later chapters.

terms therefore go beyond standard – and observable – measures of resource provision or the level of violence in a community. Instead, co-optation and coercion encompass a more holistic view that incorporates bureaucratic discretion and interpretation.[10]

What are the relative costs and benefits of pursuing co-optation versus coercion? Co-optation tends to be more effective at preventing popular threats, whereas coercion is more useful for addressing popular threats that are already underway. Separately, each strategy has drawbacks that make it difficult to implement uniformly across the country. Co-optation is expensive, and most leaders lack the necessary resources to co-opt all groups within a society. And, more importantly, to the extent that co-optation entails convincing a group that the leader is looking out for their best interests over those of other groups, a leader cannot co-opt all groups at the same time: the tactic is at least partly zero sum and requires that only some receive preferential treatment. Relying solely on coercion is dangerous for a leader as well, as too much coercion can jeopardize his legitimacy at home and abroad. While visible acts of state coercion may put down a popular threat, they may spur higher levels of domestic mobilization (Hafner-Burton, Hyde, and Jablonski 2014) or destabilizing international actions such as the imposition of sanctions, diplomatic isolation, or arrest warrants through international courts (Nielsen 2013; Carter n.d.).

2.3.5 The Bureaucrats Who Carry Out the Co-optation and Coercion the Leader Demands

This book focuses on "street-level" or "field" bureaucrats who execute the functions of their office in the periphery and speaks less about "desk" bureaucrats operating in the headquarters of the capital city. Leaders rely on field bureaucrats for social control since they work and live in the sub-national jurisdiction to which they are assigned, and therefore regularly interact with citizens. In Weberian terms, field officials have fixed and official jurisdictional areas; an official's actions within her position are paramount both in the territorial area in which she physically serves and in the specific duties she is tasked with completing (Weber, 1958, 196).

---

[10] In this way, my definitions of co-optation and coercion are similar to the definition of bias in Prendergast (2007): deviations from *de jure* practices (what Prendergast (2007) defines as mistakes) can either serve to benefit or hurt clients.

Put simply, these bureaucrats have the authority to both execute the mandate of their position and to punish citizens who object.

Bureaucrats vary in their ability to co-opt or coerce on behalf of the leader based on their formal duties. Those tasked with administration and distributing public goods – such as local water engineers, district education officers, or county health inspectors – are better equipped to co-opt an area. These officials can use their discretion to privilege some local residents with extra subsidies, waive taxes and fees, or implement central directives in a manner that benefits the area. State officials tasked with maintaining law and order – police officers, members of the gendarmerie, or paramilitary officers – are well equipped to coerce. These officers can instead use their discretion to jail local dissidents, seize "illegally acquired" funds, create administrative hurdles for known opposition supporters, or prevent local attempts at collective action. Other bureaucrats, including members of Kenya's Provincial Administration and dozens of other similar executive bureaucracies around the world, have formal duties that allow them to both co-opt and coerce well. While my theory is based on a bureaucracy whose agents can do either, it can be adapted to agencies that are better equipped to carry out only one of these strategies.

I make two additional simplifying assumptions about bureaucrats and their behavior to streamline the theory. First, I assume that bureaucrats' utility is affected by only two factors: (1) the bureaucrat's relationship with the leader and (2) the bureaucrat's social relationship with residents of the area to which she is posted. In practice, a bureaucrat's behavior will also be affected by other factors – perhaps most notably by her agency's culture or the type of relational contracts within an organization (Gibbons and Henderson 2012). I do not analyze agency culture, however, because my focus is on field bureaucrats, whose day-to-day interactions are with citizens as opposed to other bureaucrats in their organization. The second simplifying assumption is that the theory discusses a bureaucrat's compliance as deterministic based on those two previously mentioned factors. Realistically, bureaucratic behavior is probabilistic, and the variables I study do not perfectly predict behavior. But theorizing behavior as deterministic yields clearer observable implications and cleaner testable hypotheses.

2.3.6 Reliance on Bureaucrats Creates a Principal-Agent Problem

A leader relies on bureaucrats to limit popular threats to his rule, but faces a *principal-agent problem* in eliciting compliance. The survival of

Managing the State

the leader (the principal) depends on the behavior of the bureaucrats (agents) he employs. Yet a bureaucrat's preferences may diverge from those of the leader. After endowing bureaucrats with state authority, how can a leader ensure they act in line with his demands as opposed to their own preferences?

There are three primary ways in which officials can shirk from their duties. First, and most damaging to the leader, a bureaucrat's preferences might be completely in opposition to the leader's such that she would prefer a different leader take power. Just as the leader demands that bureaucrats use their authority to benefit him, bureaucrats can use their authority to aid his political rival. Bureaucrats who do not exert sufficient effort or who engage only in their formal, state-mandated tasks when asked to act politically are also shirking: refusing to augment the leader's local support is a veiled way of keeping that support in check.

Second, a bureaucrat's preferences might align with those of residents in the jurisdiction to which she is posted. A field officer's behavior affects the livelihoods of residents. A lingering danger in their deployment, therefore, is that they become too *locally embedded* in the community in which they live and let their social relationships dictate compliance. This embeddedness can be "innate" if the state official is a co-ethnic of the area. "Native" state officials are enmeshed in local networks, are familiar with local customs, and know local elites. But embeddedness can also be learned or acquired through an officer's long tenure in a station as the official establishes deep social ties with area residents. Herbert Kaufman (1960, 76) describes the dangers of embeddedness through long tenure in the U.S. Forest Service:

The danger is really twofold. On the one hand, there is the risk that field men, regarded by their chiefs as emissaries sent to live among local populaces and represent the agency to the people, become so identified with the communities in which they reside that they become community delegates to headquarters rather than the reverse ... though devoted to their leaders, rangers might be cowed by local pressures. On the other hand, there is the possibility that the field men, though devoted to their leaders, might be cowed by local pressures.

Locally embedded officers no longer act as agents of the leader, but as agents of the area in which they serve. A bureaucrat's decisions in these cases are made with the area's best interests in mind.

Third, bureaucrats may use their authority to benefit themselves by predating. More often than not, citizens are the most negatively affected by bureaucratic predation, as officers extract from the community in which they work. But predation can be costly for the leader as well, if high levels of predation from his agents substantially worsen his support in an area, or if a bureaucrat amasses sufficient local clout and resources to challenge his power (Migdal 1988; Barkey 1994). Overall, however, predation is less of a concern for leaders than the other two forms of noncompliance. In many cases, the leader turns a blind eye to low or moderate levels of officer predation or even encourages modest levels of predation in an attempt to incentivize compliance with more pressing orders. As such, the theory prioritizes the prevention of noncompliance on behalf of another elite or the local area over the prevention of predation.

The three forms of shirking are interrelated. Each problem can bleed into the next, and an officer may succumb to multiple forms of shirking at once. For instance, local embeddedness can make it easier for an officer to predate. Or an officer may be so embedded that she is more susceptible to becoming an agent of local political elites who are the leader's rivals. While I recognize these empirical realities, each form of shirking is conceptually distinct in that the officer becomes an agent of another principal – an elite rival, the local community, or the bureaucrat herself.

2.4 THE INSUFFICIENCY OF EXISTING SOLUTIONS TO THE PRINCIPAL-AGENT PROBLEM

Research on principal-agent dynamics suggests three broad categories of solutions to ensure bureaucratic compliance. First, a leader can improve monitoring. Second, he can create neopatrimonial bonds with bureaucrats to ensure that they benefit from him staying in office and therefore have a personal incentive to comply with his orders. Third, a leader can reduce officers' ability to shirk. These three classes of solutions, however, are insufficient to explain how leaders manage bureaucrats for two reasons. First, each strategy has negative costs that inhibit the leader's tenure independently of ensuring compliance. If a leader were to fully implement any of these solutions, the now higher levels of bureaucratic compliance would not outweigh the increased likelihood of elite or popular threats that the solution creates. Second, the latter two solutions focus only on the relationship between the leader and a bureaucrat or between a bureaucrat and a local area, and therefore do not fully prevent noncompliance on behalf of another principal. I discuss each class of solutions and their respective insufficiencies in turn.

2.4.1 Improving Monitoring

Many previous studies suggest that monitoring bureaucrats can reduce noncompliance (Olken and Pande 2012). Well-monitored bureaucrats will fear getting caught and reprimanded, and thus be incentivized to comply.[11] One common monitoring tactic is to measure quantifiable outputs of the bureaucrat's actions against projected targets. Another typical monitoring strategy is to increase the leader's oversight of the organization.

Improving Monitoring Decreases Bureaucrats' Effectiveness
Monitoring through the use of quantifiable targets or by increasing the level of oversight is liable to decrease bureaucrats' effectiveness. The introduction of quantifiable project targets is almost sure to backfire within bureaucracies whose outcomes are hard to quantify.[12] When the discrete outputs that bureaucrats can point to do not perfectly correlate with the outcomes that they are mandated to fulfill, attempts to introduce reporting criteria will change the bureaucrat's behavior such that they work to meet output targets instead of doing what they were hired to do. For instance, James Q. Wilson (1989, 162) described this pitfall with reference to the FBI under J. Edgar Hoover. Agents were expected to increase the recovery of stolen vehicles, so officers "[retrieved] lists from local police departments of stolen cars that had been found so that the agents could claim them as 'recoveries' even though the agents had done little or nothing to find the cars." The distortionary effects of monitoring are higher in the developing world, where the terrain is unpredictable (Honig 2018). Indeed, recent evidence from West Africa suggests that managerial techniques meant to increase bureaucratic monitoring are negatively correlated with project completion rates (Rasul and Rogger 2018; Rasul, Rogger, and Williams 2018).[13]

2.4.2 Developing Neopatrimonial Ties with Bureaucrats: Patronage and Packing

Another class of solutions to the principal-agent problem is to create neopatrimonial links between the leader and bureaucrats. If a bureaucrat

---

[11] In game theoretic terms, monitoring reduces hidden action. In response, a principal can better contract on performance.

[12] This includes officers in Kenya's Provincial Administration, who are expected to engage in low-intensity coercion or to improve poorly specified local development outcomes.

[13] Separately, monitored bureaucrats may lower their productivity due to perceptions of distrust (Frey 1993; Falk and Kosfeld 2006).

believes that her livelihood is tied to the leader staying in office, then she has a personal incentive to comply with his directives, even absent monitoring.

Previous studies suggest that a leader can create these neopatrimonial bonds by distributing vast amounts of *patronage* to bureaucrats and directly showering them with resources.[14] For instance, a leader can give bureaucrats additional compensation (bonuses), buy officers new uniforms and equipment, grant them access to preferential loans or state benefits, and importantly, link internal promotions to their compliance with the leader's orders instead of to the formal mandate of their position. Further, leaders can allow a bureaucrat to use their position to predate with impunity. In forging a direct monetary relationship between himself and state officials, the leader turns them into his clients from whom he expects compliance (Bratton and van de Walle 1997). The distribution of patronage makes it clear that the bureaucrat's favorable financial situation is directly attributable to the leader.[15]

Alternatively, the leader can build neopatrimonial bonds with bureaucrats by *packing* the institution with in-group members.[16] In-group bureaucrats are, by definition, given preference in hiring and promotion decisions. The bureaucrat's entry into the state and the progression of her career is therefore directly tied to the leader staying in power. Thus, a leader can trust that bureaucrats will not favor a rival elite because they are likely to lose their job if the leader is ousted. Packing helps to

---

[14] Jackson and Rosberg (1982), Clapham (1985), Chabal and Daloz (1999), Brownlee (2002), van de Walle (2003), and Pitcher, Moran, and Johnston (2009).

[15] Patronage is thus especially useful to buy the loyalty of the leader's out-group bureaucrats. More often than not, these bureaucrats made it into the state through the lobbying of their own incorporated elite. Absent patronage from the leader, these out-group officers are likely to be loyal to their own in-group elite, not necessarily the leader, and to use their authority on that elite's behalf. But as the leader delivers more and more patronage to an officer, she begins to re-align her interests away from her elite and toward the leader.

[16] A large literature argues that we should expect the leader's in-group state officials to be the most loyal. For instance, see Enloe (1973), Jackson and Rosberg (1982), Horowitz (1985), Brown (1994), Quinlivan (1999), Slater (2003), Bellin (2004), McLauchlin (2010), Sassoon (2011), Bellin (2012), Decalo (2012), and Nepstad (2013). Much of the packing literature has specifically examined the coercive apparatus. Yet many of the lessons apply to less coercive state bodies as well. A similar strategy is to pack the state, and especially the security forces, with a minority group separate from that of the leader's. By wedding the fate of a minority group to the regime or labeling a group a "martial class" or a "community of trust," the leader re-creates many of the same material and symbolic logics for in-group loyalty (see Enloe 1973; Migdal 1988; Makara 2013; Osborne 2015; Wilkinson 2015; and Greitens 2016).

convince bureaucrats that their fate is intrinsically linked to the leader's (Bellin 2004).

Creating Neopatrimonial Relationships Reduces the Potential for Elite Incorporation

Although creating neopatrimonial institutions through bonds of money or blood induces bureaucrats to comply, it can create even worse political challenges for a leader by instigating new elite or popular threats. The leader's ability to stave off elite threats is directly at odds with his ability to create neopatrimonial state institutions. Leaders incorporate elites to pre-emptively share resources with them. Elites demand this incorporation because they need to reinforce *their own* popular support among their in-group through clientelistic appeals, in part by distributing state resources and jobs (Chabal and Daloz 1999; Roessler 2017). Moreover, in weak party contexts, elites value the ability to place their supporters in important bureaucratic positions so as to siphon off money from state coffers (Sigman 2017). In sum, resources used to buy officer loyalty reduce the total amount available that the leader can use to placate elites. And a leader who packs the state is unable to distribute state positions to the in-group members of incorporated elites.

A leader may refrain from creating neopatrimonial state institutions for other reasons. For instance, neopatrimonial states are thought to be less efficient at carrying out their goals (Evans and Rauch 1999; Xu 2018). Further, the creation of patrimonial institutions can disrupt bureaucratic norms. Bureaucrats may resist abrupt changes to their agency's autonomy or long-standing compensation and hiring practices. And because state jobs are perceived to be desirable, a leader who privileges his own co-ethnics will be perceived as disproportionately channeling state resources to his own group. This perception increases other groups' popular dissatisfaction with the leader.

2.4.3 Reducing Bureaucrats' Embeddedness

A third strategy to ensure bureaucratic compliance is to deliberately decrease the embeddedness of bureaucrats within the area they serve by frequently shuffling bureaucrats across stations and/or avoiding the assignment of bureaucrats to their "home" areas.[17] Either way, decreasing

---

[17] A separate but related literature explores how leaders shuffle top elites within different top posts (e.g., cabinet members, army commanders) to reduce embeddedness within an

embeddedness is less about realigning the incentives of a bureaucrat such that she has a personal stake in keeping the leader in office and more about lowering the level of damage that a shirking bureaucrat can do.

Lowering embeddedness reduces the damage of bureaucratic shirking through a *knowledge* mechanism. Unembedded bureaucrats have less knowledge about the area, so their noncompliance will have less of an effect on the leader's local support. Reducing embeddedness also helps prevent a bureaucrat from using her social connections to become a threat to the leader himself. For example, during the Ottoman Empire, "the rotation of officials prevented an alliance between [officials] and peasants against the central state, explaining the absence of peasant rebellions in the 17th century" (Debs 2007). Likewise, China enforces strict term limits for any state administrative officers and prevents top administrative cadres from working in their "home" province in order to reduce corruption and to diminish the risk of officials colluding with local elites due to their knowledge of local dynamics.[18]

Lowering embeddedness can also increase compliance with orders to coerce through a *social* mechanism. Constantly rotating bureaucrats or appointing officers who hail from another in-group reduces the social connections that a bureaucrat has or may develop over time. These officers are more willing to enforce the administrative hurdles intended to weaken rivals and to inflict violence on regime opponents on behalf of the leader precisely because they are socially detached (Arriola 2013; Saha 2014; Greitens 2016; Carter and Hassan Forthcoming)

Reducing Bureaucrats' Embeddedness Threatens Their Ability to Govern Well

Attempts to decrease a bureaucrat's ability to shirk through artificial changes to local embeddedness are costly. This class of solutions reduces bureaucrats' ability to carry out the leader's demands, therefore making bureaucrats less effective at pre-empting popular threats.

---

agency. The logic behind this elite shuffle is similar, albeit more attuned to the coup risk that elites present. Namely, leaders weigh the efficiency gains of having an elite serve a long tenure in a post against the increased potential that the elite can create a following within the agency. See, among others, Tordoff and Molteno (1974), Migdal (1988), Bayart (1993), Chabal and Daloz (1999), Hashim (2003), Huber and Martinez-Gallardo (2008), Bethke (2012), Francois, Rainer, and Trebbi (2015), Woldense (2018), Kroeger (2018), Carter (n.d.).

[18] For instance, see Miyazaki (1976), Huang (2002), Landry (2008), McCulloch and Malesky (2014), and Zeng (2015).

Reducing local embeddedness through constant shuffling or the deliberate posting of out-group officers has negative effects on the officer's knowledge of the local area and therefore her ability to effectively carry out the leader's orders.[19] This is partly due to the same knowledge mechanism that makes embeddedness dangerous. A bureaucrat's general training provides a foundational understanding of the agency's mission and an overview of the basic tasks she is expected to carry out. But all jurisdictions are different and will require bureaucrats to adapt general mandates to specific situations (Scott 1998). An embedded officer knows the local power players and which wheels to grease to get societal approval (e.g., to get local buy-in when she launches a new program or needs to call an important meeting), can more efficiently use the available resources (e.g., by hiring the best contractors for a job), and can identify recipient beneficiaries who are either the most in need or the most loyal to the leader. During Kenya's colonial era, for instance, regime elites extolled the benefits of long tenure on a bureaucrat's ability to implement local development:

[the officer] entered upon his third year as District Agricultural Officer and the District is now beginning to reap the profits of the continuity of his three year direction of agricultural affairs. The benefits accruing from this continuity of staff are to be seen also in the progress of coffee [cultivation] in the District and in the agricultural advance of the hitherto backward Western Division.[20]

Similarly, in Mobutu Sese Seko's Zaire, Young and Turner (1985, 226) find that "a number of sub-regional commissioners were assigned to their own ethnic areas, on a tribal basis, on the ground that they would better understand local problems." Relatedly, evidence from China suggests that bureaucrats who have short tenures are less willing to invest effort in projects that will likely have the greatest impact on an area's development, and will instead restrict themselves to smaller activities with more limited – but observable – short-term effects (Eaton and Kostka 2014).

The reduction of contextual knowledge by limiting embeddedness negatively affects a bureaucrat's ability to coerce. An embedded bureaucrat has a better sense of who is liable to instigate a popular threat, as well as a deep network of informants who alert her to new community organizers, and a sense of which symbolic events or religious celebrations people are

---

19 There is a large body of literature on the merits and pitfalls of embeddedness. See, for example, Meier and Nigro (1976), Evans (1995), Tsai (2007a), Pepinsky, Pierskalla, and Sacks (2017), Bhavnani and Lee (2018), and Carter and Hassan (Forthcoming).
20 Elgon Nyanza 1959 Annual Report, p. 15.

likely to use as a cover to protest.[21] Moreover, greater knowledge of the area means that an embedded bureaucrat can apply targeted, discriminate coercion that quickly ends a popular threat, as opposed to indiscriminate violence across the entire jurisdiction that decreases the leader's popular support unnecessarily.[22]

Decreasing local embeddedness also hinders the social channel bureaucrats can use to co-opt the jurisdiction to which they are posted. Officers with innate embeddedness are members of the local group, and those with learned embeddedness in a sense *become* members of the local group. Either way, embedded bureaucrats have a sense of obligation to residents in the jurisdiction and are emotionally invested in their livelihoods. Evidence on Chinese bureaucrats finds that embedded officers are more likely to provide local public goods because they receive moral standing from the community for their actions (Tsai 2007a). Regime elites in the Ottoman Empire found that locally embedded officers were more just in their rulings: "the governor-general [should] be appointed for longer periods of time, because without permanent secure positions, the [state officials] are liable to resort to injustice and when injustice prevails the people are in discomfort and the country is in distress and disorder" (Barkey, 1994, 79). Residents and local stakeholders have also been found to trust locally embedded officers more, and are thus more willing to cooperate with the state, as this excerpt from the Kenyan colonial record suggests:

Continuity in the form of a District Commissioner is essential if a district is to develop in any particular way ... a personal loyalty tends to develop between the African and the [officer], but it does take some time to do so. If changes are made too quickly, suspicion inevitably grows and nothing is achieved.[23]

This trust compounds. The community is more willing to contribute to local public goods, or even engage with the government at all, if they trust the bureaucrat stationed there (Carter and Hassan Forthcoming).

In sum, this section's discussion of a leader's principal-agent problems and how to solve them – by increasing monitoring, creating

---

[21] The ability of in-group officers to better coerce an area even holds during wartime. Lyall (2010) finds that co-ethnic soldiers are more effective at weeding out counterinsurgents than non-co-ethnics for the same reasons described here.

[22] For instance, Deng and O'Brien (2013) find that officers with social ties to protesters are able to talk them out of protesting without resorting to violence. On higher levels of violence by unembedded officers or combatants, see Kalyvas (2006), Lyall (2010), Arriola (2013), Greitens (2016), and Lewis (2017).

[23] North Nyanza 1958 Annual Report, p. 8.

neopatrimonial relationships to induce officer loyalty, or efforts to reduce bureaucrats' ability to shirk – shows that leaders are reticent to fully implement any single solution. Each broad category of solutions risks worsening a leader's grip on power in a manner separate from bureaucratic noncompliance. In Section 2.5 I present a theory of how leaders manage bureaucrats by partially implementing each solution intended to alleviate the principal-agent problem.

2.5 MANAGING THE STATE TO STAY IN POWER

Leaders make decisions about managing bureaucrats – who to hire, where to post them, how often to shuffle them, and who to promote – based on a desire to avert both elite and popular threats. This section discusses each of these goals in turn. It then considers the role of regime type in determining which parts of the country the leader deems most important in his attempt to stay in power.

2.5.1 Reliance on the State to Prevent Elite Threats

A leader needs to address both elite and popular challenges, but he is liable to prioritize the former for two reasons. First, elite threats are more dangerous. Second, solving elite threats can sometimes temper grassroots discontent among the elite's followers, and thus prevent popular threats from emerging.

Many leaders preempt elite threats by incorporating elites through a party, legislature, or directly into the state through the cabinet or state-owned enterprises. To solidify the incorporation, the elite often requires the leader to offer the elite's followers government jobs. Incorporated elites need to reinforce their own level of popular support through clientelistic appeals such as distributing state resources to their followers. An elite rival is viewed as a threat to the leader that needs to be bought off only if she has sufficient support among her own base and therefore can credibly mount a challenge against him. And a loyal elite supporter can guarantee her future incorporation if she has a personal base of political power.

Some leaders find it too dangerous to incorporate their most powerful rivals. Providing rivals with resources increases the likelihood of that elite's success should she decide to challenge the leader in a coup attempt or an electoral campaign. As such, some leaders exclude elites who are perceived as too powerful, or will refuse to incorporate those who are unwilling to trade regime incorporation for acquiescence.[24]

2.5.2 Reliance on the State to Prevent Popular Threats

A leader can rely on the state to co-opt or coerce groups in an attempt to forestall popular threats. Decisions about the management of bureaucrats to ensure compliance require the leader to consider the relationships between the leader himself, a bureaucrat, and the area to which the bureaucrat is posted. An area's *alignment* with the leader determines the likelihood of a popular threat emerging, and in response, whether the leader chooses to co-opt or coerce the area; the *loyalty* of a bureaucrat to the leader determines her willingness to comply with orders; a bureaucrat's *embeddedness* in her post affects her ability, and to an extent her willingness, to carry out the leader's directives.

Alignment with Leader: Sub-National Variation in Popular Threats

A group's *alignment* toward the leader depends on its perceptions about whether the current leader or a viable replacement will credibly co-opt the group in the future. Alignment is important because it reflects the risk of the group launching or sustaining a popular threat.

Alignment between the leader and an area falls along a spectrum. At one end, the leader's *aligned* groups expect state resources and state resources and preferential treatment. These groups are content with the status quo and their expected future stream of resources. A popular threat is unlikely to launch in or spread to areas they inhabit, and they support the leader at high levels because they realize that their situation would be worse under a different leader whose promises about resource distribution are less credible (Padro i Miquel 2007). The leader's own in-group tends to form the base of his aligned groups. In weak party contexts, it is difficult for a leader to credibly build support among other groups, which are reluctant to preemptively support the leader as he cannot guarantee their co-optation in the future. That said, societal groups that have long-standing historic or symbolic linkages with the

---

[24] Much of the literature on authoritarian regimes has noted this catch-22 about the dual necessity and danger of elite incorporation. See, for instance, Magaloni (2006), Gandhi and Przeworski (2007), Frantz and Kendall-Taylor (2014), Harkness (2016), and Roessler (2017).

leader, such as the in-group of the leader's spouse (Adida et al. 2016), may perceive his promises of co-optation as credible, encouraging them to support the leader and thus be considered aligned.

Misaligned groups occupy the opposite end of the spectrum. These groups are often the in-groups of excluded elites. Though an excluded elite will try to sow dissatisfaction among the entire population by promising a future stream of resources should she take office, these promises are most credible within her own in-group. The high level of dissatisfaction with the leader among misaligned groups, and the willingness of their respective in-group elite to coordinate them, make them the most likely to launch popular threats. One implication of identifying misaligned groups according to their potential to launch a popular threat is that they must surpass a minimum size and be politically relevant. The exclusion of an elite from a micro-ethnic group, on its own, is unlikely to instigate a large and destabilizing popular threat.

There are also *unaligned* groups. Their level of expected resources in the future from the current leader relative to a viable replacement is uncertain or in between that of aligned and misaligned groups. These groups are unlikely to be dissatisfied enough with the regime to launch their own popular threat, but threats from elsewhere are more likely to spread to the areas they inhabit than to aligned areas. In electoral regimes, unaligned groups are the country's swing voters. Whereas the votes of aligned and misaligned groups are locked in for the leader and opposition respectively, unaligned groups can provide critical electoral support to help the leader or an opposition candidate create a minimum-winning coalition.

A group's alignment affects how the leader attempts to govern it. Aligned groups will be co-opted; they will continue to support the leader at high levels and are unlikely to launch a popular threat as long as the leader continues to co-opt them. Misaligned groups are coerced. They are unwilling to be bought off by the leader because they expect to benefit should their in-group elite come to power. Unaligned groups can theoretically expect either strategy: the leader may try to co-opt them, judging that they will be more receptive to co-option than misaligned groups. Alternatively, the leader may coerce unaligned groups (Robinson and Torvik 2009), which may hesitate to fully trade their support for state resources since the leader can renege on his promises if he no longer needs their support or finds another unaligned group willing to be co-opted for less.

Bureaucratic Loyalty toward the Leader: Variation in Officers' Willingness to Comply

A bureaucrat's *loyalty* to the leader depends on her career prospects. Loyalty, in turn, affects a bureaucrat's willingness to comply with the leader's demands. All else being equal, bureaucrats prefer to materially gain from their position. The leader's most *loyal* bureaucrats are those who have a neopatrimonial relationship with him. More often than not, an organization's highest-ranking bureaucrats are considered the most loyal. Regardless of their group alignment with the leader, high-ranking bureaucrats are showered with resources or are allowed to use their position to predate significantly more than their lower-level counterparts. Senior bureaucrats can expect to do worse if the leader leaves office; a new leader is likely to dismiss his predecessor's high-level appointments because they are loyal to the old leader, and these bureaucrats are likely to be punished for carrying out the old leader's politicized actions.

But the vast majority of bureaucrats occupy lower-level positions, and their loyalty to the leader is more variable. This is in large part because they owe their position to the lobbying efforts of an incorporated elite rather than the leader himself. Yet the leader can still cultivate perceptions of favoritism with some lower-level bureaucrats. Specifically, lower-level bureaucrats from the leader's in-group expect some degree of favoritism in promotions to cushy, high-ranking posts for at least two reasons. First, to the extent that a leader believes bureaucrats from his own group are inherently loyal, there is a self-fulfilling cycle in which those bureaucrats will be promoted because of their group match with the leader. Second, lower-level bureaucrats who hail from the same group as the leader expect more favoritism through their incorporated political elites. The leader's in-group elites are often incorporated into the state in high numbers and have special access to the leader. Their incorporation is relatively stable, whereas rival elites are always at risk of being excluded. For these reasons, lower-level in-group bureaucrats expect to benefit from the leader staying in power, which gives them an incentive to comply with his orders.

Loyalty, like alignment, can also be placed on a spectrum. I expect the leader's most *disloyal* bureaucrats to be those who have the highest expected benefit from the leader losing office. An out-group, lower-level bureaucrat – which the majority of officers are likely to be when the agency is not packed – expects to fare better if her in-group elite unseats the current leader, because the new leader will instead privilege her group for promotions. Not all elites have a viable path to the presidency (or have uniform expectations about future incorporation by other political elites), however, and thus not all bureaucrats have equally misaligned incentives with the leader. Instead, lower-level bureaucrats whose in-group elite is a viable rival of the leader are likely to be the most disloyal to the current leader. They have a strong incentive to shirk from the leader's demands, and instead use their authority to increase their patron's chances of coming to power.

Bureaucratic Embeddedness within a Jurisdiction: Variation in Ability to Govern

Officers differ in their degree of *embeddedness* within a jurisdiction. Embeddedness matters because it affects the bureaucrat's ability, and at times willingness, to carry out the leader's orders.

Whether innate or learned, locally embedded bureaucrats are better able to carry out the leader's demands. The knowledge mechanism of local embeddedness suggests that bureaucrats who are members of the same in-group as locals, or who have been posted there for a long period, are best able to adapt central mandates to local conditions. The social mechanism of local embeddedness, however, suggests that bureaucrats' willingness to comply will depend on the nature of the task. Embedded bureaucrats are more willing to co-opt the area because they have a sense of obligation to residents and are emotionally vested in the area's development. Co-optation by an embedded bureaucrat is independent of her (dis)loyalty to the leader: she co-opts because she is an agent of the local area. But embedded bureaucrats are less willing to coerce precisely because they have social incentives to use their authority on behalf of, not against, locals.

2.5.3 Regime Type and the Relative Importance of Different Areas

The presence or absence of multiparty elections affects the leader's perception of where the most damaging popular threats will emerge. Autocrats consider aligned and misaligned areas to be more important for their survival than unaligned areas. Aligned groups are critical to maintaining power, as they provide the popular legitimacy and support necessary to sustain the regime. At the same time, an autocrat assumes that any popular threats will originate in misaligned areas. Misaligned groups are liable to be mobilized for collective action by their elites, or may be dissatisfied enough with the autocrat that they mobilize on their own.

The leader's calculus about the importance of different areas changes if he must contest in multiparty elections. In electoral regimes, the leader needs to build a minimum-winning coalition and therefore counts on his aligned groups to provide the core of his votes. But they might not have sufficient numbers to reelect the leader on their own. Indeed, in sub-Saharan Africa, the largest ethnic group only comprises a majority in 28 percent of countries (Fearon 2003). Determining the relative importance of misaligned versus unaligned areas in electoral regimes is less clear-cut. In some cases, a leader may perceive that misaligned groups are unlikely to vote for him absent large amounts of costly co-optation or coercion, and instead focus on unaligned areas. In others, the leader may perceive it to be easier to coerce misaligned areas to depress their turnout than to target unaligned areas. Whether a leader considers unaligned or misaligned areas more important is country-specific, and is likely to be affected by factors such as electoral rules, the relative size of groups, and the level of coercion the leader can realistically expect from security agencies.

In sum, regime type affects the relative importance of different areas. All leaders will consider their aligned areas to be important. Autocratic leaders consider misaligned areas important for regime stability, and electoral leaders will consider either, but not both, misaligned or unaligned areas to be important.

2.6 EMPIRICAL IMPLICATIONS OF THE THEORY

This section describes the theory's empirical implications for the hiring, posting, shuffling, and promotion of bureaucrats. Whereas hiring and promotion patterns are dictated by elite threats, posting and shuffling decisions are made in response to perceptions of the leader's popular threats, which change fundamentally between autocratic and electoral regimes. I split the hypotheses for posting and shuffling bureaucrats by regime type. I note that two aspects of the theory are case-specific: (1) whether the leader intends to co-opt or coerce unaligned groups and (2) whether the leader of an electoral regime believes misaligned or unaligned areas are more important for his political survival. I discuss predictions for these two aspects of the theory based on the Kenyan case.

2.6.1 Hiring and Promotion

I assume that higher ranks of an agency are populated by bureaucrats who have been promoted from lower ranks. This simplification means that the composition of lower- or entry-level positions is a function of hiring decisions and the composition of higher-level positions is a function of promotion decisions.

We should expect the composition of the state through hiring and promotion to reflect the leader's degree of elite incorporation. Countries with low levels of elite incorporation will have a packed state precisely because the leader does not need to solidify bonds with out-group elites. Countries in which the leader does incorporate elites will have a diverse state: the breakdown of the state by group will resemble the breakdown of elite incorporation. The empirical observations for posting and shuffling bureaucrats assume some degree of ethnic diversity in the state, as in the Kenyan case.

Promotion decisions are liable to be affected by other concerns as well because the center has better information about the current crop of bureaucrats than new recruits. Competence is likely to matter: to the extent that a leader cares about technocratic skill, he may seek to fill important high-ranking positions with competent (Brierley Forthcoming) or experienced individuals (Woldense 2018). In addition, Chapter 8 examines promotions in situations where monitoring is possible and the center has observed credible signals about a bureaucrat's loyalty toward the leader and compliance with politicized orders. During a period of (observable) political violence, bureaucrats can prove their loyalty to the president by carrying out very visible acts of political violence that benefit the leader or his supporters. In these contexts we should expect bureaucrats who acted loyally to be promoted. Their advancement, first, ensures compliance among high-ranking bureaucrats in the future – bureaucrats who advanced after acting loyally in the past are likely to act loyally in the future. And second, it incentivizes compliance with politicized orders among lower-level bureaucrats, as it shows that any bureaucrat, regardless of in-group identity, can be promoted.

2.6.2 Governance under Autocracy: Posting and Shuffling Patterns

Table 2.1 illustrates posting and shuffling strategies in an autocratic regime. Aligned areas are considered strategic. The leader must maintain support in these areas to retain some semblance of popular legitimacy. The autocrat will therefore disproportionately post loyal bureaucrats who can be expected to comply with his orders to these locations. Bureaucrats in aligned areas will be asked to co-opt residents. The leader

TABLE 2.1 *Predictions for Autocratic Regimes*

Alignment	Importance	Posting Strategy	Governance Strategy	Embeddedness Strategy
Aligned	High	Loyalists	Co-optation	High
Misaligned	High	Loyalists	Coercion	Low
Unaligned	Low	Others	Coercion	Low

will try to maximize co-optation by embedding bureaucrats. He will post bureaucrats who are members of the same group as residents and will refrain from shuffling bureaucrats posted in these jurisdictions. (An autocrat's most closely aligned areas will be those inhabited by his in-group. Therefore, the posting of loyal bureaucrats simultaneously allows for the posting of an innately embedded officer).

Misaligned areas are also strategic for the autocrat's survival because they are likely to launch a popular threat. The autocrat will therefore post loyal bureaucrats to these areas. Unlike aligned areas, however, the autocrat wants misaligned areas coerced. As such, the autocrat will refrain from posting loyal officers who are in-group members with the misaligned group, and he will frequently shuffle officers between these posts to deter the formation of social relationships that could reduce officers' willingness to coerce.

Unaligned areas are the least strategic under autocracy. Unaligned groups may sustain a popular threat launched by misaligned groups, but are unlikely to instigate one on their own. The autocrat will therefore be willing to assign officers with suspect loyalties – including bureaucrats hired to appease rival elites – to unaligned areas. The leader will manipulate the embeddedness of bureaucrats posted in unaligned areas based on whether co-optation or coercion is seen as more effective at preventing popular threats. Within Kenya's Provincial Administration, I expect unaligned areas to be coerced because these bureaucrats have a comparative advantage at coercion. As such, I expect low embeddedness for bureaucrats in unaligned areas.

I note that leaders are likely to use a double strategy of reducing embeddedness – posting non-co-ethnics and shuffling bureaucrats quickly – in areas they want to coerce when the state is not packed and they cannot guarantee coercion through neopatrimonial bonds with the leader. The lack of loyal officers is heightened because many of them will be assigned to aligned areas to ensure high levels of co-optation.

TABLE 2.2 *Predictions for Electoral Regimes*

Alignment	Importance	Posting Strategy	Governance Strategy	Embeddedness Strategy
Aligned	High	Loyalists	Co-optation	High
Misaligned	Low	Others	Coercion	Low
Unaligned	High	Loyalists	Coercion	Low

2.6.3 Governance under Electoral Regimes: Posting and Shuffling Patterns

Table 2.2 illustrates posting and shuffling strategies under electoral regimes. Similar to autocratic regimes, a leader who faces multiparty elections will consider aligned areas strategic and will govern them through co-optation. Posting and shuffling patterns in aligned areas will therefore resemble those under autocracy.

The relative importance of misaligned versus unaligned areas in electoral regimes is case-specific. In Kenya, unaligned areas are seen as valuable, while misaligned areas, according to President Moi's Permanent Secretary of Provincial Administration, are a "lost cause."[25] Since the leader only needs to create a minimum-winning coalition, he can therefore write off misaligned areas. The theory thus expects leaders to post officers with questionable loyalty to misaligned areas. Despite their lower strategic value, the leader would still prefer these areas to be coerced. The leader will ensure that bureaucrats in misaligned areas are unembedded – that they are not co-ethnics of residents and are shuffled frequently.

Given the importance of unaligned groups to winning an upcoming election in the Kenyan case, the leader considers unaligned areas to be strategic, and will send loyal bureaucrats to these locations. And given the Provincial Administration's comparative advantage in coercion, especially during electoral campaigns, we should expect bureaucrats in unaligned areas to exhibit low levels of bureaucratic embeddedness. As under autocracy, we should expect to see this double strategy of posting non-co-ethnics and shuffling them quickly in areas that the leader wants to coerce. Not all officers are loyal to the leader. Instead, the leader will attempt to prevent shirking by reducing the social bonds that the officer shares with local residents.

[25] Interview with former Permanent Secretary of Provincial Administration, July 1, 2012, Nairobi, Kenya.

In Section 2.6, I lay out a theory about how leaders manage bureaucrats to prevent elite and popular threats. Here, I extend the theory in several directions. I briefly examine countries in which strategically valuable areas are determined by other criteria and the management of bureaucracies that do not report to the leader.

2.7.1 Political Value Along Different Dimensions

I discuss management of the state with regards to a leader's politically valuable areas. However, areas that seem less politically valuable may in fact be strategically important in other ways. For instance, urban areas may be considered strategic because of their political significance or the decreased costs of collective action (Bates 1981; Wallace 2014; Thomson et al. 2019). Other areas of high economic value – such as those with high levels of natural resources, important cash crops, or vital industries – may also be considered strategic regardless of regime type and the area's political alignment.

My theory can be modified to take other valuable areas into account as long as we have a prior about where these areas are, and whether the leader intends to govern them through co-optation or coercion. Previous studies have indeed found that areas with economic extraction potential are governed in an attempt to maximize officer compliance. For example, Belgian rubber companies purposefully recruited African "sentries" from outside a concession area to coercively enforce rubber quotas (Harms 1974; Lowes and Montero 2016). Similarly in Namibia, the German colonial government staffed police stations in economically important areas with "young and fresh recruits" who could devote more attention to their job, instead of deploying men with families (De Juan, Krautwald, and Pierskalla 2017).

2.7.2 Bureaucracies Headed by Other Elites

The theory examines how a country's leader manages the state in order to preempt elite and popular threats. Yet there are two situations in which a country's leader may not be at the helm of every state bureaucracy. First, and as I argue in Section 2.5, a leader willingly incorporates rival elites into the state by making a rival the head of an important ministry (Arriola 2009). These ministries manage their own street-level bureaucrats.[26] Second, in federal countries, sub-national governors are in charge of federal bureaucracies within their unit.

Either way, one can adapt the contours of the theory to the "leader" of the state bureaucracy in question. A rival elite at the helm of a national ministry is likely to hire and promote bureaucrats with an eye toward solidifying her alliances with other elites, and can be expected to manage bureaucrats in a way that aligns subnational areas with herself (as opposed to the leader). Similarly, federal-level elites will hire and manage bureaucrats in an attempt to balance horizontal and vertical elite threats alongside their popular threats. In the Conclusion, I apply the logic of the theory to China and Russia, two federal countries.

2.8 SUMMARY

The state can prove the most powerful tool in a leader's arsenal (Slater and Fenner 2011). However, wielding the state for political survival requires that the leader rely on bureaucrats to carry out his most politicized orders. This chapter has laid out a theory of how a central leader manages bureaucrats in a way that seeks to maximize their compliance. A leader will decide *who* should staff the state to address pressing elite threats, and how to *post and shuffle* bureaucrats in an effort to temper popular threats. The rest of the book examines this theory in Kenya.

---

[26] An alternative explanation of the management patterns I find in Kenya may be that bureaucrats are managed to stave off threats against important elites. I find little quantitative support for this explanation in Chapters 5–8.

3

The Origins of the Kenyan State

3.1 INTRODUCTION

This book examines a leader's management of bureaucrats to temper elite and popular threats by going inside the Kenyan state for the first five decades after independence. Before beginning the empirical analyses, I provide necessary background information on Kenya.

Three factors have shaped the elite and popular threats against Kenyan leaders: the country's ethnic cleavages, the distribution of resources and especially land (the policy issue that has caused the most tension between ethnic groups), and formal bureaucratic institutions. The threats to each president have largely emerged from outside his own ethnic group, from groups who are incensed about land politics. In response, presidents have relied on the state to ward off threats to their rule.

This chapter explores the overlapping connections between ethnicity, land conflict, and policy administration. I first provide a brief overview of the country's colonial era, as all three factors can trace their politicization to this period. Second, I present background information on Kenya's administrative and political institutions after independence. In these first two sections, I focus on the Provincial Administration – the country's executive bureaucracy in charge of security, administration, and development – which is analyzed in the empirical chapters that follow. I describe the agency's emergence and expansion during colonization, as well as formal trends in its basic management after independence. Third, I outline the incentives of officers within the Provincial Administration to inform discussions of their behavior in subsequent empirical chapters.

3.2 COLONIAL KENYA: LINKING ETHNICITY, LAND, ADMINISTRATION, AND CONFLICT

British colonialism linked ethnicity, land conflict, and policy adminis-tration in Kenya. Colonization entailed the forced, state-led relocation of indigenous Africans to small, outlying areas reserved solely for their ethnic group. Colonialism therefore formally reshaped the perceived boundaries of ethnic "homelands" and made previously inconsequential differences in identity salient for territory. The colonial regime relied on the Provincial Administration to deal with the popular threats that emerged from these ethnicized land struggles, including the anticolonial *Mau Mau* Rebellion. By independence, the Provincial Administration had grown so large in size and scope that it was the clear choice for social control by subsequent postindependence presidents.

3.2.1 Colonization, Ethnicity, and Land

The British established the East African Protectorate in 1895 and officially made Kenya a colony by 1920. Administratively, the colony was divided into provinces, with lower-level units cascading below them (Table 3.1 illustrates the colony's administrative structure). The colonial government began to dole out large tracts of the most fertile land in Central and Rift Valley Provinces to European settlers with little regard for the indigenous Kenyans who had occupied that land (Kanogo 1987; Okoth-Ogendo 1991; Kanyinga 2000b). Indigenous Kenyans were legally prohibited from owning land in these "White Highlands." Kenyans were instead relegated to their specific ethnic group's "Native Reserves," land set aside for each of the colony's forty-plus ethnic groups on a fraction of their historic homeland.[1]

As they did in other colonies around the world, the British colonial administration demarcated the reserves, and thus sub-national units, along perceived ethnic boundaries to reduce unnecessary ethnic tension and improve the ability of local administrative and social elites to maintain order (Mamdani 1996). Native Reserves largely fell within individual districts (one tier below administrative provinces, as seen in Table 3.1). Africans' movements between reserves and districts were

---

[1] Some of the country's larger ethnic groups had multiple reserves. Some of the colony's smaller ethnic groups were not large enough to warrant their own reserve. They were administered with other neighboring groups.

TABLE 3.1 *Kenya's Administrative Structure*

Unit	Administrator
Province	Provincial Commissioner (PC)
District	District Commissioner (DC)
Division	Division Officer (DO)
Location	Chief
Sub-Location	Assistant (or Sub-) Chief

This table lists Kenya's administrative units in order of descending size and the provincial administrator for that unit. The positions above the dotted line are considered "trained officers." They are the main focus of this book because they can serve in almost any jurisdiction across the country.

restricted through the use of the *kipande* (identification card), which further homogenized units by limiting migration, and as Karuti Kanyinga (2000b, 38) explains, "set the stage for the construction of ethnic identities and ... for, administratively, relating ethnic identities to the control of land."[2] In this way, the British administered Kenya by explicitly linking ethnicity and land, and politicizing the link between the two.

Arguably, the relegation of Kenyans to Native Reserves most directly affected the country's plurality ethnic group – the Kikuyu – who continue to comprise about 20 percent of the population. The fertile land west of Mount Kenya that the Kikuyu ethnic group historically farmed was largely incorporated into Central Province during colonization and became a large portion of the White Highlands.

Demand for land among this ethnic group grew during colonization. The group's population grew from about 1 million in 1948 to 1.6 million by 1962 without any real increase in the size of their reserves.[3] This population growth relegated many Kikuyu farmers to smaller and smaller plots of land within their reserves. Average landholdings fell from 8.1 acres in 1931 to 6.7 acres a decade later, with population density in some

[2] The Native Reserve system also homogenized units through the assimilation of migrants. Many in overcrowded reserves were allowed to migrate to less crowded reserves so long as they officially adopted their host community's ethnic identity (Parsons 2012). This practice helped maintain the fiction of tribes as primordial identities that allowed for the introduction of the Native Reserve system in the first place (Parsons 2011).

[3] There are no accurate estimates of the population of each ethnic group prior to 1948, though the colony as a whole grew from 2.8 million in 1921 (Colony & Protectorate of Kenya Annual Report, 1921) to 8 million by 1962 (1962 Census).

parts of Central Province increasing from an already dense 463 per square mile to 542 per square mile during this time (Anderson 2005a). Many found it financially impossible to continue farming their own land. By 1950 around 25 percent of this group were working as "squatters," or tenant farmers without formal title deed, on European land.[4] Not all Kikuyu farmers were this land poor, however. A small minority of affluent Kikuyus bought large tracts of land within the reserves. Wealthy Kikuyu reinvested their gains into buying more land and educating their children, further widening the inequality gap within the community (Njonjo 1977; Throup 1987; Branch 2009).

The Kikuyu land issue also affected neighboring areas – and the ethnic groups that lived there. As the landed Kikuyu elite "grabbed" more of the group's reserves, more and more poorer members of this group were forced to squat for white farmers in neighboring Rift Valley Province (Kanogo 1987; Kershaw 1997). Rift Valley is considered the ancestral homeland of various pastoralist ethnic groups, but white settlers there preferred to recruit Kikuyu squatters because of their farming (as opposed to pastoral) traditions. On the eve of independence around 40 percent of the Kikuyu ethnic group lived outside their native reserves; they comprised 27 percent of the population of Rift Valley in 1962.[5]

The colonial regime came to rely heavily on the country's territorial administrative bureaucracy – the Provincial Administration – to maintain control over the colony amid unrest by the indigenous population.

3.2.2 Governing Colonial Kenya: The Birth of the Provincial Administration

The Provincial Administration was the colonial regime's main organ of security, administration, and development. Colonial power officially originated in London, but the colony's governor had effective control, which was executed by the Provincial Administration. The Provincial Administration had sweeping powers and a broad mandate that spanned from maintaining law and order to coordinating development, including oversight of other colonial bureaucracies. The colonial regime gave it such a broad mandate for two reasons.[6] First, security and development were

---

[4] 1962 Census.
[5] Ibid
[6] For other prefectural administration systems, see Fesler (1965), Smith (1967), and De Juan, Krautwald, and Pierskalla (2017).

considered two sides of the same coin. Local development promised to reduce hostility against the colonial regime, so it was a crucial component of maintaining order. Second, vesting that much authority in a single agency was cheap and practical. Consolidating administration into one body was cost effective. Moreover, the time lags involved in communicating orders to and from London made it necessary to give officers executive authority in their jurisdictions to respond to fast-moving situations (Berman 1992). Although technology has improved since the colonial era, officers still govern without continuous, direct oversight from the center as it is more efficient.

What, specifically, did the colonial Provincial Administration do? It carried out nearly all necessary administrative tasks. For instance, officers enforced the *kipande* system and collected colonial taxes. They helped regulate farm labor and forcibly recruited men to serve for the British effort during both world wars (Savage and Munro 1966). Administrators allocated the colonial government's resources, disseminated information about and oversaw the implementation of new agricultural programs, coordinated development policy between local stakeholders, and helped determine where to build new infrastructure projects. They also adjudicated land disputes both among indigenous Kenyans and between Kenyans and white settlers. After elections were introduced to the colony, the Provincial Administration approved candidacy papers, supervised campaigns, determined voter eligibility, and tabulated the results. It is no wonder that colonial administrators referred to themselves as "Johnny on the spot."[7]

The Crown created other service bureaucracies to help govern the colony, but they were all subservient to the Provincial Administration: "while agricultural officers, veterinary officers and those technical officers concerned with economic development of the district had their role to play, it was the [Provincial] Administration with whom the final responsibility lay for development (Gertzel, 1970, 26)."[8] And because the colony tried to cut costs by understaffing the state, bureaucrats in the Provincial Administration were expected to take on the mandates of vacant positions within other bureaucracies across the jurisdiction. One colonial administrator warned his successor, "You are the local [council]

---

[7] Interview with colonial DO, July 13, 2017, Nairobi, Kenya.

[8] Gertzel (1970) describes Kenya in the run-up to and soon after independence. This conflation of regimes is not a problem because the Provincial Administration's formal duties after independence were the same as in the colonial era, as I describe in this chapter.

authority" because he did not expect those positions to be filled by the time he left his station.[9]

Similarly, even though numerous colonial coercive organs helped maintain law and order, British colonial governors demanded that the Provincial Administration coordinate these other bodies. These included local policing units (the Tribal Police and Home Guard), which were confined to individual Native Reserves, as well as the army and the paramilitary (the General Service Unit, GSU), which had countrywide jurisdiction.

The colonial Provincial Administration's hierarchy mapped onto the colony's administrative structure. The colony was run as a centralized, unitary state with five administrative tiers. The provinces were similar to U.S. states, districts to U.S. counties (within states), divisions to towns, and locations to wards, sub-locations to census tracts. Each tier had, and continues to have, its own administrator who served as the unit's executive (see Table 3.1). "Trained" officers – Provincial Commissioners (PCs), District Commissioners (DCs), and District Officers (DOs) – were initially British bureaucrats. DCs and DOs had similar powers as their PC. They were simply in charge of smaller jurisdictions and beneath the PC (and for DOs, beneath the DC) in the chain of command. Though this book focuses primarily on these trained officers, I note that Chiefs and Assistant (or Sub-) Chiefs, the most local administrators, served a wholly bureaucratic function and were most comparable to local-level, African state administrators in other colonies. Chiefs and Assistant Chiefs had to be from the local jurisdiction in which they served. They were never rotated, to ensure they had the local context that trained officers lacked. DOs had around a dozen Chiefs and Assistant Chiefs in their jurisdiction, and PCs could have upwards of a hundred.

Trained officers were so called because they received intense training in administration, security logistics, and development to equip them to implement colonial policy in all types of areas. Local knowledge was not considered as important. Indeed, by 1962, only forty of these officers had some fluency in a Kenyan language.[10] Officers were promoted according to rational-legal criteria after the introduction of colonial civil service reforms in the 1930s (Xu 2018). Promotion depended on practical experience, one's tenure within the organization, and the number and variety of posts held. Trained officers were compensated well. As of 1962,

---

9 1959 Handing Over Notes, Kapsabet (Nandi) District, Kenya National Archives, Nairobi.
10 1962 Staff List of the Colony and Protectorate of Kenya.

top-level PCs officers earned a base salary of £3,500, equivalent to about $95,000 today and much more than the average British salary of £800 at the time (~ $22,000 today). Lower-level DOs still earned a sizable £2,175 (~ $60,000 today). Moreover, all officers got an "overseas addition" of £700–1,000 per year (~ $19,000–$27,000 today) and a personal allowance of £345 (~ $ 9,500 today).[11]

The Africanization of the Provincial Administration began in 1947. This process initially involved educated Kenyans working as aides to trained (British) Provincial Administration bureaucrats. But in 1962, on the eve of independence, nearly 30 percent of DOs were Kenyan.[12]

3.2.3 Growth of the Provincial Administration during the *Mau Mau* Rebellion

Demand for land among Kikuyu squatters sparked a violent insurgency that threatened the colonial regime and led to the growth in the size and scope of the Provincial Administration, which made it Kenyan presidents' institution of choice to put down popular threats after independence.

The *Mau Mau* Rebellion (1952–1960) began as an anticolonial rebellion in which rebels promised their supporters *ithaka na wiathi* ("land and freedom").[13] The colonial regime officially called the rebellion "The Emergency," reflecting the state of emergency that was declared in Kenya during those years. The conflict morphed into a Kikuyu civil war fought along class lines, with landless squatters who supported the rebels on one side and landed "loyalists" who backed the colonial regime on the other. An estimated 30,000 members of the Kikuyu ethnic group in and around Central Province aided the rebels in some capacity, while the British recruited more than 60,000 Kikuyu loyalists to aid the colonial regime. Between 25,000 (Branch 2009) and 50,000 (Blacker 2007) Kenyans, including 1,500 loyalists, were killed.[14]

---

[11] Ibid. By comparison, Chiefs and Assistant Chiefs earned £60–110 per year (~ $1,600–$2,500 today).

[12] 1962 Staff List.

[13] *Mau Mau* was largely a Kikuyu rebellion, though some members of the Embu and Meru ethnic groups – who comprised the other third of colonial Central Province, and resided to the south and east of Mount Kenya, respectively – participated in smaller aggregate numbers.

[14] Elkins (2005) suggests as many as 300,000 were killed during *Mau Mau*, though these figures have been disputed, especially by Blacker (2007).

The Provincial Administration's scope of duties grew as it led the fight against *Mau Mau*. It increased its use of low-intensity coercion, especially in areas with substantial rebel populations. The Provincial Administration expanded its intelligence network to find men who had "oathed" their loyalty to *Mau Mau* or were rebel sympathizers. As many as 25 percent of Kikuyu men were detained at some point during the Emergency (Branch 2009). The Provincial Administration used its authority to reallocate land from suspected rebels or sympathizers to loyalists. The agency's authority over the *kipande* system and interdistrict movement was used to clamp down on members of the Kikuyu ethnic group in particular. One DC explained in 1957 that the movement of Kikuyus "is still subject to the Emergency Regulations and I have tightened up on this to a considerable extent. I feel that one should be jealous over the issue of passes and severe in cases where the regulations have been infringed."[15] His successor noted, "all [Kikuyu] should be known to the Police, whom I have personally told to keep a register ... Any nonsense from any [of them] results in his removal to Eldoret, whence he disappears."[16]

In a preview of how postindependence elected leaders would later use the Provincial Administration, bureaucrats in this organization repurposed their formal mandate to oversee electoral competition to prevent anticolonial candidates from winning. It enforced a ban on all political organizations within Central Province and against cross-district political organizations across the rest of the colony during the Emergency. When political organizations were not convincingly supportive of the colonial regime, the Provincial Administration severely limited their actions by, for instance, restricting fundraising efforts and refusing to grant meeting permits (Branch and Cheeseman 2006). The Provincial Administration also tilted elections away from perceived *Mau Mau* sympathizers and Kikuyu candidates in general through voter registration. Only individuals with sufficient wealth or landholdings were allowed to register to vote, two factors that strongly signaled loyalty to the colonial regime. Moreover, this loyalty test was made explicit in Central Province – voters were only registered after the DC affirmed their loyalty. The loyalty provision was applied so stringently that only 7.4 percent of the adult population was registered to vote in Central Province, compared with about 30 percent across the country (Branch 2009).

[15] 1957 Handing Over Notes, Kapsabet (Nandi) District, Kenya National Archives, Nairobi. This report originally referred to the Kikuyu, Embu, and Meru (see Footnote 13).
[16] Ibid.

Further, bureaucrats in Kikuyu areas were allocated special powers to violently repress locals to stop this popular threat from spreading. Officers gained the authority to detain residents without probable cause, force villagization and labor, lead military battalions against rebels, and shoot to kill Africans in restricted areas (Anderson 2005b; Elkins 2005).

The growth in the scope of the Provincial Administration's authority led to a surge in its resources and authority; field officers had reason to request increases in office staff and budgets.[17] In 1954 the DC of Kitui District, which bordered Central Province, demanded an increase in the number of administrators and the security units they oversaw by arguing that they were the sole defense against *Mau Mau* and that "[s]ecurity in the district, administratively, is run on a shoe string":

the level of effective safari [scouting] work has fallen way below the danger mark. Contact with the people is being lost, and with the Kikuyu reserves as an example I cannot think of any more potentially dangerous trend than that could develop ... I reiterate that delay [in increasing the district's staff] is in my opinion danger- ous ... without [more] staff, in the long run, it will become impossible. The alter- native to success is unpleasant to think upon ... if my requirements seem excessive, which they are not, let them be weighed against the security of the future not of this Kamba Reserve alone.[18]

The PC of Rift Valley in 1954, the largest site of *Mau Mau* activity outside Central Province, similarly wrote to headquarters in Nairobi to request more office staff – including revenue officers, foremen, and stenographers – "owing to the fact that the Emergency takes up 80% of [the] time" of trained officers who should not be expected to do office work on top of their field work.[19]

The number of (trained) officers in the Provincial Administration increased from 180 in 1951 (Berman 1992) to 433 in 1962.[20] By 1961, Central Province had more than 300 administrators, including 65 trained officers – or 1 administrator for every 7,000 people.[21] This ratio was significantly higher than that of other African colonies at the time, including French West Africa (1:27,000), Congo (1:35,000), and Nigeria (1:54,000) (Crowder 1970; Kirk-Greene 1980). Security staff

---

[17] Throup (1987) and Berman (1992) argue that elites within the Provincial Administration successfully succeeded in creating the "myth of *Mau Mau*" and overestimated the *Mau Mau* threat in order to justify this expansion.

[18] DC Kitui to PC Southern, July 20, 1954, BB/1/142, Kenya National Archives, Nairobi.

[19] Rift Valley PC to Chief Native Commissioner, March 9, 1954, BB/1/142, Kenya National Archives, Nairobi.

[20] 1962 Staff List.

[21] 1961 Central Province Annual Report.

were significantly augmented during this time as well. By 1961, provincial administrators in Kikuyu-majority districts in Central Province and Rift Valley oversaw some 130 GSU officers and 2,500 police officers.[22] Daniel Branch (2009, 165) summarizes the growth in the organization's size and scope due to the Emergency, claiming that "[a]t no other time in the past had district or provincial commissioners' effective control over law and order within their territorial boundaries been so important."

Two related implications of the growth of the Provincial Administration lasted long after *Mau Mau*. First, the agency refused to give up its newfound resources and authorities after *Mau Mau* was put down: it "fiercely protected its rediscovered importance, successfully fending off any suggestion of significant reform or devolution of powers to decolonization" (Branch, 2009, 165). Second, the country's first president, Jomo Kenyatta (who himself had been imprisoned for almost a decade by the Provincial Administration during the Emergency), turned to the same institution for social control when he took office, since it had proven itself able to temper popular threats.

3.3 THE POSTINDEPENDENCE LANDSCAPE

The Provincial Administration was the country's primary organ of social control at the time of independence. It continued performing many of the same functions as during the colonial era. This section outlines elements of Kenya's postindependence landscape to set the scene for the Provincial Administration's utility. I begin with Kenya's formal administrative institutions. Second, I provide an overview of how this bureaucracy has been run since independence. I describe the formal mandates of its bureaucrats, as well as the *de jure* criteria for hiring, posting, shuffling, and promoting officers, in order to identify politicized deviations in future chapters. Third, I briefly discuss the country's political institutions to introduce the political players with whom administrators interact.

3.3.1 Kenya's Formal Administrative Institutions

Kenya initially adopted a federal, or *majimbo* (meaning "region" in Swahili), state structure upon independence. In this setup, bureaucrats were expected to serve their respective provincial (or regional) assemblies

---

[22] Calculated from data in Vanden Eynde, Kuhn, and Moradi (2017). I thank the authors for sharing their data.

Kenyan Provinces and Five Largest Ethnic Groups

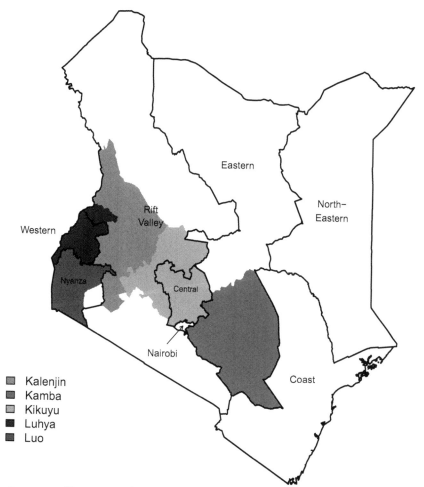

FIGURE 3.1 Kenyan provinces in the postcolonial period. The shaded areas indicate districts in which each of Kenya's five largest ethnic groups comprise a majority.

rather than the president. But by 1964, and as I describe in Chapter 4, *majimboism* had been abolished and Kenya was governed as a unitary state. During the vast majority of the study period, policy was determined in the center, cascaded down the chain of command, and was implemented by administrators in their respective jurisdictions.

Figure 3.1 maps Kenya's postindependence provincial boundaries, which are largely similar to the colonial-era administrative (and Native

TABLE 3.2 *Ethnic Breakdown by Province*

Province	Largest Group	Percent (Province)(%)	Percent (Country)(%)
Central	Kikuyu	95.9	19.6
Coast	Mijikenda	54.7	4.5
Eastern	Kamba	54.5	10.9
Nairobi	Kikuyu	37.6	19.6
Northeastern	Ogaden	35.6	0.9
Nyanza	Luo	62.5	14.1
Rift Valley	Kalenjin[†]	51.0	11.6
Western	Luhya	88.0	13.5

† I aggregate the Kalenjin subgroups that were counted separately in the 1969 census. This table lists the country's postcolonial administrative provinces. It also indicates the largest ethnic group in each province and the group's provincial and national size. Ethnicity figures are from the 1969 census, the first census after the demarcation of Kenya's provinces.

Reserve) boundaries.[23] Figure 3.1 displays the administrative districts in which each of the country's five largest ethnic groups – the Kalenjin, Kamba, Kikuyu, Luhya, and Luo – comprised a majority of residents. These five groups together comprise almost 70 percent of the country's population.[24] Their homelands cover nearly all of the country's arable land, an important factor given that Kenya remains a largely agrarian nation.[25] Unsurprisingly, these five groups have dominated the postindependence political conversation. Table 3.2 details the ethnic breakdown of the country's eight postindependence provinces.

As before, Central Province continues to be considered the homeland of the Kikuyu ethnic group, who comprised almost 96 percent of the province's population by 1969. But two districts with Kikuyu majorities that are contiguous to Central Province – Laikipia and Nakuru – were placed within Rift Valley Province. This ethnic group has comprised roughly 20 percent of Rift Valley's population since independence. Rift Valley's "indigenous" pastoralist groups – the KAMATUSA, the

---

23 The changes are detailed in the 1962 *Report of the Regional Boundaries Commission.*
24 These figures are from the 1969 Census, the first census after independence.
25 While Nathan (2019) correctly points to the urban transition across much of sub-Saharan Africa, East Africa remains mostly rural.

KAlenjin, MAasai, TUrkana, and SAmburu – comprise about 60 percent of the province's population, the largest of which is the Kalenjin. The majority of Kenya's Luo population live on the shores of Lake Victoria, in Nyanza Province, though urban Nairobi and Mombasa have large Luo communities. The Luhya ethnic group comprises the vast majority of Western Province. Trans-Nzoia District in Rift Valley is also majority Luhya. And the Kamba ethnic group populates the lower half of Eastern Province, while the Embu and Meru ethnic groups – two groups that are closely related to the Kikuyu – reside in the part of Eastern Province that borders Mount Kenya.

3.3.2 The Provincial Administration after Independence

Kenya's Provincial Administration remains the country's executive bureaucracy and the bureaucracy most closely associated with the presidency. It is housed under the equivalent of an interior ministry. At the beginning of the study period it fell under the Ministry of Home Affairs, but by the end of the study period it had been renamed the Ministry of State for Provincial Administration and Internal Security.[26] The ministry's official headquarters is in Harambee House in Nairobi, but each provincial and district capital houses its own headquarters. The interior ministry is one of the select few that is part of the "Office of the President" that meets regularly with the president.

The Provincial Administration is structured as it was during the colonial period (see Table 3.1). Each administrative unit is staffed by the officer of its associated tier (e.g., each province is staffed by one PC, each division by one DO). Each provincial and district headquarters can employ up to a dozen additional trained officers to help with office work. It has always been one of the country's largest coercive organs, growing

---

[26] Since the promulgation of the 2010 constitution, the Provincial Administration and its ministry have seen numerous superficial changes. It is now called the National Administration, but its inner workings remain relatively unchanged. Except for slight changes in position titles, officer positions today are nearly identical to what they were before 2010. The National Administration has also retained many of the same functions as under the old constitution. The largest organizational difference is that it now has a position between the PC and DC, the Regional Commissioner (RC). The jurisdictions of RCs are similar to those of DCs before the proliferation of administrative districts from 1992–2009. I use the terminology from the pre-2010 era, as the majority of the study period occurred before then.

from 400 trained officers (PCs, DCs, DOs) at independence to approximately 1,200 by 2012.[27]

The Provincial Administration has retained many of the same duties it carried out during the colonial period. First, provincial administrators remain fundamental for maintaining law and order. Officers are expected to catch local criminals, stop illegal activity, and monitor seditious activity. They have wide latitude to implement their preferred course of action within their jurisdiction, except for matters that the center is aware of and for which explicit instructions are given. Officers run security committees that bring together lower-level officers, informants, and local elites to address pressing security issues. The PC's version is termed the Provincial Security and Intelligence Committee (PSIC), and parallel security committees are replicated at the district (DSIC) and division (sub-DSIC) levels. Lower-tiered committees report their most important findings up the chain of command, but have executive authority over certain local matters such as the power to forcibly relocate people from land that is owned by others.[28] Further, Provincial Administration officers all have a deployment of Administrative Police (AP) officers to help them maintain law and order. By 2012, an administrator working in the headquarters of Rift Valley claimed that each DO averaged thirty-four APs in their command. In effect, this means that a PC has thousands of APs at their command, since APs can be called upon by their officer's senior in the Provincial Administration.[29]

The nature of an officer's security work depends on her jurisdiction. For example, in pastoralist areas, provincial administrators are expected to curtail cattle rustling between warring ethnic groups, subgroups, or clans, as explained in this 2008 excerpt from the Provincial Administration's internal newsletter, *The Administrator*:

> The Pokot community has occasionally raided the Tugen community from Baringo District stealing their livestock and injuring their people ... Among the roles that the Provincial Administration plays in reconciliation has been but not limited to: Bringing the communities together through public barazas [community meetings] which draw together elders and opinion leaders from the two communities, Voluntary disarmament whereby the communities have been

---

[27] These figures do not include Chiefs and Assistant Chiefs, who are managed differently. Including these lower-level officers increases the size of the Provincial Administration to about 15,000 by 2012. "Ethnic Diversity and Audit of the Civil Service," National Cohesion and Integration Commission, 2012.

[28] Kenya Truth and Commission (2013, 188, 201–203).

[29] Interview with then DO, January 30, 2012, Nakuru, Kenya.

encouraged to surrender illegal firearms in their possession voluntarily and many have complied, Coordinating all the peace stakeholders in both communities and transmitting information in liaison with the DSICs and sub-DSICs, Arbitration and reconciliation – which has involved bringing the warring parties together to ventilate on the sources of conflict and durable solutions ...[30]

In border districts, officers are expected to "be vigilant [against smuggling]. You will also have to pay close attention to the Customs Officer at the border to make sure that duty is paid, for all the goods exported and imported out and into the country."[31] Provincial administrators in ethnically heterogeneous areas that are considered prone to violence are expected to lead sensitization campaigns and resolve ethnic grievances.[32] This task has become more important after multiple bouts of electoral violence since the country's return to multiparty elections. In recent years, officers have cracked down on illicit drug use and the brewing of *changa'a* (home-brewed spirits). A 2010 issue of *The Administrator* discussed these efforts in coastal Kilifi District, where the tourism industry has been associated with high levels of drug and substance abuse: "We have conducted several raids targeting illicit brews and drug peddlers in the district and have also pinpointed night clubs in the district that allow access to underage youths and raided them in order to deter the perpetuation of these vices."[33]

Second, Provincial Administration officials continue to play a large role in basic administration, as they did during the colonial era. They officially document births and deaths in their jurisdictions, and administer ID cards – the postindependence equivalent of the *kipande*.[34] Provincial Administration officers also sanction public assemblies by issuing (or denying) permits for local meetings and campaign rallies. Local branches of civil society organizations and political parties must register with the Provincial Administration before holding meetings or running programs. These bureaucrats also solve local disputes between warring factions, businesses, or ethnic groups. Multiple provincial administrators

---

[30] "Building Architecture for Peace," *The Administrator*, July–September 2008, p. 10.
[31] "Minutes of Busia DC's Meeting with DOs, Chiefs, and Assistant Chiefs," March 19, 1991, DB/1/37, Western Provincial Archives, Kakamega, Kenya.
[32] Interview with then PC, October 31, 2011, Nakuru, Kenya.
[33] "Drug Abuse and Child Prostitution," *The Administrator*, June–October 2010, p. 27.
[34] The distribution of ID cards is especially important because these documents are necessary for a citizen to undertake any official, formal state activity, from transferring land to voting to entering government buildings. Since ID cards document individuals' ethnicity and birthplace, their issuance provides the state with a running ethnic census.

interviewed for this study described their persistent role in resolving intrafamilial disputes, at times even providing marriage counseling for couples in the jurisdiction.

Land administration remains one of the organization's most important roles. In the immediate postindependence years, when successive governments were allocating former Crown- or settler-owned land, administrators helped identify which applicants would get resettled, determine who was eligible for special financing terms, and evict illegal squatters who did not have formal claims over land. Today, these bureaucrats continue to enforce land claims, oversee land titling, and help resolve local boundary disputes.

Third, the Provincial Administration is deeply involved in local development. Just as during the colonial era, officers are expected to coordinate local development projects within their jurisdiction. Bureaucrats are considered so crucial to development that, for much of the study period, they had the sole authority to approve monetary disbursements from the central government. When money is needed for a project, Provincial Administration officers organize a *harambee* (meaning "let's all pull together"), in which community members and local elites contribute funds. After a project has been approved or the funds have been raised, officers choose local contractors and monitor its progress. Until 2003, DCs led development committees comprised of local political elites, business leaders, and government bureaucrats to allocate unit-wide funds distributed from the center. Since 2003, each Member of Parliament (MP) has received her own Constituency Development Fund (CDF)[35] with which she can allocate money to development projects within her constituency, but the relevant administrators continue to hold important seats on the allocation committee.[36]

Much of the development work carried out by provincial administrators involves upholding livelihood standards and sensitizing the population on important issues. In Coast Province, for instance, the Provincial Administration led a campaign to increase primary school enrollment rates through the following interventions:

---

35 See Harris (2016) and Harris and Posner (2019) on the CDF.
36 These bureaucrats still play a central role in development even after the adoption of the new constitution.

A register system whereby every chief acquires details about a drop out pupil, the name of the parent or guardian of such a pupil, class and reason for the drop-out, as well as recommended remedial action to be taken to ensure that such a pupil resumes classes ... Video hall raids to flush out pupils idling in such hideouts, Partnership with NGOs [nongovernmental organizations] and CBOs [community-based organizations] to promote health and sanitation standards in schools, Provision of school feeding programme by the Ministry of Education and other partners .... Enforcement of Anti-Drug and Substance Abuse including the Liquor Licensing Act to reduce incidences of Drug Abuse.[37]

While the mandates of other state bureaucracies overlap with that of the Provincial Administration, no other agency has nearly as comprehensive or varied a mandate, or is as important to the country's day-to-day administration. The Provincial Administration does not maintain law and order alone; it coordinates the country's other security agencies. In addition to the intertwined Administrative Police, Kenya's other internal security agencies are the Kenya Police and the GSU. The Kenya Police is the country's conventional police force, responsible for investigating crime, protecting life and property, and apprehending criminals. The GSU is the paramilitary branch of the Kenya Police that is called in for special operations. These organizations work closely with the Provincial Administration, and for much of Kenya's history were directed by the respective administrator in their jurisdiction.

The Provincial Administration coordinates the development activities of service, or line, ministries (e.g., Health, Education, Roads), as the example of primary school enrollment on the coast suggests. Each line ministry has field bureaucrats at the provincial and district levels to help carry out projects. Provincial Administration officials organize meetings for relevant subsets of the staff working in their jurisdiction between once a month to once a quarter in an attempt to connect bureaucrats from service ministries with local leaders, stakeholders, and political elites and to ensure that work is not replicated unnecessarily.[38] Once work has started, these bureaucrats oversee implementation to ensure the project adheres to central government standards.

De Jure *Management of the Provincial Administration*

Recruitment into the trained ranks of the Provincial Administration (PCs, DCs, DOs) has become highly competitive. Recruits for entry-level DO

---

[37] "Working in Partnership for the Benefit of Children's Education – Coast Province," *The Administrator*, July–September 2008, p. 23.
[38] Interview with then DC, February 16, 2012, Nyeri, Kenya.

positions must hold a college degree in a relevant field and pass a rigorous interview process. Many candidates meet these qualifications: by 2010, only an estimated 3–5 percent of qualified applicants were selected as DOs.[39] Chapter 4 describes how individuals have a much greater chance of being recruited if an elite lobbies on their behalf.

The Provincial Administration maintains strict advancement procedures for its officers. Promotion within one's rank – i.e., within the rank of a DO or DC – is linear. A new recruit must start as a DO Cadet, regardless of her neopatrimonial connections. Her potential promotion ladder is to become a DO3, DO2, DO1, and then a Senior DO. Advancements to a presidentially appointed position – a DC or a PC – are clearly subjective. But similar to promotions within one's rank, advancements are only possible after having achieved the necessary requisite position.[40] One can only be chosen to serve as a DC2 (the lowest DC rank) after having served as a Senior DO (the highest DO rank); one can only be promoted to PC (there are no ranks among PCs) after having served as a Senior DC (the highest DC rank). Officers cannot be demoted.

Certain informal norms regarding officer assignment are strongly followed. For instance, officers are not allowed to serve in their home jurisdiction. PCs do not serve in their home province, and DCs and DOs do not serve in their home district.[41] Elites within the Provincial Administration claim that this rule has been strictly upheld since at least Moi's presidency. In recent years, regime elites have rotated officials after three years for the majority of posts, and every two years for hardship posts in rural, far-flung areas.

The Permanent Secretary for Provincial Administration is formally in charge of managing the posting and shuffling of officers. He makes his decisions in close consultation with the president and other regime elites. PCs in particular have a large say over where DOs within their respective provinces get posted. There is a perception among officers that elite legislators can affect transfers as well. I control for this possibility in all

---

39 Interview with then DO, February 1, 2012, Nairobi.
40 The advancement criteria were necessarily lax in the independence era, when there were not enough qualified officers to fill the agency's highest positions. The country's first PCs was promoted straight from the ranks of DOs – the highest rank Africans had held during the colonial period.
41 All of the ethnicities that are well represented in the Provincial Administration are among the country's largest ethnic groups and comprise the ethnic majority in more than one district. This means that officers who are members of large ethnic groups, whose officers collectively comprise the majority of Provincial Administration officers, can still serve in a co-ethnic, if not home, district.

quantitative analyses, but do not find systematic evidence of this assertion. Once a transfer has been made, they have a few weeks to pack their belongings and report to their new post.

A small minority of Provincial Administration "desk" officers are stationed in Nairobi and work in the headquarters of other line ministries. They are expected to carry out basic administrative duties in their posted ministry, such as balancing district-level budgets and preparing material for Parliament. In theory, field officers and desk officers are interchangeable: They all receive the same training upon entering the Provincial Administration. But bureaucrats who have spent too much time in the ministries are unlikely to be deployed back to the field.

3.3.3 Kenyan Political Institutions

The country's political institutions changed little between its transition away from federalism in 1964 and the passage of the 2010 constitution. For the majority of the study period, the country had a unicameral national legislature. MPs were elected from single-member districts through plurality rules. From the country's return to multiparty elections through the 2007 election, presidents were chosen through a system that combined elements of an electoral college and plurality rules.

Administrative and political units do not have overlapping boundaries. Individual constituencies have always nested within larger administrative districts; however, each administrative district could be home to as many as a dozen constituencies. For the years in which I examine DOs (1992–2007), constituencies span multiple divisions (which are similar to U.S. municipalities). To demonstrate these relationships, Figure 3.2 shows how administrative and political units within Laikipia District nested circa 1997. The six DOs stationed in each of Laikipia's six divisions all reported directly to the Laikipia DC, Solomon Sirma Boit. And in turn, Boit reported directly to the Rift Valley PC, Mohamed Yusuf Haji. I do not map out location and sub-location boundaries, but for the sake of completeness, the twenty-five Chiefs all reported directly to their respective DO, and the fifty Assistant Chiefs reported to their respective Chief.

In 1997 Festus Mwangi Kiunjuri was elected MP in Laikipia East constituency. We can assume he held numerous rallies across his constituency in the run-up to that election. Each rally would have required a permit and approval from the respective DO for Central, Lamuria, or Mukogodo

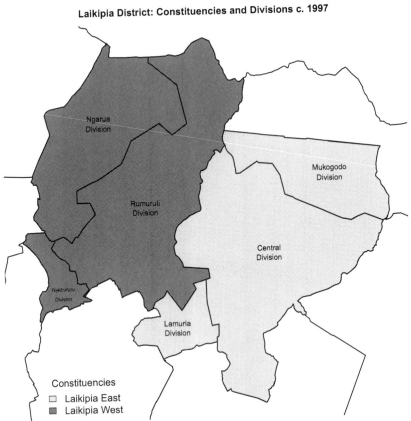

Laikipia District: Constituencies and Divisions c. 1997

FIGURE 3.2 Laikipia District administrative and political boundaries circa 1997.

divisions. For instance, if Kiunjuri had wanted to hold a rally in Central Division, he would have needed written approval from the DO of Central Division, J. Elung'ata. However, given the Provincial Administration's chain of command, all political rally approvals were forwarded to superior officers. In this case, Kiunjuri's request would have been decided by Elung'ata, but Boit and then Haji each had the authority to overturn Elung'ata's decision.

Kenya also had local political institutions during these years. Upon independence, the country was organized into numerous "county councils," which were renamed "local authorities" in the late 1990s.[42]

---

[42] Local authorities were designated based on their population, from densely populated "municipalities" to less populated "townships" and rural "counties."

The number of councils increased from around 40 during independence to 177 by 2012. County councils were expected to raise local taxes to provide local services in primary education, health care, and road maintenance.

Since the overlap between legislative constituencies and administrative units may affect the management of bureaucrats, I control for the presence of influential MPs. That said, it is unlikely that the center would have managed bureaucrats in the Provincial Administration with the primary goal of controlling Kenya's local-level political institutions. County councils and the subsequent local authorities were weak and have had little effect on national-level politics.[43] The vast majority of county councils were unable to carry out their basic responsibilities after independence, so Kenyatta scaled back their duties. Donors forced the country's second president, Daniel arap Moi, to rehabilitate local authorities in the 1990s. But local authorities lacked the capacity to carry out basic duties, and largely became vehicles through which local politicians distributed low-level patronage.

3.4 UNPACKING OFFICER INCENTIVES

The behavior of Provincial Administration bureaucrats is shaped by numerous motivations and concerns. This section elaborates on how two such motivations have become politicized. First, bureaucrats have a strong incentive to climb the ranks. Second, most bureaucrats have an intrinsic desire to improve citizens' livelihoods, and this concern grows stronger as the bureaucrat becomes more deeply embedded in her jurisdiction. Taken together, these discussions lay the groundwork for assessing how Kenyan presidents have manipulated bureaucratic *loyalty* and *embeddedness* to ensure compliance despite weak monitoring. Each of these motivations is discussed in turn.

There are additional motivations and concerns that affect bureaucratic behavior but are not inherently political or have not been politicized. The third part of this section discusses the concerns of this nature that were mentioned most frequently during my interviews – postings to far-flung areas and different posting preferences by gender.

---

[43] This is in part because the Provincial Administration was used to subjugate Kenya's local governments. See Davey (1971), Akivaga, Kulundu-Bitonye, and Opi (1985), and Burbidge (2019).

3.4.1 Officer Motivation to Climb the Ranks

Positions in the Provincial Administration come with many benefits, but higher positions receive more benefits. Understandably, then, officers want to climb the ranks. As later chapters will show, subsequent presidents have used this motivation to develop neopatrimonial relationships with some officers in an attempt to better elicit bureaucratic loyalty.

While all trained positions within the Provincial Administration are associated with significant prestige, higher positions are that much more respected. Provincial Administration officers are among the most prestigious in the entire Kenyan state precisely because they outrank other bureaucrats working in service ministries in their jurisdiction. Further, these officers have high visibility within their jurisdiction. The vast majority of citizens in rural areas know the name of their PC and DC. Further, some PCs, and even some DCs, have national-level name recognition. During some parts of the study period, these officers were as prominent as cabinet ministers.

In addition, though officers have historically been among the most well-compensated state employees, senior positions earn a higher formal salary and receive better benefits.[44] By 2003, the salary of the highest-ranking DOs was only 10–15 percent of the salary of PCs. Further, PCs and DCs receive free housing, a government vehicle, and in some cases a hosting account.[45] Officers also get bonuses for special tours or additional work, with compensation dependent on rank. For instance, in the wake of the 2007–2008 postelection violence, DOs received an additional 4,000 KSH (approximately $40) a day for helping internal displaced people; DCs received an additional 10,000 KSH (approximately $100) a day.[46]

Provincial Administration officers of all ranks are notorious for supplementing their official paycheck by using their position to predate, or "eat." Some of this predation is simply a misuse of government funds. For instance, one MP complained: "While some of [the DC's] trips to Nakuru may be official, others I believe are not and made to look official so that he can take advantage of free government resources, the vehicle with free petrol, the driver and escorts (APs); which is a misuse of government resources for personal gain or to satisfy his own interest ... at

---

44 The private sector was small for much of the study period, meaning that recent college graduates often preferred guaranteed salaries from the state to those outside the state.
45 DOs received some of these benefits during the early days of the republic.
46 Ministry of Internal Security Internal Memo, July 2, 2008, HT/1/90, Nyanza National Archives, Kisumu, Kenya.

government expense."[47] Other archival records suggest that bureaucrats used their authority to carry out vendettas against local enemies, including against individuals who had "stolen" the bureaucrat's significant other or did not show the officer due respect.[48] The biggest potential for predation involves using one's authority to procure valuable resources for oneself. This type of predation was possible across jurisdictions, given that bureaucrats have immense power that is shaped by the area's needs. According to an officer who served under the country's one-party regime:

Mombasa can be pretty good because of the port. And borders. Malaba with the Uganda border, Namanga with Tanzania, Logitotio in Turkana. Places like Northeastern were pretty good because you can hunt, hunt elephants and get tusks. ... Nairobi can be pretty good because of the plots. The officer is in charge of the land adjudication committee. And there could be plots in the slums. There are government lands awaiting allocation. He either allocates himself or allocates them to his favorites. The inner districts can be good for land as well. When land is going for sale, the officer begins to empower himself by owning property. Or takes a fee for transferring things ... you can be an officer and a business person.[49]

Yet levels of predation, and wealth, rise exponentially as officials rose through the ranks.[50] Consider this stark example of separate cases of predation by a DC and his DO and their respective punishments: one group of citizens complained about how their DC had "grabbed" 200 acres of land in an area meant to settle poorer local farmers on small (~ 5-acre) plots. The PC and his intelligence committee discovered that "the allocations were exaggerated" – he only grabbed 100 acres.[51] However, the same PC oversaw the investigation of petty cases of predation by lower-level DOs in his province. One DO shut down his wife's business because civilians complained to the PC that he improperly used government vehicles to take her to work and to transport merchandise to her store.[52]

---

[47] MP Isiolo to Permanent Secretary of Provincial Administration, February 18, 1992, BB/1/250, Kenya National Archives, Nairobi.

[48] See KA/6/18 - 20, Kenya National Archives, Nairobi.

[49] Interview with former DO, November 7, 2011, Nairobi.

[50] I noted clear differences in the levels of wealth between high-ranking PCs and DCs versus DOs during my interviews. Many of my interviews with DOs occurred over tea and *chapati* that I paid for at a local cafe. Many of the PCs and DCs I interviewed insisted we take lunch at expensive restaurants that they paid for; whereas DOs talked about their *shamba*, or farm, back in their home district, PCs and DCs talked about the various *shambas* they owned in multiple districts.

[51] Provincial Security Intelligence Officer (Central Province) to PC Central, May 7, 1985, VQ/1/133, Kenya National Archives, Nairobi.

[52] DC Kirinyaga to PC Central, October 7, 1986, VQ/1/133, Kenya National Archives, Nairobi.

Predation by senior officers (PCs and DCs) was permitted because these officers were considered among the most loyal in the state.[53] These officers comply with the vast majority of political orders from above, so their superiors look the other way when there is predation. Indeed, a former editor at *The Daily Nation*, Kenya's premier newspaper, estimated that long-serving PCs under Moi and Kibaki were worth at least $5 million USD each, "and that is a gross understatement." PC salaries topped out at around $800 USD per month in 2003. That PCs can amass so much wealth on a relatively humble formal salary is a testament to their ability to predate at high levels with the implicit approval of Harambee House. While many DOs used their authority to predate and were not reprimanded, the scale of their predation was nowhere near as large as that of their senior officers.

Bureaucrats also value rising through the ranks, and staying in the service longer to better position their postadministration careers. Indeed, many PCs and DCs launched political careers after their tenure in the Provincial Administration. For example, when I interviewed him, Peter Kiilu, a former PC under Moi, was serving as an MP from Makueni in Eastern Province. His position in the Provincial Administration gave him an electoral advantage nearly a decade before he even ran for office. While Kiilu never served in his home province, he continuously wrote to the Eastern PC and the Makueni DC to divert resources to his home area: "We [in Makueni] have so many stalled Government projects ... which seriously need priority in funding."[54] Kiilu claimed that his ability to steer resources to Makueni during his tenure in the Provincial Administration helped get him elected in 2007. Likewise, Mohamed Yusuf Haji was the most prominent provincial administrator from the Somali community under President Moi. Haji stepped down as PC of Rift Valley in 1997 after Moi nominated him as an MP (Parliament at the time reserved some seats for presidentially nominated MPs). He has remained an elected representative since then. Another DC I interviewed in 2011 discussed his political aspirations while he was still serving as an administrator. He eventually ran for an MP seat in his home constituency in 2017. Though he does not

---

53 As I show in Chapter 8, officers are promoted after showing loyalty to the president during rare instances when their actions are observable. And even those who are promoted due to their elite connections recognize the benefit of the incumbent staying in office.
54 Letter from PC Nyanza to DC Makueni, July 17, 1992, Folio BB/11/140, Kenya National Archives, Nairobi.

come from a wealthy family, he self-funded his $50,000 campaign. I find that (at least) four of Kenyatta's PCs sought elected office after serving in the Provincial Administration, as did three from Moi's autocratic regime, three from Moi's electoral regime, and at least two from Kibaki's.

Similarly, many PCs and DCs parlay their contacts and networks into private business. One DC I met in 2011, who had retired by the time I interviewed him again in 2017, told me about his new business venture. He consulted with some private firms to help them register with the government and helped others win government contracts. Business was steady, he claimed, because of his extensive knowledge of formal procurement policies and his wide network of administrators within the state. DOs can also use their position to launch a political career or successful business venture; however, it is easier for PCs and DCs to do so. High-ranking officers have a higher status, greater name recognition, deeper networks within the state, and are likely to have amassed more money during their tenure in office.

3.4.2 Public Spirit among Bureaucrats

Throughout the course of my field research, it became abundantly clear that officials who joined the Provincial Administration were deeply committed to helping Kenyans. While this was not their only motivation, it would be remiss to overlook the public spirit of those working in this agency.

For instance, one British officer who served in Central Province during the Emergency, arguably the period in which the Provincial Administration was the most violent towards Kenyans, recalled how he felt a social obligation to go beyond the coercive mandate of his office and instead use his authority to better the livelihoods of those he lived among:

> By [1956] I was building hospital wards in Nyeri General Hospital and odd jobs like putting water supplies in the villages because you had to do something. We had the money from the Emergency grants so this is where it went. And also, with the legislation you could say, 'right - you're doing bench terracing here.' And [the local residents] would do the bench terracing. Of course that was authoritarian you might say, those wicked colonial administrators ... But it was for their own good.[55]

---

[55] Interview with former DO, July 13, 2017, Nairobi.

A bureaucrat who served during Moi's more repressive years explained, "we didn't work for Moi. We work for government. You work with *wananchi* [the people] to solve their problems. We work for Kenya."[56]

This civic-mindedness to help residents increases with an officer's embeddedness in a station, as their willingness to help is driven by the social bonds that officers have or make with the local community. In Busia District, locals lamented the transfer of a DC who had served in the district for years: "We hope that this new gentlemen [sic] will be as genuinely committed to peace and total co-operation as their previous colleagues."[57] Many administrators described how they continue to visit former stations where they served for many years. Some even continue to donate to *harambee* projects out of a sense of social obligation. In addition, bureaucrats are more knowledgeable about what the area needs if they are more deeply embedded. One officer explained:

by people knowing you and you knowing the people its easier to do your work. You know how to solve these problems, you know virtually everybody. You've built your networks and institutions. You have chiefs and assistant chiefs and village elders and civil society and they are your friends. And you know the church leaders ... There are civil servants and you know all of them. It's easier on you when you have a small problem. If you want to sort out something, you know exactly who to involve. ... Now that you really know so much about the area, you have institutional memory.[58]

The officer was clear to note that he is better able to help out with development projects as well as maintaining security on behalf of all residents if he has been in a post for a few years: "the people no longer misinform you. When people deliberately lie to you so that they can make you behave in a manner favorable to them ... You know as much as they know. They can no longer misinform you."[59]

3.4.3 Nonpoliticized Concerns of Provincial Administrators

In Sections 3.4.1 and 3.4.2 I discussed two motivations of administrators – a desire to advance within the ranks (or to keep one's job if one is already in a high-ranking position) and public spirit. Future chapters will show how these motivations feed into the concepts of loyalty and

---

56　Interview with former DC, June 29, 2017, Nairobi.
57　Minutes of DDC Busia Meeting, March 19, 1991, DB/1/37, Western Provincial Archives, Kakamega.
58　Interview with former DC, July 15, 2017, Nakuru.
59　Ibid.

embeddedness, respectively, and the ways in which presidents manipulated these relationships to maximize social control. There are other concerns that also affect bureaucratic behavior and incentives but have not been politicized. In particular, the bureaucrats I interviewed expressed a strong preference for serving in urban areas. And bureaucrats of different genders had different preferences with regard to postings.

As with any field bureaucracy, officers tend to prefer some stations over others. By and large, officials in the Provincial Administration prefer positions in urban areas, in part because these areas have more and higher-quality services. Young and unmarried recruits prefer urban areas, where they have a better chance of meeting and dating other young, educated single people. And older, married recruits prefer urban areas for the sake of their spouse's job and the opportunity to enroll their children in good local schools.

For these same reasons, officials especially dislike posts in the country's arid north. This includes Northeastern Province (Garissa, Mandera, and Wajir districts) alongside the top halves of Eastern (Isiolo and Marsabit districts) and Rift Valley Provinces (Samburu and Turkana districts). Unlike other rural areas that are between population centers, the far reaches of the north are geographically remote and have significantly worse amenities than the rest of the country. For instance, a bus ticket from Mandera, in the topmost corner of Northeastern, to Nairobi costs the equivalent of $40 USD and can take two days. As recently as 2013, the Kenya National Highways Authority noted that the entire Northeastern Province had only twenty kilometers of paved road.[60] Northern districts consistently rank last in development, and the area has become a hotspot of terrorist activity. While the severity of the security and economic situation in the north means that even small improvements in governance outcomes are likely to be noticed by one's superiors and lead to promotions,[61] most of the bureaucrats interviewed for this study suggested a strong aversion to assignments in the arid north.

A potential concern is that this preference for urban areas may confound my empirical analysis. Bureaucrats who have connections with

---

[60] "Sorry State of Mandera-Garissa Road," *The Star*, June 27, 2013.
[61] One officer I interviewed attributed his recent presidential appointment to DC to having served well in Northeastern Province. Another officer claimed that the challenges he overcame during his time in Northeastern prepared him for the rest of his career. Still another talked about how his posting to the part of Garissa District that is home to Dadaab, Africa's largest refugee camp at the time, allowed him to hone his administrative skills.

political elites may lobby for urban posts. Or perhaps all officers, including those whom I code as being disloyal to a president because of ethnicity and rank, have a strong incentive to comply with politicized orders to avoid being sent to Turkana. Yet unlike agencies in which bureaucrats can languish in a remote post for decades, the Provincial Administration's formalized system of officer rotations protects them from serving too long in rural areas. Stints in hardship posts are formally limited to two years, and officers cannot be moved from one hardship post to another. Further, during much of the study period, DOs were required to serve in a hardship post before they were eligible to advance.

The one avenue in which this urban preference may affect my results is through gender bias. Because of the lack of amenities in rural areas, men administrators posted to these areas tend to live apart from their families during the week and travel home over the weekend. But because of gender norms about motherhood and spousal obligations, woman are expected to live with their families. Many women officers I spoke with tried to preempt a rural transfer by requesting a post at the headquarters in Nairobi or other urban centers. Those requests were overwhelmingly likely to be approved.[62]

I control for the possibility that women officers had different posting patterns than their men counterparts in the analyses for which I have gender data.[63] The small number of women in the Provincial Administration both confirms the presence of strong gender norms within this bureaucracy and alleviates concerns about the magnitude of this confounding. By 1990, only 25 of 574 positions (4 percent) were filled by women. The country's first woman DC was only appointed in 1996, and the first woman PC in 1999.[64] By 2012, women comprised only 232 of 1,186 officers (20 percent).

3.5 SUMMARY

This chapter introduced the Kenyan case. It opened by examining the interplay between ethnicity, land conflict, and policy administration.

---

[62] Interview with then Secretary of Provincial Administration, July 17, 2012, Nairobi; Interview with then DO, January 16, 2012, Nyeri.

[63] Controlling for gender also allows me to control for differences in posting assignments based on an area's perceived gender norms.

[64] According to a former Secretary of Provincial Administration, women were hired only on temporary contracts through the 1980s.

Each of these factors originated in the colonial era, and has persisted throughout the presidencies of each postindependence leader. The chapter then pivoted to the country's administrative and political institutions. The next chapter examines elite politics in Kenya, and how each of Kenya's first three presidents dealt with elite threats to their rule through incorporation. It then shows the ramifications of elite incorporation on the ethnic composition of the Provincial Administration.

4

Elite Incorporation and the Diversity of the State

4.1 INTRODUCTION

This chapter introduces the *elite* threats that Kenya's first three presidents faced and begins to trace the downstream implications of how each president addressed those threats on available strategies for confronting *popular* threats.

Kenyan presidents faced numerous elite threats that they tried to alleviate by incorporating elites into their regime. The goal of incorporation is to "purchase elite cooperation ... if not exactly support, and thus extend [the leader's] time in office" (Wright, Frantz, and Geddes 2015, 289).[1] Not all elites were incorporated, however, because not all of them were willing to be bought off. Presidents did not incorporate those who were genuinely unwilling to trade incorporation for acquiescence. This reluctance makes sense: it is not in the president's interest to empower an elite rival with state resources if the opponent is intent on using those resources against him.

Patterns of successful elite incorporation had two downstream implications for popular threats. First, as documented in later chapters, each president faced popular threats that were a direct consequence of failed elite incorporation. Popular threats arose in areas inhabited by followers of elites who were excluded from the state, as these elites mobilized their followers for collective action. Second, the ways in which presidents addressed elite threats helped shape which strategies were available to

---

[1] Wright et al. (2015) reference autocracies in particular, but the goal of this strategy is the same across regime types.

manage popular threats. Incorporated elites used their position to lobby their respective president to hire their co-ethnics as state bureaucrats and promote them to higher positions. Therefore no president was able to rely on a packed state, in which bureaucrats were loyal due to co-ethnicity with the leader, to put down popular threats. Subsequent chapters examine how each president was instead forced to strategically manage the posting and shuffling of bureaucrats to ensure compliance where it mattered most. We cannot understand *how* bureaucrats are managed without first knowing *who* they are. And who gets hired to important state institutions is an outcome of the elite-level bargains examined in this chapter.

This chapter deepens our understanding of regime durability by conceptualizing a leader's threat landscape more holistically. Work in authoritarian politics largely focuses on how autocrats resolve challenges from other elites through incorporation. This focus makes sense – elite threats have led to the downfall of approximately two-thirds of the world's autocrats (Svolik 2012). In line with these findings, I show that Kenyan presidents' first course of action was to respond to elite challenges. However, I show why a focus on elite-level politics is not enough. Since responses to elite threats have downstream implications for durability (Greitens 2016), we must examine elite and popular threats in tandem to understand political survival.

This chapter contributes to our understanding of principal-agent dynamics. Prior studies tend to assume that principals always try to hire good types, and that they only hire bad types when it is difficult to screen candidates. According to this logic, the principal-agent problem can be attributed to hiring mistakes based on incomplete information. Yet this chapter discusses the conditions under which principals purposefully hire bad types in order to solve other, more pressing, problems.

The following sections describe each president's elite threat landscape in turn. I then empirically examine the effects of elite incorporation on the make-up of the Provincial Administration from 1964–2012.

4.2 KENYATTA'S POLITICAL LANDSCAPE

At first blush, it may seem that Kenya's first president – Jomo Kenyatta – faced no serious elite threats to his rule. He formed alliances with elites from other large ethnic groups to secure the electoral dominance of his party – the Kenya African National Union (KANU) – in the elections leading up to independence. The victory installed Kenyatta not only as the country's first executive but as *Baba Taifa*, "father of the nation." He drew moral support from both KANU and the opposition during the transition to independence, which made it hard for rival elites to separate attacks on his policies from attacks against Kenyatta himself. And indeed, he ruled Kenya from independence until his peaceful death in 1978.

However, Kenyatta faced numerous elite threats that prevented him from immediately consolidating his one-party regime. In this section, I first recap the political threats he faced that had elite components. I then describe Kenyatta's attempts at elite incorporation.

4.2.1 Kenyatta's Elite Challenges

This section details the two largest elite threats to Kenyatta's presidency. The first originated from Kenya's *majimbo*, or federal, state structure upon independence. The second stemmed from elites within his own party who defected to create a new political party.

Kenyatta's first elite threat originated in the colonial era. In the run-up to independence, the British oversaw negotiations between the two largest political parties, KANU and the Kenya African Democratic Union (KADU), about the country's postindependence administrative structure. Each party had strong support from distinct ethnic groups. KANU was seen as the party of the Kikuyu and Luo ethnic groups. Kenyatta, alongside other Kikuyu elites, became KANU's leader upon his release from detention in 1961. Luo elites with organizational experience in urban trade unions filled out the remainder of KANU's initial leadership team. This included the prominent radical Oginga Odinga, who became the party's vice president, and Tom Mboya, who served as its chairman.[2] KADU, led by Daniel arap Moi (Kalenjin) and Ronald Ngala (Mijikenda), was an amalgamation of smaller ethnic associations in Rift Valley and Coast Provinces. The country's other large ethnic groups were split between these two parties.

Despite KANU's dominance in preindependence elections, the British favored KADU's proposal for *majimboism* during the transition period. Kenya adopted a devolved federal state based on the country's provinces (to be renamed regions). Under this new federal arrangement, regional parliaments held significant power over policy, including the authority to tax, determine the allocation of public services, and maintain law

---

[2] See LeBas (2011).

and order. Kenyatta and the national parliament only had authority over issues of foreign affairs, macroeconomic policy, and national defense.

Majimboism aggravated the elite threat Kenyatta faced from KADU because it institutionally safeguarded KADU elites despite their smaller electoral base. By 1962, KANU's two core ethnic groups were the country's largest, comprising one-third of the population. And KANU had won a clear majority of seats in the colonial multiparty elections. But *majimobism*, combined with the distribution of ethnic groups across the country, helped KADU retain more strength than would be expected by the size of its base or its election results. Further, with majority control over the Coast and Rift Valley legislatures, KADU elites hoped to implement meaningful regional policies that helped make up ground among elites from unaligned ethnic groups in other regional legislatures.[3] Most notably, KADU tried to win support from elites from the Luhya community, the country's third-largest ethnic group at the time, through its stance on the "Kitale Question." The majority of the country's Luhya population was split between four districts. Three were combined to form Western Province, but the colonial regime placed Trans-Nzoia district (the capital of which is Kitale) in Rift Valley. Moi promised to use KADU's control over the Rift Valley legislature to negotiate a transfer of Trans-Nzoia to Western Province in an attempt to attract Luhya elites to KADU. Many of Moi's co-ethnic Kalenjin followers opposed this policy, and wanted to keep this fertile district in Rift Valley (Lynch 2011a).

Kenyatta's second elite threat originated from ideological differences within his own party.[4] KANU's radical wing, led by Odinga, had advocated socialist-leaning policies – including the nationalization of settler-owned land (Harbeson 1971) – since before independence. Yet Kenyatta and other moderates obstructed Odinga's efforts to use his influence within KANU to change the party's position on certain issues. Nonetheless, Odinga's platform was popular among many Kenyans, particularly in areas inhabited by his co-ethnic Luo community. It was also strong in areas sympathetic to *Mau Mau* as well as in parts of the country dominated by other groups.

Importantly, Odinga's socialist leanings allowed him to establish ties with the Soviet Union and China, which gave him access to independent

---

[3] See Riedl and Dickovick (2013).

[4] This elite tension was not due to the incorporation of KADU (see Section 4.2.2). KADU elites had fairly similar policy preferences as Kenyatta and his faction with regards to policies that fell along class lines (Leys 1975).

financing. He was therefore able to establish a separate power base without being incorporated into the state. Many KANU Members of Parliament (MPs) flocked to Odinga's radical faction given his popularity and financial clout. Odinga had thus cultivated a large and diverse elite coalition that could challenge Kenyatta and the moderates in the immediate postindependence period.

4.2.2 Elite Incorporation under Kenyatta

Kenyatta addressed the elite KADU threat through incorporation. He initially tried to temper the elite threat from the radical wing of KANU using this strategy, but was unsuccessful: some radicals defected to form a new opposition party.

Kenyatta tried to weaken KADU leaders' power in the regions by dismantling *majimboism*. Under the pretense of preventing the waste of government resources, the national government refused to relinquish central control of civil servants or to transfer funds until the regions developed sufficient capacity to administer themselves. This was effectively a catch-22: with no funds or personnel, the regions could not exhibit the required capacity.

Undercutting *majimboism* frayed the bonds between KADU's leaders and their followers. Without the dispersal of the devolved funds, KADU leaders lacked the necessary resources to maintain personal levels of popular support. The KANU-dominated central government favored areas inhabited by their supporters in allocation decisions. KADU MPs realized that being in the opposition could cost them their positions, as upstart candidates in their constituencies were likely to challenge them for their seats. Kenyatta's cabinet also interfered in regional affairs to fray the bonds between KADU elites. The Ministry of Home Affairs, overseen by Odinga at that point, would not sanction the proposal to transfer Trans-Nzoia during the Kitale Question debate, "until the people affected by the transfer were first consulted."[5] Recognizing that many citizens in Rift Valley would disapprove of this transfer, KADU elites dropped the matter and lost ground with Luhya elites.

As *majimboism* was weakening, Kenyatta sought to eliminate the KADU threat entirely by incorporating its leaders into KANU. Kenyatta offered KADU leaders large tracts of land and high-ranking positions

---

5 As seen in Anderson (2005b, 562). Also see Throup (1987) and Kanyinga (1998).

within his party that they could use to channel resources to their respective bases in return for disbanding KADU (Leys 1975), which they agreed to do by late 1964. Parliament changed the constitution to formally end *majimboism* and establish a unitary state. Daniel arap Moi was appointed Vice President, and Ronald Ngala and other prominent KADU elites joined the cabinet.

Kenyatta also attempted to temper the elite threat from within his own party by incorporating potential opponents. KANU became a true "catchall" party after the incorporation of KADU elites (Widner 1992), similar to other independence-era parties across sub-Saharan Africa that represented the spectrum of the country's ethnic groups and policy positions (Zolberg 1966). Initially, this "one-party democracy" resulted in significant legislative independence (Opalo 2019); the legislature had "lively, critical debate" (Gertzel, 1970, 9) about the country's most important policy issues in an attempt to incorporate elites' disparate policy proposals.

But with so many factions, it was difficult to use the party or legislature to appease all sides through policy, or to effectively use any mechanism other than patronage. Since Kenyatta leaned toward the moderate and conservative factions, he blocked many of Odinga's formal attempts to move KANU leftwards. For instance, Kenyatta adopted a "willing buyer, willing seller" land management model and reassured white settlers that their land would not be expropriated, and they would be compensated for any land for which they held the title.[6] Kenyatta charted a path that was closely aligned with capitalism and the West, and criticized Odinga's connections with the Soviet Union and China.

Kenyatta initially attempted to compensate the radicals for their policy losses by increasing their access to state resources. Odinga was shuffled between powerful (and lucrative) posts such as Vice President and Minister of Home Affairs. Achieng Oneko, another Luo radical, was appointed Minister of Information. Radicals from other groups were appointed as Assistant Ministers or served as heads of important parastatals that gave them easy access to state resources. Kenyatta aimed to sideline the radicals out of policy debates but ensure their cooperation through patronage, as he had successfully done with KADU elites.

But this type of incorporation proved insufficient. Compelled in part by a reorganization of KANU, Odinga exploited his cross-ethnic support to

---

[6] This model also helped address the popular threat from some parts of the Kikuyu community, as I discuss in the next chapter.

create his own party in 1966 (Okoth-Ogendo 1972): the Kenya's People's Union (KPU). Twenty-nine KANU MPs from across the country – more than a quarter of the legislature at the time – left KANU to join the KPU upon its formation. An additional twenty to thirty MPs had promised to defect as well (Mueller 1984).[7] Odinga sought to challenge Kenyatta for the presidency and implement his left-leaning agenda.

4.2.3 Other Elite Threats against Kenyatta and Later Patterns of Elite Incorporation

In Sections 4.2.2 and 4.2.3 I describe two of the elite challenges that Kenyatta faced and how he tried to manage them through incorporation. As the next chapter shows, his popular threats were tied to these elite threats, and he would ultimately rely on the Provincial Administration to put them down. In this section I describe Kenyatta's other elite threats and patterns of incorporation that did not systematically change his popular threat landscape.

Kenyatta continued to face some level of elite discontent within KANU throughout his presidency. The legislature remained relatively independent and strong under Kenyatta; parliamentarians attempted to use formal parliamentary procedures to increase their authority (Opalo 2019). He maintained control over elites in part through *harambee*. *Harambee* began as a local development strategy whereby local communities were expected to identify and begin providing the local public goods they needed. In practice, communities often invited their MP as a keynote guest to events, with the expectation that she contribute generously to the fundraiser. Kenyatta increased the political salience of MP contributions by urging communities to judge their representatives by their level of *harambee* giving (Widner 1992), which became expensive for MPs. Kenyatta then provided donations to favored MPs or as a carrot to win support for his legislative agenda. MPs who did not receive visits from Kenyatta were less likely to meet the demands of their constituents, and more likely to get voted out. In addition, Kenyatta relied on the Provincial Administration to keep tabs on recalcitrant elites within KANU before they could incite their followers to popular action (Opalo 2019). He also used the institution to rig the elections of some elites or hinder their efforts to connect with their followers.

---

7 These MPs did not defect after it became clear that Kenyatta was intent on using the Provincial Administration to rig KANU defectors out of office.

As Kenyatta consolidated power, he increasingly looked to his in-group elites to fill the most important positions within the cabinet. These insiders included many Kikuyu elites, and especially those from his home Kiambu District and other parts of southern Central Province ("south of the River Chania," a river running through Central Province). Kenyatta also relied heavily on elites from the Embu and Meru communities, which are closely related to the Kikuyu ethnic group.[8] By 1971, elites from these ethnic groups formalized their political ties through the Gikuyu, Embu, and Meru Association (GEMA).

Separately, Kenyatta addressed the coup threat from his armed forces upon coming to office through a mix of patronage and formal institutions. The army mutinied in January 1964 due to poor pay and conditions (Parsons 2003). Loyal regiments quickly put down the mutiny, and Kenyatta court-martialed the coup's leaders to deter further unrest from the armed forces (Hornsby 2011). Kenyatta began to build a patrimonial relationship with the army in an attempt to secure their loyalty. He improved the military's pay and conditions and installed Kikuyu officers in top leadership positions. When he uncovered an assassination plot against him in 1971, he used the military trial to prevent other elites from defecting (Shen-Bayh 2018).

4.3 MOI'S POLITICAL LANDSCAPE DURING HIS AUTOCRATIC REGIME

After Kenyatta's death in 1978, Vice President Daniel arap Moi took over the presidency. Throughout his nearly fourteen-year one-party regime, Moi faced elite threats that were the lasting institutional legacy of Kenyatta's reign in many of the same ways that Kenyatta faced some elite threats that had their roots in colonialism. In this section I first outline the elite threats that Moi faced during his one-party regime. Second, I evaluate the degree and success of elite incorporation intended to deal with these threats.

4.3.1 Moi's Elite Challenges

Moi faced powerful Kikuyu elites at the beginning of his tenure. Kikuyu leaders only became stronger as Kenyatta neared the end of his life,

---

[8] Whereas the Kikuyu have historically resided to the west of Mount Kenya, the Embu reside to the south and the Meru to the west.

precisely because of the degree of incorporation he allowed his co-ethnic elites. The strength of Kikuyu, and more broadly GEMA, elites during this time is best exemplified by the "change-the-constitution" movement. According to the country's constitution at the time, the vice president becomes interim president upon the death of a sitting president and has ninety days to call new presidential elections.[9] Even though Moi's elite support was fractured by the mid-1970s, GEMA elites thought ninety days would be long enough for Moi to consolidate sufficient control to win the election. The change-the-constitution movement wanted the interim presidency to go to the speaker of the National Assembly, whose support GEMA elites could secure. While this movement was never put to a vote, it had the support of one-third of parliament, including MPs outside of GEMA areas (Widner 1992).

Odinga and other prominent Luo leaders also continued to challenge Moi. Odinga had sufficient international ties and personal popularity that he remained popular with his base, despite his exclusion from the state for the last decade of Kenyatta's presidency. His continued strength gave him an advantageous position during the transition period; GEMA elites tried to get him to join the push to change the constitution.

4.3.2 Elite Incorporation under Moi

Moi sought to incorporate Kikuyu elites to prevent them from attempting another plot to force him out of the presidency. One of Moi's former regime elites summarized his precarious position upon assuming the presidency, "you couldn't deny Kikuyus all positions within politics. They were already the business elite, so all deals – such as government contracts, and remember that the government is the biggest company – ended up benefiting Central Province somehow. They had economic power. This meant they had political power."[10] The strong position of many Kikuyu elites secured this community nearly 30 percent of the appointments in Moi's first 1979 cabinet, despite representing only 20 percent of the general population. In fact, Moi's initial cabinet during his interim presidency did not change substantially from Kenyatta's, save the reshuffling of Mbiyu Koinage, Kenyatta's brother-in-law and Moi's "nemesis," away

---

9 See Meng (2018) on the Kenyatta-Moi succession.
10 Interview with former Permanent Secretary of Provincial Administration, July 1, 2012, Nairobi, Kenya.

from the Ministry of Provincial Administration (Hornsby, 2011, 331). Other Kikuyu elites were incorporated through state-owned banking institutions, which allowed them to make preferential loans to themselves and their constituents (Arriola 2012).

The continuation of Kikuyu elite co-optation, however, did not mean that Moi had sufficiently bought off all Kikuyu elites. After the initial transition period, Moi downgraded Kikuyu elites to a junior partner in the ruling coalition; under Kenyatta they were considered senior partners. Moi's incorporation of Kikuyu elites was therefore less than what a Kikuyu successor would have accomplished. Moreover, Moi did not incorporate Kenyatta's closest allies, who had largely hailed from southern Central Province. Kenyatta's inner circle arguably lost the most after Kenyatta's death, and had the strongest incentives to use their incorporation to unseat Moi. Moi therefore sought to exclude this faction in favor of other Kikuyu elites. He elevated Mwai Kibaki, a Kikuyu from Nyeri district, the north of Central Province and very much outside Kenyatta's inner circle, to Vice President over many other Kikuyu leaders who were closely tied to the former president.

Moi initially tried to incorporate Odinga and other prominent Luo elites as well. Odinga accepted a post in the Cotton Lint and Seed Marketing Board, and some of his closest allies were appointed to other parastatals or the cabinet. As Charles Hornsby (2011, 354) summarizes, "Moi seemed to be leading a new accommodation, in return for which Odinga would help him sustain power." But Odinga used his new position within the state to criticize KANU. After it quickly became clear that he would not trade state resources for acquiescence, Odinga's access to the state was once again cut off. Odinga responded in May 1982 by creating and attempting to register the Kenya African Socialist Alliance (KASA), a new political party to challenge KANU and Moi. Some Kikuyu elites talked of defecting from KANU to join KASA, and new fears arose of a revitalized Kikuyu-Luo alliance that sought to unseat Moi. Soon after Odinga went public with his plans to register KASA, however, Moi pushed constitutional amendment Section 2(A) through the legislature to ban all non-KANU parties and make Kenya a *de jure* one-party regime.

Elite discontent boiled over with the August 1, 1982 coup attempt, which was launched by Luo members of the Kenya Air Force who had strong ties to Odinga and his son Raila. This coup attempt was poorly organized, with little communication between the coordinating regiments; yet the low-level officers managed to gain control of the country for six hours.[11] Their (short-lived) success was in part because top Kikuyu leaders in various internal security apparatuses had not acted immediately or decisively against the coup plotters. Some senior Kikuyu elites even claimed that they were aware of these plans beforehand, but did not arrest suspected mutineers in the hopes that Moi would fall. There is also evidence of two other coups by security forces planned for early August by Kikuyu elites; it seems that Luo officers launched the hasty attempt to preempt a Kikuyu coup and another Kikuyu presidency (Decalo 1990; Hornsby 2011).

4.3.3 Other Elite Threats against Moi and Later Patterns of Elite Incorporation

Moi's political threats from Kikuyu and Luo elites, described in Section 4.3.2, affected the nature of his popular threats. Chapter 6 shows how Moi managed bureaucrats in the Provincial Administration to put down those elite threats. Moi faced other elite threats that he was able to handle without affecting his popular threats.

Moi responded to the initial potential for unrest from the armed forces upon coming to office by installing loyalists at the head of some coercive organs. He was careful not to quickly turn over all of Kenyatta's personnel for fear of triggering another coup (Harkness 2018). After the coup attempt, he replaced many top security leaders with loyalists (Hornsby 2011) and relied more heavily on KANU to incorporate – and control – elites. Whereas Kenyatta was willing to allow infighting in KANU and the legislature, Moi restricted it and instead sought to control policy and elite debate (Widner 1992; Opalo 2019). His tight grip over elites helped Moi weaken many of his most vocal critics. As he consolidated power throughout the 1980s, he began to exclude rival elites from the regime. He demoted Kibaki from the Vice Presidency in 1988, and later kicked him and other prominent rival elites out of the cabinet entirely. Moi instead began to incorporate elite supporters including more co-ethnic Kalenjin and other Rift Valley pastoralist elites.

The country's poor financial situation amplified the level of elite (and popular) discontent even if it did not lead directly to action against Moi. Like many African leaders, Kenyatta and Moi intentionally distorted markets to prevent urban unrest (Bates 1981), despite the implications

---

[11] See Singh (2014) on coup success rates as a function of the plotters' rank in the armed forces across Africa.

for macroeconomic health (Ballard-Rosa 2016). Kenya experienced two of its most severe droughts during the new government's first decade of office, first in 1979–1980 and then in 1984–1985 (Bates 1989), further worsening the country's economic situation. Kenya became one of the first countries in sub-Saharan African to take on structural adjustment programs. Some reforms were economic, which had political implications (Herbst 1990; van de Walle 2001), while others were purely political. As I describe in Section 4.4, the country's precarious financial position helped pave the way for the country's return to multiparty elections.

4.4 MOI'S POLITICAL LANDSCAPE DURING HIS ELECTORAL REGIME

The nature of elite threats fundamentally changed after Kenya's return to multiparty elections. As discussed theoretically in Chapter 2, if leaders must win office through multiparty elections, the most damaging elite threats come from viable opposition campaigns.[12]

The final decade of Moi's tenure (1992–2002), after Kenya transitioned to an electoral regime, illustrates this changing nature of political threats. Moi successfully contested the 1992 and 1997 elections. These elections represented a dual elite and popular threat because Moi's most prominent elite rivals galvanized their co-ethnic bases alongside other segments of the population in an attempt to vote Moi out of office. In the end, opposition elites had difficulty coordinating their campaigns and producing a unified opposition, but Moi still faced the real possibility of losing power. In this section, I briefly discuss Kenya's transition to an electoral regime. I then describe Moi's political threats, and his attempts to incorporate elites and win the elections.

4.4.1 Kenya's Return to an Electoral Regime

Excluded Kikuyu and Luo elites mobilized their co-ethnics to fight against Moi's autocracy in the open around the time of the fall of the Berlin

---

[12] I make no judgement about the difficulty of coordinating an elite challenge to the president under autocratic versus electoral regimes. While the consequences of a failed coup plot are disastrous for the elite plotters, the coordination problem that elites face in organizing against the leader under electoral competition is also difficult to solve, both because building a multi-ethnic opposition coalition requires many more elites and resources than a small coup coalition and because electoral coalitions are created publicly (Arriola 2012; Gandhi and Buckles 2017).

Wall. Two former Kikuyu ministers, Kenneth Matiba and Charles Rubia, alongside Oginga Odinga and others, called for a mass rally in Nairobi's Uhuru Park on July 7, 1990. The elite organizers were arrested days before the rally, but thousands of civilians still gathered in the park, and simultaneous rallies were held in other major cities.[13] Security forces violently repressed protesters, killing dozens and injuring hundreds, which sparked three days of civilian riots around Nairobi. July 7, or *Saba Saba* ("seven seven") is still commemorated as an important day in the country's transition toward multiparty elections.

By May 1991, excluded elites joined with business owners, lawyers and religious leaders who were committed to repealing the constitutional ban on opposition parties (Kanyinga 1998). Together, they launched a new civil society organization, the Forum for the Restoration of Democracy (FORD). FORD's push for multiparty elections included tactics such as holding large-scale rallies in Nairobi and other areas, fighting arrests and administrative blockages through the courts and, more broadly, linking together various anti-KANU civil society groups.

Kenya transitioned to an electoral regime later that year due to both domestic pressure and international leverage. Popular agitation for a transition was clearly high, but the final push to lift the ban on opposition parties came from the international donor community. Kenya's aid donors met to discuss their future relationship with the country and decided to suspend $350 million in monetary aid for six months in solidarity with the fervor shown by civil society and opposition elites. These donors made the resumption of aid contingent on political and economic reforms.[14] Moi felt compelled to enact the reforms in order to secure the short-term loans that would allow him to incorporate elites (Arriola 2012). He called a special meeting of KANU one week after the donors' decision and announced his intention to repeal the constitutional ban on opposition parties. The country held its first multiparty elections since the independence era the following year. Elections have since been held roughly every five years.

4.4.2 Moi's Elite Challenges during His Electoral Regime

Moi's most severe elite challenges during his electoral regime came from elites who mounted viable opposition campaigns against him. FORD,

---

13 These pro-democracy rallies were similar to the wave of pro-democracy movements across Africa at that time (Bratton and van de Walle 1992).
14 World Bank, "Press Release of the Meeting of the Consultative Group for Kenya" (Paris, November 26, 1991), 3–4. As cited in Barkan (1993).

the opposition movement that spearheaded the move toward democratization, split into two factions in the run-up to the 1992 election. Kenneth Matiba headed FORD-Asili (FORD-A) and Oginga Odinga headed FORD-Kenya (FORD-K). The 1992 election also featured Mwai Kibaki under the Democratic Party; he became Moi's most serious opponent in the subsequent election.

Though these rival elites did not unseat Moi, they comprised a strong and vocal minority in parliament and gave the legislature real power over Moi's executive authority. Since many of the presidential aspirants won their parliamentary seats in concurrent elections, they were able to lead opposition factions in the legislature. They found many opposition MPs, as many long-standing KANU legislators were voted out in 1992 and 1997.[15] Further, Moi had to contend with several KANU defections: of the 111 MPs who ran for reelection in 1992, 30 (27 percent) did so on another ticket.[16] Of the fifty-five MPs who won on the KANU ticket in 1992 and stood for reelection in 1997, five (9 percent) defected to the opposition.[17]

The opposition's rise in parliament increased its veto power. Parliament implemented reforms to increase its authority over budgeting (Barkan 2008; Opalo 2019) and attempted to formally legislate demands made by active parts of civil society. Most notably, it passed the Constitution of Kenya Review Act and oversaw multiple waves of constitutional review that sought to constrain executive power. Parliament also prevented attempts to overturn the constitution's two-term limit for presidents.

4.4.3 Elite Incorporation during Moi's Electoral Regime

For the most part, Moi focused his incorporation efforts during these years on elites from aligned and unaligned communities. Under his autocratic regime, he was mostly concerned about rival elites who might launch a coup. But after the introduction of multiparty elections, Moi sought to build bonds with elites who were willing to back him and to mobilize support from their communities to help him sustain a winning electoral coalition.

---

[15] Despite unfair and unfree parliamentary elections, alongside malapportionment that favored rural KANU zones over urban opposition areas (Fox 1996; Boone and Wahman 2015), KANU barely sustained a parliamentary majority. It retained 53 percent of parliamentary seats in 1992 and 50 percent in 1997.

[16] Figures calculated using data from Hassan and Sheely (2017).

[17] See Opalo (2019) for the low reelection rates of Kenyan MPs more generally.

These elites were incorporated in part through the use of state resources. Many elites who considered defecting to the opposition were willing to be bought off with material rewards. They calculated that immediate tangible benefits were better than risking regime ire, all in the hopes that the opposition would follow through on its promise to distribute benefits if it won (van de Walle 2006; Arriola 2012). For instance, Moi created hundreds of new administrative locations and sublocations in jurisdictions of MPs who were at risk of defecting. This lower-level unit creation automatically resulted in the hiring of hundreds of new Chiefs and Assistant Chiefs for those new units who, in turn, served as brokers for their respective MPs (Hassan and Sheely 2017).

Elite incorporation during Moi's electoral years excluded the strongest Kikuyu and Luo elites in the run-up to his reelection campaigns. Prominent elites from these communities had defected to the opposition, and it became increasingly clear that their constituents were unlikely to support his reelection bids.[18] Unsurprisingly, the number of Kikuyu elites in the cabinet dropped from eight in 1988 to one in 1993. The number of Luo elites dropped from five to one.[19] However, as Parliament became increasingly hostile toward Moi, he sought to cautiously incorporate willing Kikuyu and Luo elites, including Raila Odinga, who ran for president in 1997 on the National Democratic Party ticket.[20] Moi incorporated the younger Odinga into a parliamentary coalition with KANU during his final term. Raila Odinga and MPs affiliated with him received patronage goods in exchange for their support in Parliament, including their votes against legislation and constitutional changes that were intended to limit Moi's executive power.

4.5 KIBAKI'S POLITICAL LANDSCAPE

Kenya's third president, Mwai Kibaki, beat Moi's anointed successor in 2002. Kibaki won because he put together a multi-ethnic coalition that bought off elites from most of the country's politically relevant groups

---

[18] Indeed, no Kikuyu or Luo MPs who contested on the KANU ticket in 1992 won reelection. The 1992 highest vote total for a KANU candidate in Central Province was 14 percent, and 16 percent in Luo parts of Nyanza.

[19] Cabinet ministers at this time had to be MPs. No Kikuyu or Luo MP candidates won election during the 1990s on the KANU ticket. Kikuyu and Luo elites who served as ministers were first nominated to Parliament by Moi.

[20] As I discuss in Chapter 7, Raila Odinga proved even less viable than his father, winning only 10 percent of the vote and not even being able to consolidate support from his co-ethnics.

(Arriola 2012). His coalition broke down before his 2007 reelection campaign, however, and he faced a formidable opposition campaign led by Raila Odinga.

In this section, I lay out Kibaki's initial elite coalition, the attempts to keep the coalition intact through elite incorporation, and the eventual defection of some elites.

4.5.1 Uniting the Opposition: Kibaki's 2002 Election Victory

Moi signaled that he would not seek a third term early in his second elected term. Many of his closest advisors were implicated in election-related violence during the 1990s and thus seen as unviable presidential candidates. Moi chose Uhuru Kenyatta, Jomo Kenyatta's son and a relative newcomer to politics, to succeed him. This move fractured what was left of KANU as other elites had been angling to succeed Moi.

A number of opposition leaders coalesced behind Mwai Kibaki soon after his 1997 defeat. Kibaki's growing ties to the business community allowed him to buy off many of the same political elites that the state had incorporated in the past (Arriola 2012). By 2002, he had convinced some of the last holdouts – including Raila Odinga and his elite supporters, who at that point had been incorporated into Moi's government – to join the opposition. The multi-ethnic coalition was fittingly called the National Alliance Rainbow Coalition - Kenya (NARC, or the "rainbow coalition").[21]

Kibaki and Raila Odinga formalized the alliance in a Memorandum of Understanding, which stipulated that Odinga and his elite followers (and presumably their co-ethnic followers) would support Kibaki in 2002. In return, Kibaki agreed to 1) draft a new constitution that devolved authority along a *majimbo* framework, 2) create the post of Prime Minister for Odinga, 3) equitably split cabinet positions between Kibaki's and Odinga's elite supporters, and 4) to step down after one term, allowing another member of the coalition (likely Odinga) to run in 2007. Kibaki easily won the 2002 election with more than 60 percent of the vote.

4.5.2 Elite Incorporation after Kibaki Took Office

Kibaki reneged on many of his promises to Odinga after taking office. Even though elites affiliated with Odinga won more parliamentary seats

---

[21] See Elischer (2013) for a more detailed discussion of the formation of NARC.

than those affiliated with Kibaki, Odinga's faction received only eight of twenty-three ministerial positions, and were denied high-profile and lucrative positions (Hornsby 2011). Odinga was appointed Minister of Public Works, while GEMA elites filled the most important ministerial appointments, including Minister for Provincial Administration and Internal Security (2003–2008) and Minister of Finance (2006–2008).

The low levels of incorporation of elites who hailed from outside the Kikuyu (and broader GEMA) community at the beginning of Kibaki's presidency created tension within NARC. Many elites eventually defected from Kibaki's coalition during the campaign for a new constitution, which he had promised to draft in his 2002 Memorandum of Understanding. By 2005, Kibaki's government called on 600+ delegates from across the country to begin drafting a new constitution – later named the Bomas draft constitution, after the name of the meeting space in which the conference was held – that proposed a ceremonial President, a strong Prime Minister, and power devolved to the district level. But the Bomas draft was never put to a vote: President Kibaki and those around him amended the draft after the conference ended. This new Wako draft, named after the then-Attorney General, watered down many aspects of the Bomas draft, including the powers of the Prime Minister and the clauses on devolution.[22] The subversion of the constitution-drafting process, on top of the disregard for ethnic balancing that was promised before the 2002 election, led Raila Odinga, Kalonzo Musyoka (Kamba) and others to defect from NARC in 2005.

Elites opposed to the Wako draft led a strong, organized campaign against its ratification. The country was set to vote on the Wako draft in a November 2005 referendum. Musyoka and Odinga jointly campaigned against the proposed constitution through their newly formed Orange Democratic Movement (ODM). They argued that ratification of the Wako draft would end the push for constitutional reform without making significant changes to executive power or institutionalizing a more equitable sharing of resources across the country. Instead, they encouraged citizens to vote against the Wako draft and then mobilize to demand a new constitutional referendum. The referendum was increasingly viewed as a poll on Kibaki's performance and a litmus test for his upcoming reelection campaign. The referendum failed, garnering only 42 percent of

---

22 See Cottrell and Ghai (2007) and Kramon and Posner (2011).

the vote. Ethnic groups' voting patterns followed their respective elites' endorsement of, or opposition to, the Wako draft (Kimenyi and Shughart 2010).

ODM elites continued mobilizing popular resistance against Kibaki after the failed referendum and in anticipation of the 2007 election. Initially, ODM rallied across the country to demand the immediate dissolution of Parliament and the calling of snap elections. They argued that the referendum results showed that the administration had lost its mandate to rule.[23] These rallies later morphed into campaign rallies ahead of the 2007 election.

ODM eventually split in August 2007 because both Musyoka and Odinga wanted to represent the party in the December presidential election. In the end, Musyoka ran under ODM-Kenya and Odinga under ODM. Odinga was considered the more viable candidate from the beginning, in part because he managed to create a diverse, multi-ethnic coalition. Most prominent in this coalition was William Ruto. Musyoka was unable to build a diverse multi-ethnic coalition, and even had difficulty consolidating support among his own co-ethnics. In September 2007, after ODM split and just months before the election, 94 percent of Luo ethnic group members intended to vote for Odinga while only 59 percent of Kamba ethnic group members intended to vote for Musyoka (Horowitz 2012).[24] Kibaki's most viable contender leading up to the 2007 election was thus Odinga.

4.6 THE DIVERSITY OF THE STATE

Sections 4.2–4.5 have described each president's elite challenges. Despite variation in regime type and ethnic identity, all three faced elite threats that they tried to solve through incorporation. Yet this strategy could not temper all elite threats. And further, failed incorporation helped spark popular threats – the co-ethnics of nonincorporated elites were the most likely to launch a popular threat. The subsequent chapters of the book detail each president's popular challenges and empirically investigate how each one relied on the state – specifically the Provincial Administration – to solve them.

Reliance on the state to put down popular threats posed a principal-agent problem for each president, especially because the state was not packed with loyal bureaucrats who could be expected to comply without

---

[23] See *The Daily Nation*, "Orange Group to Defy Rallies Ban," November 29, 2005.
[24] Horowitz (2012) finds that 90 percent of members of the Kikuyu ethnic group intended to vote for Kibaki.

monitoring.[25] Instead, as outlined in Chapter 2, decisions about who is hired for state jobs are made in part through a process of elite-level bargaining and elite incorporation. Elites are expected to distribute state resources to their followers after they are incorporated into the state. One of the most valued resources that a Kenyan elite can secure for a constituent is a position in the Provincial Administration. As such, and given the importance of elite incorporation, Kenya's presidents should have been unwilling to pack the state with their own co-ethnics, because doing so would limit their ability to incorporate rival elites through the distribution of state jobs to those elites' followers.

The rest of this chapter evaluates the ethnic composition of the Provincial Administration and empirically demonstrates the lack of packing within this organization. I first present qualitative evidence that supports the elite incorporation mechanism: incorporated elites demanded that their own co-ethnics be hired into, and later promoted within, the Provincial Administration. Separately, I present qualitative evidence to suggest that some leaders tried to hire non-co-ethnic bureaucrats to prevent the appearance of a packed state, and to quell popular discontent that may arise due to perceptions of ethnic favoritism. In a second step, I evaluate these arguments using data on the ethnic make-up of the Provincial Administration.

4.6.1 Diverse Ethnic Composition to Appease Regime Elites

Elites have strong incentives to ensure their co-ethnics are hired into the Provincial Administration and rise through the ranks. Since they provide both formal and informal benefits, these jobs are highly sought after. Ethnic communities keep track of how many top administrators are from their group, which serves as a visible sign that an elite has procured benefits for her followers and signals her ability to secure other state resources for the group.

The selective process for recruitment into the Provincial Administration, as described in Chapter 3, has allowed regime elites to intervene in the process and lobby in favor of their preferred candidates. MPs have consistently asked each president for more positions for their co-ethnics. In 1970 an MP wrote the following to the Permanent Secretary of Provincial Administration about the underrepresentation of his co-ethnics in this agency:

---

25 None of the three presidents examined had adequate financing to buy off all bureaucrats.

It is an established fact that there is no Mkuria at all in the Provincial Administration Senior civil service and very very few indeed even in the junior grades of
the civil service – particularly in the Provincial Administration. Clearly this makes
my constituents feel that the Government is neglecting them and that they are not
being given a fair share in the "fruits of Independence." There is no point claiming
that Kuria people do not apply for jobs, or that there are no suitable ones.[26]

The rest of the letter contained demands for more development, which
suggests the MP equated central government positions with development
for his constituency.

While any MP could make such requests, those who were incorporated
into the cabinet were most successful in securing positions for co-ethnic
constituents. One officer explained how having an elite patron helped
some of his colleagues get hired:

There are those [administrators] who have short cuts ... Maybe because of political patronage. There are others who were at the university who didn't want to go
through the normal processes. They would use their godfathers, their patron ...
political leaders who were patronizing the right party. So they go to [the god-
father] and [the godfather] goes to Moi .... Moi had godfathers, kingpins, key
personalities from the different areas.[27]

One interviewee similarly told me about his ability to get his friends hired
into the Provincial Administration in the past, saying "it was easy: dad
was a minister."[28]

Cabinet ministers and other prominent elites also ask presidents
to promote lower-level administrators to higher-profile positions. The
officer quoted in the previous paragraph continued, "[There are some
who] become senior early .... [The godfather] would say 'you see this
girl, she can work for three years as a DO and then give her a DC. At
around [age] 30! You still have to be smart. But there are promotional
interviews that favor them."[29] Unsurprisingly, officers who did not have
a co-ethnic minister discussed their career stagnation: "there was no one
who pushed for me [to get promoted]";[30] "other people [had] been using
their political affiliations to be appointed [as a District Commissioner]
but I had nothing."[31]

[26] MP Kuria to Permanent Secretary of Provincial Administration, June 24, 1970, KA/6/18,
Kenya National Archives, Nairobi.
[27] Interview with then DC, June 29, 2017, Nairobi.
[28] Interview with then MP candidate, July 2, 2017, Nairobi.
[29] Interview with then DC, June 29, 2017, Nairobi.
[30] Interview with former DC, January 8, 2012, Nairobi.
[31] Interview with then DC, January 25, 2012, Kerugoya, Kenya.

4.6.2 Diverse Ethnic Composition to Appease Population

Hiring a diverse officer corps promises to temper popular threats through two related mechanisms. First, an ethnically diverse state is able to distribute state spoils more equitably. High-ranking PCs and DCs in particular have access to state funds that they are expected to disperse to their own communities. Given the visibility of these positions, presidents could ensure that some state resources trickled down to the country's various ethnic groups simply by having a diverse bureaucratic corps. One DC recalled how he was frequently called to be the guest of honor at *harambees* in his home area, even though he served elsewhere:

It was assumed that it was them who had the money, maybe a senior civil servant, a DC, a district head, a provincial head, or a senior officer in the central government. I would be a victim, for example. I had to [give money]. Because in your home area, where I come from, if I don't attend these *harambees*, they will think that I'm mean. They have their son. They have assumedly educated this son. Maybe while he was going to college they raised resources for him to go and pay college fees. Now he's deployed and refusing to give back …. [I gave] maybe 10000 KSH [around $100] each. You feel kind of guilty about [not contributing].[32]

Civil society groups would even ask each president directly for positions for their members. Consider the following request letter to President Moi during his one-party regime. The letter was entitled "Development Priorities By Meru People Resident in Nairobi" and equated their group's potential to develop with more appointments:

There was a time when Meru District had two Provincial Commissioners and three Permanent Secretaries, now there is one Provincial Commissioner and two Permanent Secretaries. We recommend that the Officer[s] removed be reinstated. We also recommend that we get one more District Commissioner.[33]

Precisely because of the benefits of having an administrator from one's community, presidents in the multiparty era used positions to reward ethnic groups that were part of the winning coalition. At a meeting between Moi and a delegation of Isiolo leaders in 1994, the delegation members first asserted their loyalty to Moi:

Your Excellency, this is the first time for a delegation from Isiolo to be availed an opportunity of meeting you since the last multi-party general elections of 29th

---

32 Interview with then Senior DC, October 13, 2012, Nairobi.
33 Nairobi Meru Residents to Unspecified Recipient, February 7, 1991, BB/11/138, Kenya National Archives, Nairobi.

December 1992, in which Isiolo District came out clearly as a purely KANU zone. We wish to assure you, Your Excellency, that Isiolo district is and has always been and will remain a KANU zone.

The meeting quickly shifted to a list of requests, including the recruitment of officers into the state and their advancement:

Your Excellency, we now have qualified people from Isiolo District who can serve our Country in various capacities. It is our humble request that you appoint such people to serve ... Your Excellency, you can recall, that in your effort to give equal opportunities to all Kenyans to serve as Administrative Officers [within the Provincial Administration], a number of Kenyans from previously disadvantaged Districts were appointed as Administrative Officers, this District did not benefit much from this kind gesture. We also note that there has never been an appointment of a District Commissioner from Isiolo District. We, therefore, kindly request you to appoint Administrative Officers from this District to serve the Government in various Administrative capacities.[34]

This logic persists up to the current presidency of Uhuru Kenyatta (2013–present), son of Jomo Kenyatta. One senior Somali administrator explained that the Somali community has recently tended to split its vote between the incumbent and viable opposition candidates. Their strong support of all major candidates has helped ensure their inclusion in the state. A senior official from a coastal tribe explained that few of his co-ethnics were represented in the Provincial Administration because "we are in the opposition. The first family [the Kenyattas] has taken our land and Uhuru knows that we can never vote for him. Uhuru knows that we can never vote for him and so we pay."[35,36]

Second, and relatedly, diversifying the state promises to reduce popular threats by limiting overt favoritism and historical inequities between groups. Since the Provincial Administration is the "face of Kenya," over-representation by one's co-ethnics – or any ethnic group – is visible, and is liable to create resentment among other tribes. Instead, the Provincial Administration has adopted a policy of descriptive representation: "Beginning with Moi there came to be other considerations. Where do you come from? Are there other senior officers from there?"[37]

---

[34] Minutes from Meeting of Isiolo Delegation with President Moi, March 28, 1994, Kabarak, Kenya, BB/11/140, Kenya National Archives, Nairobi.
[35] Interview with former DC, June 7, 2018, Nairobi.
[36] It is rumored that the Kenyatta family is the single largest owner of land in former Coast Province, including 30 percent of arable land in some districts.
[37] Interview with then DC, December 3, 2011, Nairobi.

Ethnicity, alongside qualifications, became a factor in hiring and promotion decisions.

To be sure, Moi implemented this philosophy of "ethnic balance" to justify dealing with Kikuyu over-representation in the Provincial Administration after Kenyatta's death by lowering the number of Kikuyu administrators and increasing the representation of administrators from other communities.[38] Moi's former Permanent Secretary of Provincial Administration summarized this logic, "Moi had equalized representation in government after Kenyatta died because the Kikuyus had centralized it. He let so many smaller tribes in. It was about status."[39]

But ethnic balancing was an informal policy of this agency even under Kibaki's presidency, a Kikuyu whose ethnic community stood to gain from moving away from this policy. One objective of the policy was to rectify long-standing inequalities in hiring and promotions. For instance, during my field research, many officers stated that there are forty-one districts in Kenya, so each should have their own DC. Others claimed that there are more than forty tribes in Kenya, so why should one tribe (referring here to the Kikuyu) get more than their fair share of DCs? One administrator explained how promotion decisions took into account ethnic balancing:

It might happen that you have three brothers [a euphemism for members of the same ethnic group]. They are all very good, but you can not post them all. We have eight provinces, and eight PCs. So that means each province has at least one PC. [And each province's new PC] are from different communities [within the province]. You will find that if the former PC came from lower Eastern, that is the Kamba, after a time the next one must come from upper Eastern – the Embu or Meru – irrespective.[40]

Another DC working under Kibaki explained:

There is tribal balance. If we are looking for one PC and there are twenty DCs who are qualified. We look at your record, and from there is tribal balance ... even the DOs. When it comes to promotion, there are some marginalized minorities. They cannot be seen. That is why, for example, some of these DOs or DCs who come from these small groups, they're advantaged. For example, appointment from DO to a DC the Kamba, Kikuyu, Kalenjin, we are the majority in that field. So, they are all qualified, but you find there is someone who comes from these

---

38 In 1978 Kikuyu administrators held about 45 percent of top Provincial Administration positions.

39 Interview with former Permanent Secretary of Provincial Administration, October 18, 2015, Nairobi.

40 Interview with then DC, December 3, 2011, Nairobi.

small communities, so not unless you pay special attention to him, he will not get it, as compared to the other community. You find, if you are taking of a very small tribe like the Pokomo [0.3 percent of population by 1989], or Oroma [0.2 percent], you find we have promotions. The Kikuyus, who are qualified, they are more than enough. You have to pay special attention to the minority.[41]

The drive to reduce overt favoritism of a president's co-ethnics by the state was formalized with the passage of the 2010 constitution, which stipulates that no more than 30 percent of the bureaucrats in any ministry or state department can come from a single ethnic group.[42]

One implication of diversity at the top of the organization is that all lower-level officers have a chance, however small, of being promoted to a presidentially-appointed position. The path is clearly easier for co-ethnics of each respective president – each president's co-ethnics have tended to be the plurality in the Provincial Administration (see Section 4.6.3) as well as among other top state positions that administrators can move into (e.g., managing a parastatal). Yet, and as I describe in Chapter 8, the possibility of advancement was substantial enough to compel some lower-level administrators, of various ethnicities, to act loyally during periods of political violence.

4.6.3 Evaluating the Ethnic Composition of Kenya's Provincial Administration

I find that the Provincial Administration's diversity was driven by presidents' desires to incorporate rival elites. For some presidents, the diversity of the officer corps was also driven by attempts to incorporate a representative array of ethnic groups. Figure 4.1 plots the percentage of cabinet representation for each of Kenya's five largest ethnic groups (Kalenjin, Kamba, Kikuyu, Luhya, Luo) in the previous year on the percentage of PCs and DCs in the Provincial Administration. These groups are also the most well represented in the Provincial Administration. The top panels depict the representation of PCs and DCs under each president and gives a sense as to which ethnic groups saw their officers promoted. The bottom

---

[41] Interview with then DC, January 25, 2012, Kerugoya.

[42] The Provincial Administration is in compliance with this rule according to the audit carried out by the National Cohesion and Integration Commission, entitled "Ethnic Diversity and Audit of the Civil Service." The group with the largest representation in the Provincial Administration, the Kikuyu, only comprised 16.84 percent of the staff. However, this number includes all Provincial Administrators, including Chiefs and Assistant Chiefs. These lower-level officers are much more numerous than the trained officer corps, and must be from the community in which they serve.

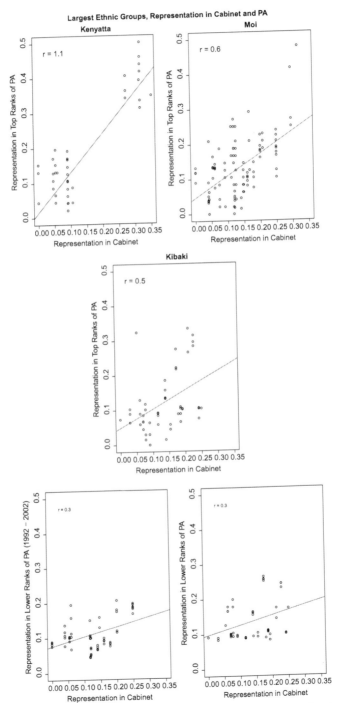

panels display the representation of DOs under Moi's electoral regime (1992–2002) and Kibaki and give us an idea as to which ethnic groups were recruited. There is a positive relationship between cabinet representation in the previous year and Provincial Administration representation in the current year across presidencies and ranks. The larger each group's cabinet representation, the larger their representation in the Provincial Administration one year later.

I also plot the percentage of officers under each president from those five ethnic groups alongside their percentage in the general population in Figure 4.2. As before, the top panels show representation for higher-level PCs and DCs; the lower panel gives representation for lower-level DOs. This second figure shows that the country's largest ethnic groups were all well represented in the Provincial Administration during all presidencies, and in levels that generally reflect their composition within the general population, albeit with considerable variation. Even in plotting basic descriptive statistics, it is clear that the Kenyan state was never packed.

I examine these relationships more systematically by running an ordinary least squares (OLS) regression in which the dependent variable is the percentage of officers from each of the country's five largest ethnic groups. The analyses of PCs and DCs span 1964–2012, while the analyses of DOs span 1992–2012. The main independent variables are the percentage of cabinet positions that a particular ethnic group held in the previous year and the percentage of the population that a particular ethnic group comprises according to the most recent census. Since this analysis is annual, I can account for frequent changes in cabinet composition. I also control for whether the country had multiparty competition in that year where appropriate.

The results are in Table 4.1. Columns 1–4 look at high-ranking PCs and DCs and are indicative of who was promoted within the Provincial Administration. Columns 5–7 look at lower-level DOs and help us understand who was hired. Columns 1 and 5 display the results from the data pooled across presidents for higher- and lower-level administrators, respectively. The remaining columns break down the analyses by president. Column 1 indicates that a one-percentage-point increase in a group's cabinet representation in the past year is associated with a 0.53-percentage-point increase in the group's representation among PCs and DCs ($p < 0.001$). The relationship holds if I look at the Kenyatta or Moi years individually (Columns 2 and 3). This suggests that during Kenya's most authoritarian years, leaders refrained from packing their state, and

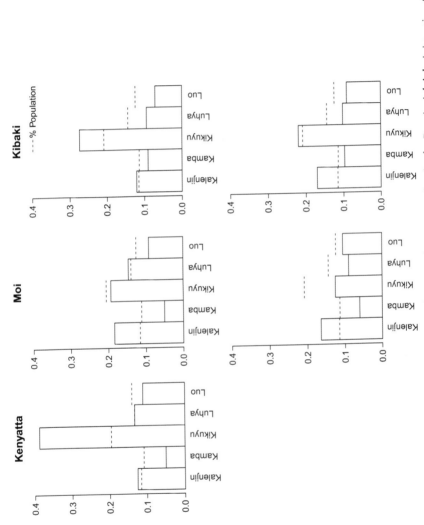

FIGURE 4.2 The relationship between the percentage of the population and representation in the Provincial Administration for the country's five largest ethnic groups. The top panels examine PCs and DCs and date from 1964–2012. The bottom panels examine DOs and date from 1992–2012. Ethnic composition of the population comes from the 1969 census for Kenyatta, 1979 census for Moi, and 1989 census for Kibaki.

TABLE 4.1 *Representation in the Provincial Administration by Cabinet Representation and Ethnic Group Size*

	PCs & DCs				DOs		
	1 All	2 Kenyatta	3 Moi	4 Kibaki	5 All	6 Moi	7 Kibaki
Percent Cabinet (previous year)	0.53***	0.50***	0.50***	−0.17	0.27***	0.31***	−0.01
	(0.07)	(0.14)	(0.10)	(0.10)	(0.06)	(0.07)	(0.12)
Percent Population	1.24***	2.25***	0.65**	2.57***	0.43**	0.28	1.05***
	(0.16)	(0.44)	(0.19)	(0.21)	(0.13)	(0.15)	(0.25)
Multiparty Elections	−0.02	0.02	−0.03*	—	—	—	—
	(0.01)	(0.01)	(0.01)	—	—	—	—
Intercept	−0.10***	−0.22***	−0.01	−0.21***	0.03	0.03	−0.01
	(0.02)	(0.05)	(0.03)	(0.02)	(0.02)	(0.03)	(0.03)
Num. obs.	245	75	120	50	105	55	50

*** $p < 0.001$, ** $p < 0.01$, * $p < 0.05$. OLS regression results on the determinants of the ethnic diversity of the Provincial Administration. The first four regressions examine the ethnic diversity of PCs and DCs. Columns 5 – 7 examine diversity among lower-level DOs. Columns 1 and 5 examine data pooled across presidencies. The remaining columns break down the analysis by president.

opened up the ranks to the co-ethnics of the elites they incorporated into the cabinet the previous year. Similarly, Column 5 indicates that a one-percentage-point increase in a group's cabinet representation in the past year is associated with a 0.27-percentage-point increase in the group's representation among DOs ($p < 0.001$), though this result is driven by Moi's electoral years.

There are at least two factors that help explain the null result for *Percent Cabinet* in Columns 4 and 7. First, the results may reflect the nature of Kibaki's coalition. Kibaki came to power through a Rainbow Coalition in 2002 that received support from most ethnic groups. He also created a "Grand Coalition" with his electoral opponents after the 2007–2008 postelection violence. Kibaki distributed state jobs not based on cabinet representation, but by general population figures. Indeed, notice the high coefficient on *Percent Population* for the Kibaki models. This logic suggests that the unique circumstances surrounding Kibaki's presidency led him to diversify the state in line with general population trends. Second, the results in Column 4 may reflect promotion decisions based on observed loyalty. As I show in Chapter 8, bureaucrats who acted loyally during the highly-visible 2007–2008 post-election violence were more likely to be promoted afterwards, regardless of their ethnic identity. Elite lobbying likely matters less when the center can monitor bureaucrats and has a credible signal about which officers would act loyally if promoted.

These results speak to other work on hiring in African bureaucracies. Most recently, Brierley (Forthcoming) finds that professional bureaucracies in Ghana are diverse. While she argues that this diversity is the result of meritocratic norms at the top ranks, I find that meritocracy and patronage can coexist. So long as there is an oversupply of qualified applicants, leaders can both hire qualified individuals and distribute jobs to cement elite bonds.

4.7 SUMMARY

This chapter has laid out the elite threats faced by Kenya's first three leaders. Each leader sought to address these threats by incorporating elites into the state, preemptively sharing state resources to temper opponents' desire to seek control. Not all elites were willing to be incorporated; in turn, co-ethnics of these nonincorporated elites were often at the forefront of popular mobilization against the president. The next four chapters trace how Kenyan presidents would come to rely on the state, and specifically the Provincial Administration, to put down these popular threats that were often sparked by failed elite incorporation.

Each president would have preferred a state packed with his own co-ethnics to combat the remaining popular threats, since members of one's own group are considered loyal and willing to comply with orders even without monitoring. However, each president oversaw a diverse state. To help explain this puzzle, I show that the Provincial Administration was never packed precisely because of successful elite incorporation. Co-ethnics of incorporated elites could expect more state resources, thereby tempering their desire to mobilize against the leader. But perhaps more importantly, incorporated elites received appointments to coveted bureaucratic positions for their co-ethnics. The second half of this chapter documented that the ethnic composition of the Provincial Administration reflected patterns of elite incorporation through the cabinet. The next chapter examines how President Kenyatta strategically managed bureaucrats within the Provincial Administration to exert social control during his administration.

5

The Provincial Administration under
President Kenyatta

5.1 INTRODUCTION

This chapter examines President Jomo Kenyatta's (1963–1978) use of Kenya's largest security and administrative apparatus, the Provincial Administration, to forestall popular threats against his rule and consolidate the country's one-party authoritarian regime.

His reliance on this agency to temper popular threats, however, gave rise to a principal-agent problem. Given the center's inability to perfectly monitor bureaucratic behavior, agents in the field were at risk of failing to follow orders. The theory in Chapter 2 hypothesizes that a leader can maximize bureaucratic compliance where it matters most, despite the inability to monitor, by jointly considering three relationships – an area's *alignment* with the leader, a bureaucrat's *loyalty* to the leader, and the *local embeddedness* of a bureaucrat to the area in which she is posted. Together, these three relationships shape how a leader governs an area, as well as a bureaucrat's ability and willingness to comply with orders in the absence of monitoring.

The chapter thus begins by outlining the alignment of different areas towards Kenyatta. I detail the popular threats he faced, including those stemming from his land allocation policies and the Kenya People's Union (KPU). Many of these threats were consequences of patterns of elite incorporation. The qualitative evidence I gathered for this study demonstrates how bureaucrats in the Provincial Administration played a crucial role in putting down those popular threats by allocating land to Kenyatta's co-ethnics as well as tilting elections against the KPU. As this section makes clear, the Provincial Administration "became the iron frame upon which Kenyatta built his political control of the country" (Leonard, 1991, 106).

I then explore how the regime maximized compliance. This chapter focuses on top-level Provincial Administration bureaucrats – Provincial Commissioners (PCs) and District Commissioners (DCs). Although most were not Kenyatta's co-ethnics, the loyalty of these high-ranking officers was sustained through patronage. They were among the highest paid in the state and were allowed to use their position to predate extensively. As such, they expected to keep benefiting from the president's continued rule, regardless of their ethnicity.

Yet their compliance was not guaranteed. The qualitative evidence suggests that PCs and DCs still posed a shirking risk if they were too embedded in the jurisdiction in which they served. Embedded bureaucrats – either through co-ethnicity with area residents or long tenure in a station – are less willing to carry out coercive demands because of their social bonds with area residents. High levels of embeddedness compel a bureaucrat to act as an agent of the local population and to use her authority to improve the livelihoods of residents. Yet given this social attachment to and better knowledge of residents, embeddedness made bureaucrats more willing and better able, respectively, to carry out orders to co-opt.

I then quantitatively evaluate my argument. Since I hold bureaucratic *loyalty* constant, I examine how differences in area *alignment* led to the center's manipulation of a bureaucrat's *embeddedness* in an attempt to ensure the co-optation or coercion of an area. I analyze annual data on the assignments of all Kenyatta's PCs and DCs, and find that administrators were managed to increase embeddedness, and therefore better co-opt, in areas inhabited by the president's co-ethnics. Embeddedness was systematically reduced elsewhere, especially in areas inhabited by misaligned groups. Moreover, the quantitative analyses find suggestive evidence of the effects of embeddedness. Specifically, Kenyatta's in-group areas that were governed by a co-ethnic administrator in a given year could expect higher levels of land allocation than similar areas without a co-ethnic administrator for that year.

This chapter highlights several components of the argument made in Chapter 2. Leaders face a principal-agent problem when relying on bureaucrats to carry out their demands. This chapter shows that strategically managing bureaucrats in order to better co-opt areas can succeed, not due to bureaucrats' loyalty to the center, but instead by aligning bureaucrats' incentives with the local area. Increasing bureaucrats' local embeddedness allows them to become agents of the jurisdiction, thereby increasing their willingness and ability to improve the livelihoods of residents. This finding is in line with recent evidence that bureaucrats perform better when they are intrinsically motivated (Besley and Ghatak 2005; Rasul and Rogger 2018). But Kenyatta was only willing to allow these benefits in areas in which his co-ethnics lived. This chapter thus gives us a new mechanism to understand the better development outcomes that African presidents' co-ethnics experience (Franck and Rainer 2012; Hodler and Raschky 2014; Burgess et al. 2015; Kramon and Posner 2016).

5.2 AREA ALIGNMENT AND THE PROVINCIAL ADMINISTRATION'S ACTIONS

This section gives an overview of Kenyatta's popular threat landscape and defines the alignment of different areas towards him. It then provides evidence that the Provincial Administration took different actions in areas with different alignments.

5.2.1 Area Alignment toward Kenyatta

Kenyatta faced numerous popular threats that persisted despite his efforts to incorporate elites. Here, I discuss three: two threats emanating from his land allocation policies and the threat stemming from the elite defection of the KPU.

The most serious popular threats to Kenyatta arguably related to the settlement of agricultural land. The first of these popular threats came from his co-ethnics. The Kikuyu community was heavily fractured after the *Mau Mau* Rebellion, which began as an anticolonial insurgency but became an intra-Kikuyu war fought between landed colonial loyalists and landless rebels (Kanogo 1987; Throup 1993; Kershaw 1997; Branch 2009). Independence implicitly addressed the loyalist/rebel cleavage, but it only aggravated the land issue. Given *Mau Mau*'s role in bringing about independence, newly repatriated rebels and their sympathizers expected to be rewarded with land. But Central Province, considered the ancestral home of the Kikuyu ethnic group, showed signs of overpopulation from the colonial era (Anderson 2005a).

Kenya's *majimbo*, or federal, state structure formally constrained Kenyatta's executive authority in allocating land outside of Central Province. The opposition Kenya African Democratic Union (KADU) party won majority control over the Coast and Rift Valley legislatures

TABLE 5.1 *Agricultural Land and Population by Province.*

Province	1962 Population	Land Potential, hectares ('000)		
		High	Medium	Low
Central	1,363,072	909	15	41
Coast	718,725	373	796	5,663
Eastern	1,475,025	503	2,189	11,453
Nairobi	63,276	16	–	38
Northeastern	269,325	–	–	12,690
Nyanza	1,266,100	1,218	34	–
Rift Valley	1,758,409	3,025	123	12,220
Western	733,731	741	–	–
Total	8,318,070	6,785	3,157	42,105

Population figures are estimated using data from the 1962 census. That census gives population figures following colonial provinces and districts; however, some of those boundaries changed after independence. Land measured in thousands of hectares. Land figures and arability definitions are from the 1972 Kenyan Statistical Abstract, the earliest year after independence for which land totals were given following postcolonial boundaries. High-potential land has an annual rainfall of 857.5 mm+ (980 mm+ in Coast Province). Medium-potential land has an annual rainfall of 735–857.5 mm (735–980 mm in Coast Province; 612.5–857.5 mm in Eastern Province). Low-potential land has an annual rainfall of 612.5 mm or less.

on a platform promising that land would be allocated through land boards headed by elites from ethnic groups considered indigenous to that province. Kenyans would therefore find it difficult to convince land boards outside their ethnic group's "home" province to allocate land to them. These policies were explicitly designed to benefit KADU's own aligned groups and disadvantage potential Kikuyu settlers. KADU's control over Coast and Rift Valley was especially problematic for Kenyatta, given their high levels of available agricultural land, as seen in Table 5.1, which classifies the land in each province by agricultural quality. Rift Valley is home to nearly half of the country's high-potential agricultural land. Coast Province contains roughly 10 percent of all high- and medium-potential land. I also provide the 1962 population figures for each province. The agricultural land in these two provinces was much less densely populated than agricultural land elsewhere.

The inability of poorer members of the Kikuyu ethnic group to acquire land upon independence led to a (short-lived) insurgency. The Kenya Land and Freedom Army, a *Mau Mau* group that never fully disbanded after the formal end of the Emergency, swore to engage in an underground guerrilla movement to force the state to distribute land to Kikuyu squatters until 1965.[1] Other *Mau Mau* rebels fought state security forces after rejecting new land allocation arrangements that they deemed unsatisfactory (Hornsby 2011).

Chapter 4 details how Kenyatta quickly dismantled *majimboism* by 1964. Under a centralized state, Kenyatta could – and did – distribute land to Kikuyu farmers across the county (see Section 5.2.3). His implementation of favorable land policies thus both subdued the *Mau Mau* popular threat and consolidated support among his co-ethnics.

Kenyatta faced a second popular threat related to land. This threat emerged among populations of incorporated KADU elites after the end of *majimboism*, and was a direct consequence of Kenyatta's favorable land policies toward Kikuyu settlers. Though Kenyatta was able to subdue KADU elites through personalized patronage, their constituents mobilized dissatisfaction against his government because they believed their land was unfairly taken away. There are numerous reports of the indigenous groups of Coast and Rift Valley provinces squatting on or informally seizing land formally allocated to Kikuyu settlers. Some of these land confrontations turned violent. For instance, one group of Kikuyu settlers in Uasin Gishu district in Rift Valley wrote to the Permanent Secretary of Provincial Administration:

Nandis [a Kalenjin sub-tribe] at prest [sic] are fighting Kikuyu to death. They usually stream throughout [the] night ... Nandis have already burnt houses and beaten ten Kikuyu. Nandis have already destroyed everything possessed by a Kikuyu, they burn the houses and everything they get inside the house. Any Kikuyu found on the way is beaten to death.[2]

In neighboring Trans-Nzoia, Kikuyu residents complained that they "bought their plots and they are now not working in these plots simply because the main holders are expelling them."[3] Likewise, a local Kikuyu women's group wrote of land and local politics woes:

Among the [Kikuyu] residents of Cherangani we have widows and other men who are never allowed to buy *shambas* [farms] by the leaders in the are [sic]. We are always told that the time for buying *shambas* is past .... During the council

---

[1] As before, they were most active in Central Province and Kikuyu-dominated areas in Rift Valley.

[2] Kikuyu Residents Kaptagat Settlement Scheme to Permanent Secretary Provincial Administration, July 18, 1969, KA/6/19, Kenya National Archives, Nairobi, Kenya.

[3] KANU Kapsara Sub-Branch to District Commissioner Trans-Nzoia, January 14, 1968, KA/6/19, Kenya National Archives, Nairobi.

elections the man we had put as a candidate was thrashed before the public by [his opponent]. This man was made to fail because he is a Kikuyu.[4]

Kenyatta would come to rely on the Provincial Administration not only to distribute land to his co-ethnic community, but to coerce out-groups who resisted Kikuyu settlement.

Separately, Kenyatta faced a popular challenge from the KPU. The KPU found its strongest support among the Luo co-ethnics of the party's leader, Oginga Odinga. But given its substantial cross-ethnic support, it posed a real popular threat to Kenyatta and his party, the Kenya African National Union (KANU). Kenyatta forced the MPs who defected to the KPU in 1966 to stand for immediate reelection. These elections were neither free nor fair due to the actions of the Provincial Administration (Mueller 1984). And these KPU MPs all lost in nationwide polls in 1969 or defected back to KANU between 1966 and 1969.[5]

Despite the disintegration of the KPU in 1969, Kenyatta experienced increased popular discontent among Luo citizens for the rest of his presidency. In Nyanza, considered the home province of the Luo, residents were accused of "being behind KPU with their full hearts."[6] One (non-Luo) backer of President Kenyatta explained that his (Luo) boss was: "telling us that as we are his laborers we must be in KPU and he was saying that if he found any laborers belonging to KANU [they] will be dismissed from [their] job."[7] More dangerous for Kenyatta was the discontent that turned violent. For instance, during his official state visit to Kisumu (the capital of Nyanza Province) in 1969 thousands of protesters surrounded his motorcade and the crowd eventually started rioting. In response, the security forces – under the command of the Nyanza PC – beat and shot into the crowd. Official reports indicate that eleven civilians were killed and dozens were injured, but the death toll was rumored to be significantly higher. Unrest heightened again after the 1969 assassination of the Luo elite Tom Mboya, allegedly by an ardent supporter of Kenyatta's. There was "near-insurrection among the Luos"

---

[4] KANU Leaders Cherangani Settlement Scheme to President's Office, November 15, 1968, KA/6/19, Kenya National Archives, Nairobi.

[5] I classify the majority of Kenyatta's regime as autocratic; however, there were elements of an electoral regime from 1966 to 1969.

[6] Private citizen to President, KA/6/18, October 30, 1969, Nyanza Provincial Archives, Kisumu, Kenya.

[7] Ministry of Works South Nyanza Employees to President, August 4, 1968, KA/6/43, Nyanza Provincial Archives, Kisumu.

(Hornsby, 2011, 208) during Mboya's state funeral when Luo protesters rioted along the procession route.

5.2.2 KANU Unable to Solve Kenyatta's Popular Threats

A strong KANU could have kept tabs on the population and swayed local opinion, but the party was weak and lacked the cohesiveness and uniting ideology to handle popular challenges. Indeed, it had been weak since its inception during the colonial era. During the Emergency, the colonial regime strictly enforced a ban on inter-district political organizations, meaning that political entrepreneurs could only create district-wide political organizations in the run-up to independence (Gertzel 1970). This helps explain the ethnic nature of KANU at independence: it was largely an amalgamation of different district political organizations. As such, it is questionable how much sway Kenyatta held in non-Kikuyu KANU areas, as the party drew its momentum largely from the personal followings of its ethnic leaders (Posner 2005). Even after Kenyatta incorporated elites from Coast and Rift Valley provinces, he did not manage to align citizens with himself or the party. Citizens in those provinces were loyal to their elites – who were expected to pass resources down to them – rather than to the party they nominally represented.

Nor did Kenyatta invest in creating a party with strong internal and vertical connections after independence. Local KANU branches were "never sufficiently cohesive or imbued with sufficient authority to help resolve local conflicts or to serve as reliable conduits for information to and from the central government" (Widner, 1992, 70). After Odinga defected and Kenyatta lost his intermediated connection to the Luo community, it became clear that the party alone could not prevent popular threats. If another elite defected, the party would be unable to keep popular threats from the elite's followers in check. The Provincial Administration, and not Kenyatta's party, would play the crucial role in maintaining social control.

5.2.3 Co-optation and Coercion to Address Land Demands from the Kikuyu Community

Kenyatta relied on the Provincial Administration to co-opt his co-ethnic community by providing them with resources. I focus here specifically on the distribution of land.[8] Provincial Administration land policies initially

---

[8] For favoritism in other resources, see Franck and Rainer (2012), Burgess et al. (2015), and Kramon and Posner (2016).

sought to temper the popular threat stemming from aggrieved *Mau Mau* elements; the objective later became to maintain popular Kikuyu support behind Kenyatta.[9] For Kikuyu settlers outside Central Province, these policies included coercing indigenous residents to ensure Kikuyu settlement. Together, this preferential treatment ensured the Kikuyu community's future support of Kenyatta.

Kenyatta hoped to alleviate land demands from his co-ethnics in part by creating state-sponsored "settlement schemes" – large tracts of land acquired from departing white settlers that the state divided into smaller plots to settle aspiring farmers.[10] Throughout his reign, Kenyatta oversaw the creation of such schemes in 21 of the country's 40 districts totaling 584,000 hectares (nearly 1.5 million acres) for more than 75,000 settlers.[11] Kenyatta distributed nearly 2.5 percent of the country's 24 million hectares of agricultural land in this way (see Table 5.1).

Settlement schemes were mostly created in poorer Kikuyu-majority areas while *majimboism* was still in place due to the political context in which they were launched. The idea to use settlement schemes to alleviate landlessness in different ethnic communities was crystallized in the immediate run-up to independence, just as political elites agreed on a *majimbo* state structure. With *majimboism*, and the associated formal authority that regional land boards had to choose settlers in their province, many presumed that an individual could only receive an allocation in the province associated with her historic homeland. Indeed, archival material indicates that administrators before 1964 would often explicitly write that the scheme was "for" the local ethnic group and reject applicants from other groups.[12]

Since the state had a fixed amount of cash to buy settler land, it made sense for Kenyatta's government to create settlement schemes in Central Province, the only province in which he could guarantee land for Kikuyu settlers (Wasserman 1973). And in fact, many of the settlement schemes created in the run-up to independence and soon afterwards were in Central Province. They were part of the "Million Acre scheme" – a collection

---

[9] While I refer to the Provincial Administration's actions towards Kikuyu communities as "co-optation," I recognize that these policies created bonds of dependence between Kikuyu settlers and Kenyatta that could be considered "coercive distribution" (Albertus, Fenner, and Slater 2018).

[10] By 2017, settlement schemes accounted for about 12 percent of all titled land in Kenya (Dyzenhaus 2018).

[11] This figure includes settlement schemes created at the beginning of the Million Acre scheme in 1962, when Kenya was still a colony but Kenyatta was set to become the country's postindependence leader.

[12] See, for instance, PC/NKU/2/16/54, Kenya National Archives, Nairobi.

of smaller schemes that sought to resettle 35,000 families from 1962–1967 (Leys, 1975, 75), largely in Nyandarua and Nyeri districts of Central Province. With *Mau Mau* elements still active at independence, Kikuyu resettlement became an important way to co-opt poorer members of this ethnic group to prevent them from becoming a threat. Though this land was not free, as *Mau Mau* supporters demanded, Kenyatta gave settlement scheme beneficiaries sufficient advantages – e.g., land at below-market rates and additional financing – that they were still highly valued by all Kenyans and contradicted Kenyatta's official rhetoric about free market principles.

Kenyatta relied on the Provincial Administration to carry out his pre-ferred land allocation policies because it was, and continues to be, well positioned to choose which residents were eligible for land allocation, make certain that beneficiaries could afford to buy the land, help set-tle boundary disputes between claimants, and ensure settlement by the formal owner against other claimants.[13] Land administration is not the agency's foremost duty, but the state agencies that do administer land are run through the central government in Nairobi and the Provincial Administration in the field. The land boards that were supposed to be run by indigenous elders under *majimboism* were never fully implemented. Instead, after Kenyatta dismantled *majimboism*, the central government oversaw the creation of land control boards at the province, district, and division levels that were chaired by their respective administrator to over-see the transfer of land.[14] And administrators continue to play a role in registering schemes and titling land after a scheme is settled.

The Provincial Administration helped settle Kikuyu farmers on newly acquired land in Central Province, both during and after the country's brief flirtation with *majimboism*. The schemes on the western side of Cen-tral Province were created in areas that were part of colonial Rift Valley Province, and thus home to many non-Kikuyu residents.[15] The Provin-cial Administration evicted many pastoralists to make room for Kikuyu settlers (Leys 1975). Administrators also showed leniency towards new Kikuyu beneficiaries in Central Province. While the Provincial Adminis-tration had the authority to seize land from beneficiaries who missed a loan repayment, it rarely did so in Central Province. According to Colin

---

13 For instance, see Kanyinga (2000b).
14 In some cases allotments were chosen by lottery. Often, land boards determined who was eligible to enter the lottery.
15 See the Regional Boundaries Commission Report of 1962.

Leys (1975, 79), by 1969 only ninety settlers had been evicted for nonre-payment despite many cases of default.[16]

At the same time, provincial administrators used their networks of local informants to prevent active *Mau Mau* elements from purchasing land in settlement schemes, much like the Provincial Administration's seizure of land from rebels during the colonial period.[17] One letter from a village in Central Province in 1968 explained that the "whole struggle … is between those who suffered during the emergency and those who enjoyed during the emergency."[18] And while the Provincial Administration did not seize much land from Kikuyu settlers, it made clear which Kikuyu settlers were at risk. One PC said, "People who criticized the government and yet had been given loans to buy farms and open businesses would forfeit them."[19] In this way, land allocation sought to quash the *Mau Mau* threat both by tempering land shortages and by increasing recipients' support for Kenyatta.

Kenyatta also used the Provincial Administration to resettle his co-ethnics on settlement schemes outside of traditional Kikuyu areas after the death of *majimboism* in 1964. As Central Province had showed signs of overpopulation even during the colonial era (Anderson 2005a), Kenyatta sought to expand Kikuyu settlement into less densely populated Coast and Rift Valley provinces, just as KADU leaders originally feared. Many landless coastal squatters were evicted, as were some with rightful titles, to make room for "upcountry," largely Kikuyu, tenants. Take Lake Kenyatta settlement scheme in Lamu, arguably Kenyatta's most infamous attempt to settle Kikuyus outside Central Province. Archival documents show that the Provincial Administration allocated land to Kikuyu settlers that had already been registered to local Bajun residents.[20] This helps explain the "fear of domination by the Kikuyu" among indigenous coastal groups – they recognized that schemes located there "were not specifically/exclusively aimed at redressing landlessness among coastal groups and yet, the upcountry ones were aimed at benefiting only the landless upcountry groups" (Kanyinga, 2000b, 100).

---

[16] Kenyatta himself was known to intervene "to ensure that settlers with lapsed loans were treated with leniency … [to keep] alive the direct political tie between [beneficiaries] and the state" (Boone, 2012, 80).

[17] See Berman and Lonsdale (1992).

[18] Ruguru residents to Vice President KANU Central Province, KA/6/43, April 9, 1968, Kenya National Archives.

[19] *East African Standard*, October 21, 1972 as seen in Leys (1975, 239).

[20] See AVS/15/132, Kenya National Archives, Nairobi.

Kikuyu resettlement also displaced indigenous ethnic groups of Rift Valley. For example, Eburu settlement scheme in Nakuru District in Rift Valley was originally planned to settle 150 Maasai families. Families were expected to pay a small fee for the land that many of these families could not afford. Rather than offering the farmers a loan – as some Kikuyu residents in the district had received for settlement on other schemes – the Nakuru DC agreed to let Kikuyu farmers from a neighboring district settle there instead.[21] In the end, the land for the scheme was allocated almost wholly to Kikuyu allottees. Elsewhere in Nakuru District, Kalenjin residents recall how some were "convicted and taken to [local] prisons. Houses were burnt down and women and children were thrown out onto the roads and their land given to the Kikuyus" (Klaus, 2016, 27).[22] As one older Kalenjin MP recalled, "all that the PA was doing then was helping [resettle Kikuyu farmers] on our land. Kenyatta used the PA to steal our land."[23]

Figure 5.1 shades districts in which Kenyatta created settlement schemes by the amount of hectares allocated. Settlement schemes in Central Province were concentrated in Nyandarua and Nyeri districts. The districts in Rift Valley with majority Kikuyu populations by 1979, Lakikipia and Nakuru, saw many schemes created. Many settlement schemes were created in other districts in Rift Valley and on the coast, in line with narratives about the in-migration of Kikuyu settlers. Taken together, Figure 5.1 illustrates the districts in which the Provincial Administration's actions related to land would have had the largest impact.

5.2.4 Coercion against the KPU and Its Supporters

The Provincial Administration selectively used its coercive capacity against KPU leaders and their supporters. Coercion was especially high in Luo-dominated areas, as the group was the base of KPU support. For example, the agency selectively enforced colonial-era laws and administrative ordinances to hinder KPU candidates during the 1966 snap elections (Mueller 1984). These include the Societies Ordinance of 1952, which was formulated in the wake of *Mau Mau* and required all district

---

21 See EC/9/60, Rift Valley Provincial Archives, Nakuru, Kenya.
22 There were also instances in which the Provincial Administration evicted Kikuyu settlers at the bequest of powerful pastoralist elites. Yet in many of these cases, administrators helped those evicted find land nearby (Kanyinga 2009, 333).
23 Interview with then MP, February 27, 2012, Nairobi.

**Settlement Scheme Allocation
under Kenyatta**

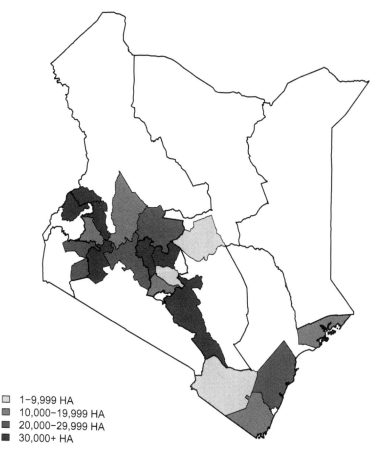

☐ 1–9,999 HA
▨ 10,000–19,999 HA
■ 20,000–29,999 HA
■ 30,000+ HA

FIGURE 5.1 Settlement scheme allocations in square hectares during Kenyatta's presidency by district. Provincial boundaries outlined in bold.

branches and sub-branches of political parties to obtain certificates of registration with the central government. The Provincial Administration also relied on the Special Districts Ordinance, again enacted during the Emergency, which forbade nonresidents from entering "Closed Districts" without prior permission from the center. Closed districts spanned parts of Central, Eastern, and Rift Valley that were affected by *Mau Mau*, but also contained several constituencies where KPU candidates were running. Other laws dictated that groups could only hold large meetings after written authorization from the area provincial administrator. Some of these laws remained on the books until Kibaki's presidency.

In addition, Kenyatta relied on the Provincial Administration to implement new laws and ordinances that prevented the KPU from gaining popular support. Official orders from Nairobi were to ban all political rallies – including those sponsored by KANU – in order to seem impartial. Yet the Provincial Administration was selective about how it implemented the order. One KPU leader wrote to his DC in 1967 about a rally in Kisumu town, Kenya's third-largest city and the heart of the Luo homeland:

Once again, we wish to draw your kind attention to the fact that KANU is holding rallies after rallies all over the country including the one which was held at the Kenyatta Sports Ground on the 5th February, 1967 under the license issued by you. We would like to know if it is your deliberate intention, Mr. [DC], to refuse only KPU permission to hold public meetings without any specific reason.[24]

Formal requests for rallies were often denied for vague "security reasons."[25] Other KPU rally requests were denied because the applicant did not give sufficient advance notice. The length of advance notice necessary seemed to vary, but was always a few days more than the length of time between the date of the rally request and the date of the proposed rally. The Provincial Administration rejected still another KPU rally request because it would likely result in monetary donations, thus violating laws on public collections. This was despite the fact that the same administrators in the same jurisdiction allowed KANU *harambees* to fill party coffers.[26] This denial of rally requests echoes the findings of Susanne Mueller's research on the ways in which the Provincial Administration used administrative ordinances to prevent the KPU from gaining popular support across the country. In the run-up to the 1966 election, the Office of the President sent the following telegram to all PCs: "Licenses to hold public meetings to be issued to KANU members only. Stop. Seven days notice required. Stop. All other applications to be referred to President's Office. Stop. Permits issued to non KANU members to be cancelled with

---

24 KPU Central Nyanza Branch Secretary to DC Nyanza, April 23, 1967, DA/1/197, Nyanza Provincial Archives, Kisumu.
25 See DA/1/197, Nyanza Provincial Archives, Kisumu and EC/1/15, Rift Valley Provincial Archives, Nakuru.
26 DC to KPU Nakuru Branch, October 5, 1967, EC/1/15, Rift Valley Provincial Archives, Nakuru.

immediate effect. Stop."[27] Unsurprisingly, the KPU received no licenses to hold public meetings in 1966, compared to an estimated 505 for KANU.[28]

Coercion by officers in the Provincial Administration against the KPU ramped up in the run-up to the national 1969 election. For instance, the KPU District Chairman of Kisumu complained that administrators had arrested his sub-branch members and sentenced them to six months in jail for holding an unlicensed committee meeting.[29] One KPU District Secretary raised the following complaint against the local administrator in 1968:

[he] had been harassing and ordering the police men to arrest and detain the KPU officials unnecessary and without grounds … During all periods [he] had failed to prove as to why that KPU Official should be detained … [he] refused the District Secretary of KPU and KPU county candidates to take 'Form N. 2' [the registration form] and other necessary information.[30]

And while the Provincial Administration slowed down the registration of branches and sub-branches in the run-up to the 1966 election, it went a step further in the run-up to the 1969 election: many KPU branches or sub-branches that had registered in 1966 were unable to renew their registration, and 43 percent of applications were rejected (Mueller 1984).[31] This number is considerably higher than the 2 percent refusal rate of KANU branch applications. KPU party secretaries received rejection letters explaining, for instance, "the interests of peace, welfare or good order in Kenya would be likely to suffer prejudice by reason of your registration as a society."[32] Administrators were instructed to check up on deregistered branches "so that we ascertain that the organization does not operate."[33] Deregistration was so ubiquitous that one DC in 1969

---

[27] As seen in Mueller (1984, 413).

[28] Also see Leys (1975), Bates (1981), and Ajulu (2002).

[29] KPU Kisumu Branch Chairman to PC Nyanza, March 11, 1969, DA/1/197, Nyanza Provincial Archives, Kisumu.

[30] KPU Machakos District Secretary to Minister of Provincial Administration, July 31, 1968, KA/6/43, Kenya National Archives, Nairobi.

[31] Mueller also correctly notes that this percentage underestimates the amount of coercion that the KPU faced in registering branches: the widespread intimidation likely prevented many local KPU branches from attempting to register, and many of the KPU branches that registered between 1966 and 1969 likely folded because of coercion by the Provincial Administration.

[32] Deputy Registrar of Societies Nakuru to KPU Molo Sub-Branch, August 13, 1969, EC/1/15, Rift Valley Provincial Archives, Nakuru.

[33] DC Nakuru to Officer Commanding Police Division Nakuru, February 24, 1969, EC/1/15, Rift Valley Provincial Archives, Nakuru.

was perplexed when he received a request to hold a meeting from the KPU, since only registered societies could make such requests. The officer demanded "documentary proof to the effect that [the] branch has not been de-registered" before he would consider the request.[34]

The Provincial Administration also used its authority over basic administration and development to prevent local residents in the jurisdiction from supporting the KPU. Since the KPU was only a popular threat if it was supported by Kenyans,

Those living in the rural areas were warned by local party and administrative officials that anyone who voted for the KPU would not get the famine-relief maize being distributed by the Government; shop-owners were threatened that if opposition supporters were found on their premises, then these would be closed; individuals who had plots in settlement schemes were told that they would lose their farms if they voted with, or supported, the KPU; DCs sometimes instructed chiefs to "write down the names of all KPU supporters in the area so that the Government would take action against them" (Mueller, 1984, 422).

In addition to economic repercussions, KPU supporters also faced real physical integrity violations at the hands of the Provincial Administration. The agency failed to prevent, and in some cases encouraged, KANU "youth wingers" – armed, ardent KANU supporters – from breaking up KPU rallies or intimidating their supporters. Other KPU supporters who protested at KANU meetings were chased off by security officers and were at times dispersed with tear gas (Gertzel 1970). One complaint letter details a local *baraza*, or community gathering, in which a local leader verbally attacked KANU MPs and spoke favorably about the KPU until the DC rebuked him and enforced censorship during the rest of the meeting.[35]

The Provincial Administration's actions eventually stamped out the KPU. Though the KPU had nationwide support upon its founding, and all of its MPs had won their previous elections, only nine (of twenty-nine) KPU candidates won reelection in 1966. The majority of these winners were in Luo-majority areas. Therefore the run-up to the 1969 election saw KPU activity predominately in Luo areas, and only Luo candidates contested on the KPU ticket (non-Luo KPU members by 1966 defected back to KANU by 1969 (Mueller 1984)). However, the KPU was officially

34 DC Nakuru to KPU Nakuru Branch, June 25, 1969, EC/1/15, Rift Valley Provincial Archives, Nakuru.
35 Residents of Marama Location to PC Western, May 2, 1969, KA/6/43, Kenya National Archives, Nairobi.

banned just before the election. Kenya remained a *de facto* one-party regime for the rest of Kenyatta's presidency.

Despite the eradication of the KPU in 1969, Odinga remained the most prominent Luo politician and Luo areas remained sources of discontent for the rest of Kenyatta's presidency. Given Odinga's exclusion from the state, he could quickly mobilize unrest among his co-ethnics against the regime. And many Luo citizens were willing to take on the costs of collective action precisely because they were not receiving a steady stream of state resources. The Provincial Administration thus remained active in Luo areas, putting down strikes, arresting KANU opponents, and neutralizing rumors against the regime even after the KPU was formally banned.

5.3 BUREAUCRATIC LOYALTY TOWARD KENYATTA

As the qualitative evidence described in Section 5.2 documents, the Provincial Administration was integral to maintaining popular control across the country. We might therefore assume that Kenyatta ensured bureaucratic compliance by packing the state. Kenyatta had consolidated his one-party regime by the 1970s, and had sufficient executive power to pack coercive agencies with in-group officers. Previous studies argue that in-group bureaucrats are the most loyal because they have neopatrimonial bonds with the leader.

Yet the top ranks of the Provincial Administration – presidentially appointed PCs and DCs – were diverse.[36] This is not to say that Kenyatta's co-ethnic administrators were not favored in appointments. Kikuyu administrators comprised 39 percent of DC-years and nearly 50 percent of PC-years. But Kenyatta ultimately chose to staff the top tiers of this agency in a manner that reflected the incorporation of elite politicians into the regime, as shown in Chapter 4. Figure 5.2 displays the representation of PCs and DCs for each of the country's five largest ethnic groups under Kenyatta.[37]

---

[36] PCs were chosen from the larger pool of DCs, and DCs from the larger pool of District Officers (DOs).

[37] There were forty-six officers from 1963–1967 and forty-eight by the end of Kenyatta's presidency. Siaya District was created in 1967 and Nairobi Province was only assigned a PC in 1970.

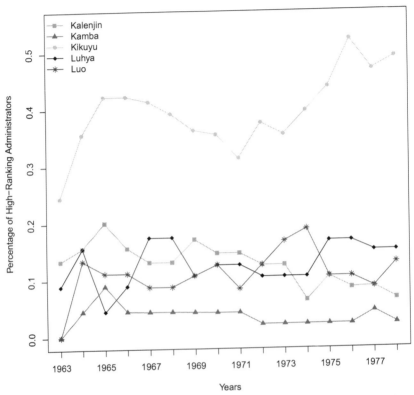

FIGURE 5.2 Percentage of Kenyatta's high-ranking provincial administrators by ethnicity. Percentages plotted for the country's five largest ethnic groups by year, who were also among the most well-represented within the Provincial Administration.

Despite variation in co-ethnicity with Kenyatta, PCs and DCs were considered among the most loyal bureaucrats in the state through patronage. These bureaucrats had strong incentives to keep Kenyatta in office. First, they owed their position to Kenyatta: even if a co-ethnic elite lobbied on their behalf, these positions were ultimately presidentially appointed. Any new leader would invariably populate these ranks with his own choices. Second, these positions were among the very best one could hope for in either the public or private sector as they were exceedingly well compensated. Further, bureaucrats received housing benefits, pension plans, and allowances for travel and hosting notable guests. And perhaps more importantly, informal compensation, for all intents and purposes, was deemed permissible after the 1971 Ndegwa Commission. The commission was led by top businessmen-politicians, which Ato Kwamena Onoma (2010, 155) compares to "assigning wolves to guard the sheep": they recommended a salary bump for top provincial administrators and, more lucratively, proclaimed that officers could engage in business on the side. For many administrators, this business took the form of predation and land grabbing. Looking at the coast, Karuti Kanyinga (2000b, 70) writes that residents:

repeatedly emphasised that the entire line of the Provincial Administration officers on the coast, from the Provincial Commissioner (PC) to the District Officers (DOs), was dominated by "land-greedy" officers who were keen to request for authority to alienate government land to settle the squatters but always turned such land into private property or sold it to rich private developers.

Kenyatta further cultivated loyalty at the top of the Provincial Administration by allowing officers to misuse their authority for personal gain, including at the expense of political elites. For instance, high-ranking administrators held immense political influence that they sometimes wielded to ensure that officers' personal opponents were not reelected (Leonard 1991). The late politician Martin Shikuku recounts the case of a PC physically assaulting an MP:

One day one of my colleagues – a man called Hon. Abu Somo – was taken to court for having alleged that the Provincial Commissioner in the Rift Valley was involved in some scandal. The poor young man was forced to withdraw his allegation and apologize. While the case was going on, the young man was beaten up by the P.C., Mr. Mathenge …. [Mathenge] hit the honourable Member in front of the judges, the police, and everyone else present, yet he was not arrested for that … Would you believe it? Mathenge was not arrested for that act, nor was he even asked to make a statement to the police, nor did any judge at that time order the arrest of Mathenge! (Shikuku, n.d., 92)

Kenyatta allowed his PCs and DCs to predate at high levels, and bestowed a high status upon them. They had few incentives to use their authority to benefit a rival elite.

But bureaucratic behavior depends on more than loyalty to the president. As Chapter 2 made clear, bureaucrats are liable to act differently depending on their embeddedness in a jurisdiction. In Section 5.4, I provide qualitative evidence to demonstrate how even loyal bureaucrats were likely to act against the center's orders if they were too embedded in their jurisdiction.

5.4 THE BENEFITS AND PITFALLS OF LOCAL EMBEDDEDNESS

Though all of Kenyatta's PCs and DCs were considered exceedingly loyal to him, their willingness and ability to either co-opt or coerce were affected by their social relationships to residents in the area in which they were posted. Most troubling for the center, bureaucrats were liable to shirk from orders to coerce if they were too locally embedded.

The strong social bonds between locally embedded bureaucrats and the communities in which they were posted had both positive and negative implications for the allocation of land. Embeddedness was helpful in areas that the regime wanted to co-opt, such as in Central Province. Officers would be willing to go above and beyond for local residents if they valued the moral standing that local residents would bestow upon them for their actions (Tsai 2007b). But an officer's embeddedness could skew the center's intended governance patterns precisely because it increased the connection between the bureaucrat and the residents in the area she served.

An example of the pitfalls of embeddedness concerns Simeon Nyachae, a Kisii administrator who was considered among the most loyal to Kenyatta. Nyachae was appointed PC of Rift Valley in 1965. As his term lengthened and his embeddedness with the majority pastoralist groups deepened, Nyachae encountered multiple situations that pitted the interests of pastoralists against those of Kikuyu farmers. Nyachae was rotated away from Rift Valley soon after an incident in which he privileged Kalenjin farmers: "Kenyatta wanted him out of the Rift Valley" because "he was not sufficiently favorable to the Kikuyu who were competing with that group for access to land" (Leonard 1991, 110). Nyachae was replaced by Isaiah Mathenge, a Kikuyu administrator. Mathenge stayed in this post for six years, until Kenyatta's death. Though he too became locally embedded through tenure, he had an innate connection to the Kikuyu community that the center sought to co-opt. He would later be considered part of the "Rift Valley Mafia" that helped resettle Kikuyu farmers deeper into historic pastoralist land (Klaus 2020).[38]

Another example comes from Kakamega District in Western Province. Kakamega had a Kikuyu population of less than 1 percent throughout Kenyatta's presidency. Local Kikuyu residents attempted to use their

---

[38] Also see Muchemi Wachira, "Mathenge was the last strongman of the Kenyatta era," *The Daily Nation*, January 22, 2006.

personal resources to buy land in the district.[39] One group of Kikuyu families argued, "we are told that everybody should be issued land in the area he lives according to his loyalty in the area he lives."[40] Even though the citizens stressed their loyalty and co-ethnicity with President Kenyatta, it seems that the local DC – who had been in his post for more than three years when this complaint letter was written – was unwilling to upset the majority Luhya population by overseeing the allocation of land to nonindigenous settlers.

My research did not reveal instances of shirking by PCs or DCs on behalf of Odinga or other elite rivals. This makes sense: high-ranking administrators would only stand to lose if Kenyatta lost power. Though their loyalty towards Kenyatta versus other elites was not in doubt, high-ranking officers may have worked on behalf of the community to which they were posted rather than on behalf of the center. For instance, one officer who worked under Kenyatta mentioned how he still visits some of his longest-serving posts, and how community members in the area have named a local transport spot in his honor. Another bureaucrat who served during these years fondly recalled being posted among his co-ethnics (though not in his home district); "I was among my people, I understood them, their problems."[41] Locally embedded bureaucrats did not purposefully work to serve another political elite. But in working on behalf of the community in which they were posted, embedded bureaucrats were at risk of increasing the local stature of Kenyatta's rivals.

5.5 QUANTITATIVE ANALYSIS: BUREAUCRATIC MANAGEMENT
UNDER KENYATTA

This section assesses the posting and shuffling patterns of provincial administrators under Kenyatta. I first recap area alignment towards Kenyatta. I then use annual data on the assignments of his PCs and DCs to examine whether bureaucrats were managed to increase the co-optation of his aligned base and to coerce misaligned areas that displayed high levels of KPU support.

---

[39] This exchange occurred after the end of *majimboism*.
[40] Private Citizens to DC Kakamega, December 28, 1965, DC/KMA/2/13/18, Kenya National Archives, Nairobi.
[41] Interview with former PC, July 3, 2017, Nairobi.

5.5.1 Area Alignment toward Kenyatta

Table 5.2 summarizes area alignment and provides descriptive statistics on posting and shuffling patterns of Kenyatta's PCs and DCs. Central Province, which was overwhelmingly populated by Kenyatta's co-ethnics, was aligned for the majority of his tenure. Though Kenyatta initially faced a resurgent *Mau Mau* threat in parts of Central, his policy proposals helped align the area's preferences with his continued tenure. Areas in Coast and Rift Valley, where Kenyatta hoped to resettle some Kikuyu farmers, were both aligned (because of the presence of his co-ethnics) and misaligned (due to the presence of indigenous groups that threatened to fight against this resettlement). Luo-majority areas in Nyanza Province were misaligned after the emergence of the KPU in 1966, during both the electoral regime of 1966–1969 and Kenyatta's subsequent autocratic regime. I also classify areas in which the KPU fielded a candidate in 1966 as misaligned for that year. However, the vast majority of the country did not participate in the Little General Election, and posed no real electoral threat to Kenyatta. By the 1969 election, only Luo areas fielded KPU candidates. The rest of the country is best classified as unaligned.

The table also adds the two measures of embeddedness I quantitatively evaluate – co-ethnicity between bureaucrat and the majority of area residents (Column 5), and length of tenure (Column 6). I list the percentage of Kikuyu administrators posted to parts of Coast and Rift Valley provinces, instead of the percentage of co-ethnic administrators, as some jurisdictions had substantial Kikuyu populations but not an outright Kikuyu majority. Together, Columns 5 and 6 lend support to the theory. The center increased embeddedness in aligned areas, through both the co-ethnicity of administrators and administrator tenure. The center decreased the embeddedness of bureaucrats elsewhere, especially in misaligned areas. The following analyses reiterate these findings more systematically after controlling for alternative explanations.

5.5.2 Bureaucratic Management and Kikuyu Settlement

Kenyatta's presidency spanned both a very brief electoral regime and a very lengthy autocratic regime. But my theory predicts that Kenyatta would have maintained the same management strategy among aligned areas across both regime types. I therefore analyze the Kenyatta years as a whole in this section. Data limitations prevent me from testing implications of the theory that have more temporal elements. For instance,

TABLE 5.2 *Management of Administrators by Area Alignment toward Kenyatta*

Alignment	Group	Location	Time Period	Percentage of Co-ethnic Administrators (%)	Average Tenure (Years)
Aligned	Kikuyu	Central Province	Post-*majimbo*	53	3.1
		Parts of Coast, Rift Valley Provinces		62*	3.2
Misaligned	Former KADU pastoralists	Parts of Coast, Rift Valley Provinces	Post-*majimbo*	—	—
	KPU supporters	Constituencies with KPU candidate	Little General Election (1966)	24	—
	Luo	Parts of Nyanza Province	1966–1978	3	3
Unaligned	Other ethnic groups	Various	Throughout	12	2.6
Total			1964–1978	18	2.6

* Percentage of Kikuyu administrators, not co-ethnic administrators, as some of these districts were not majority Kikuyu.

it would be interesting to examine if management patterns changed after the end of *majimboism* and *Mau Mau*. But the analysis begins in 1964, when both *majimboism* and *Mau Mau* were ending, as independence was only granted in December 1963. And it is difficult to hone in on management in 1964, as some administrators were still British.

The observable implications from Chapter 2 suggest that Kenyatta should manage bureaucrats to increase their local embeddedness with Kikuyu residents. PCs and DCs had strong neopatrimonial relationships with Kenyatta and were thought to comply out of personally loyalty to him. But increasing embeddedness makes bureaucrats more willing and able to co-opt a jurisdiction and its residents, regardless of loyalty towards Kenyatta.

We should therefore expect aligned Central Province to see high levels of embeddedness, both through a high percentage of co-ethnic administrators and a long tenure in office. There, the center wanted bureaucrats to create bonds with local residents and govern in their (and thus the regime's) best interests. In the parts of Coast or Rift Valley Provinces in which Kenyatta wanted to settle Kikuyu migrants, we should expect embeddedness through ethnic postings. Kikuyu bureaucrats posted to these districts would be willing to privilege Kikuyu residents at the expense of the local majority or the indigenous population. However, the theory is ambiguous when it comes to shuffling rates in areas outside Central Province with substantial Kikuyu populations. Longer tenure rates were liable to increase an administrator's embeddedness with the jurisdiction's entire population, not only its Kikuyu residents. This greater embeddedness through tenure may have helped bureaucrats better respond to the Kikuyu community's needs, or it may have allowed the bureaucrat to create bonds with the non-Kikuyu population and undermine the center's efforts to resettle Kenyatta's co-ethnics.

I examine these observable implications using data on all PCs and DCs during Kenyatta's reign. I run two regressions to examine ethnic postings. The dependent variable in the first is the percentage of years an administrative unit had a co-ethnic officer from 1964–1978, and the independent variable is an indicator for whether the majority of residents in the unit were Kikuyu. This regression captures whether Central Province and Kikuyu-majority districts in the Rift had Kikuyu officers. To better hone in on the role of officer co-ethnicity in all places with substantial Kikuyu communities, including minority communities, I run a regression in which the dependent variable is the percentage of years that a unit had a Kikuyu officer and the independent variable is an indicator variable for whether the unit's population was at least 20 percent Kikuyu by 1979 (Column 2).[42] I run two regressions to examine tenure lengths. The main independent variable in the third, as before, is an indicator variable for majority-Kikuyu districts. The main independent variable for the fourth is an indicator for whether a unit was at least 20 percent Kikuyu by 1979.

The regressions use two datasets. The time-series dataset described in Chapter 1 is used to run a Cox Proportional Hazard model on shuffling in Columns 3 and 4. Columns 1 and 2 use a collapsed version of this dataset where the observation is the administrative unit, as the variables are time invariant. All regressions control for alternative explanations. The regressions include the unit's logged 1969 population and area (in square kilometers) and 1969 ethnic heterogeneity as measured by the Herfindahl Index because larger, more populous, or more diverse jurisdictions might be more difficult to manage.[43] Further, I control for whether a jurisdiction had a cabinet minister in a particular year (Columns 3 and 4) or the average ministerial representation from that unit (Columns 1 and 2). If the ethnic composition of the bureaucracy was determined by patterns of elite incorporation, as I show in Chapter 4, the posting and shuffling decisions that affect local patterns of co-optation and coercion may have been made with elites, rather than the president, in mind.

The results in Table 5.3 provide evidence that Provincial Administration bureaucrats were posted so as to better co-opt Kikuyu populations. Column 1 indicates that Kikuyu-majority districts were likely to be administered by a co-ethnic. Substantively, Kikuyu-majority districts could expect about six years more of being governed by a co-ethnic than those without a Kikuyu majority. Column 2 shows that districts with a substantial Kikuyu population were more likely to be administered by a Kikuyu. Districts with at least a 20 percent minority population could expect an additional 4.5 years of Kikuyu administration compared with other districts (p< 0.01). Lamu District is a particularly stark example of this strategic management style. The Kikuyu population in Lamu District grew from 176 (0.8 percent of the district's population) in 1962 to 9,059 (20 percent) by 1979. This growth is tied to the introduction of Lake

---

[42] There may be a concern that using population figures by 1979 introduces post-treatment bias, since Kikuyus might have moved to a specific district because it had a Kikuyu DC. I ultimately decide to use this variable, however, in order to include Lamu District, which only gained a large Kikuyu population by 1979. Further, the results are robust to only coding districts that were 20 percent Kikuyu by 1962 or 1969.

[43] Population and ethnolinguistic fractionalization (ELF) figures from the 1969 census are post-treatment. The results are robust to dropping them.

TABLE 5.3 *Management of Administrators, Allocation of Land*

	1 Co-ethnic OLS	2 Kikuyu OLS	3 Shuffle Cox	4 Shuffle Cox
Kikuyu Jurisdiction	0.39***		−0.36†	
	(0.09)		(0.19)	
20% Kikuyu Jurisdiction		0.30**		−0.51**
		(0.11)		(0.18)
1969 Population, logged	0.03	0.02	−0.26***	−0.32***
	(0.04)	(0.05)	(0.08)	(0.08)
Area, sq. km. logged	−0.03	0.01	−0.03	−0.04
	(0.02)	(0.03)	(0.05)	(0.05)
ELF	−0.05	0.29†	−0.29	−0.31
	(0.13)	(0.16)	(0.26)	(0.25)
Minister	−0.05	0.19	0.13	0.15
	(0.10)	(0.12)	(0.17)	(0.17)
Intercept	−0.01	−0.20		
	(0.56)	(0.71)		
Num. obs.	48	48	704	704

***$p < 0.001$, **$p < 0.01$, *$p < 0.05$, †$p < 0.1$. Regressions of the management of PCs and DCs from 1964–1978. The outcome in Column 1 is the percentage of years that a jurisdiction was assigned a co-ethnic administrator, and the outcome in Column 2 is the percentage of years that a jurisdiction was assigned a Kikuyu administrator. Columns 3 and 4 look at when an administrator was shuffled from a post. Columns 1 and 2 report results from OLS regressions and Columns 3 and 4 report results from Cox Proportional Hazards models.

Kenyatta settlement scheme in 1973, referenced in Section 5.2.3, which resettled 3,500+ settlers and their families. Archival documents on this scheme indicate that the government had been planning this scheme years before it was officially opened, and that the initial waves of settlers were largely Kikuyu.[44] In line with the theory, Lamu had a Kikuyu DC nearly every year of Kenyatta's presidency.

Figure 5.3 displays the hazard ratios from Columns 5 and 6. Majority-Kikuyu jurisdictions and those with a population that was at least 20 percent Kikuyu each experienced substantially lower shuffling rates than the rest of the country. The x-axis gives the years after their initial appointment to a station. The y-axis indicates the simulated proportion

---

44 See AVS/15/132 - 134, Kenya National Archives, Nairobi.

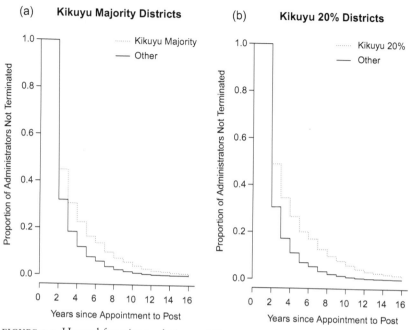

FIGURE 5.3 Hazard functions relating to Kikuyu resettlement under Kenyatta. The figures graph the hazard functions associated with Columns 3 and 4 of Table 5.3, respectively.

of administrators who remained in office. Figure 5.3a indicates that nearly 50 percent of administrators posted to a Kikuyu-majority district could be expected to stay in their district for at least two years, and about 35 percent could expect to be posted for at least three years. But outside of Kikuyu-majority districts, only 30 percent of administrators could anticipate a tenure of at least two years, and less than 20 percent could expect to stay in the post for at least three years. Figure 5.3b displays similar results. About 50 percent of administrators posted to a jurisdiction with at least a 20 percent Kikuyu population could expect to stay in their station for at least two years, and about 40 percent could expect to stay for at least three years.

The results for control variables suggest that plausible alternative explanations are not driving the posting and shuffling patterns of DCs. The results for *Area* and *Minister* are consistently insignificant. This suggests that neither traditional administrative factors nor the presence of an important, incorporated elite affected the management of administrators. The results for *Population* and *ELF* are significant in only some of the models. And the direction in which these variables point is different across the models, suggesting there is no strong relationship between these variables and management patterns.

In other analyses, I consider management of the Provincial Administration using a more expansive definition of "aligned," and find evidence of co-optation within the larger GEMA bloc. I rerun the results from Table 5.3 after considering all GEMA areas as aligned. The results are similar, albeit weaker. For instance, whereas Column 1 of Table 5.3 indicates that a Kikuyu-majority district was 39 percentage points more likely to have a co-ethnic DC than other districts ($p < 0.001$), a GEMA district was 20 percentage points more likely to have one ($p < 0.01$). Many of the other results that code GEMA areas as aligned are signed in the correct direction but do not meet conventional thresholds of significance. Separately, I find that Kiambu – Kenyatta's home district – experienced preferential management patterns compared to the rest of Central Province, even after Kenyatta consolidated his co-ethnics' support and eradicated *Mau Mau*. For the final decade of his presidency, Kiambu had only two DCs, and both were Kikuyu. The other four districts of Central Province had three to six DCs each during this period, fewer than half of whom were Kikuyus.[45] Together, these results suggest that there was favoritism within Kenyatta's aligned group, and the most preferential management practices were carried out in Kiambu.

To what extent did the increase in embeddedness in Kikuyu areas affect important development outcomes? Kikuyu-majority areas were more likely to be managed by an embedded bureaucrat, as Table 5.3 shows. But it is difficult to determine the causal effect of bureaucratic management because aligned jurisdictions were likely treated differently in other important ways (e.g., they received more resources from the center). Though I cannot overcome this inference problem, I examine correlations between subsequent levels of land allocation in areas that were managed by co-ethnic administrators. I use the time-series data to run OLS regressions in which the outcome variable is the total number of hectares of settlement scheme land, logged, that was distributed in that unit in the following year.[46] I first regress this outcome on whether the unit's administrator was a co-ethnic of the majority of locals. Substantively, districts with a co-ethnic DC saw 2.4 times as much land allocated as settlement schemes in the following year than those

45 The results from Table 5.3 are substantively similar if I drop Kiambu from the analysis.
46 Standard errors are clustered at the unit level.

that were not governed by a co-ethnic DC (p = 0.09). I then regress settlement scheme allocations on an interaction term between whether a unit had at least a 20 percent Kikuyu population and an indicator for a Kikuyu administrator. This regression thus compares land allocation across similarly aligned areas that saw different management practices. Districts with at least a 20 percent Kikuyu population that had a Kikuyu DC could expect 3.8 times as much land allocated as settlement schemes in the following year as those with a similar Kikuyu population that were not governed by a Kikuyu administrator (p < 0.001). Together, these results lend evidence to the idea that management practices affect development: jurisdictions that see more embedded bureaucrats also see better outcomes.

5.5.3 Bureaucratic Management and the KPU

I systematically evaluate the posting and shuffling patterns of provincial administrators in light of the KPU and unrest in Luo-dominated areas afterwards. High-ranking PCs and DCs were loyal to Kenyatta, and were not at risk of using their authority to benefit Odinga or any other rival elites. But an administrator may have been lenient towards KPU sympathizers, thus indirectly helping KPU elites, if she had strong social bonds with the area. After the KPU was banned in 1969, locally embedded bureaucrats may have been unwilling to clamp down on popular dissent as definitively as an unembedded bureaucrat. The theory therefore suggests that we should see lower rates of bureaucratic embeddedness in misaligned areas, both through fewer co-ethnic postings and higher rates of shuffling. This includes areas with a KPU candidate in 1966 and Luo-majority areas from 1966 onwards.

I run three regressions to examine ethnic postings. The dependent variable in the first regression is the percentage of years a unit had a co-ethnic officer from 1964 to 1978, and the independent variable is an indicator for whether the majority of residents in the unit were members of the Luo ethnic group. The dependent variables in the second and third regressions are binary indicators that denote whether the administrator in a particular year was a co-ethnic of the majority of residents. The main independent variable in the second regression is an interaction term for years after 1966 and an indicator term for a Luo-majority administrative unit. The main independent variable in the third regression is an interaction term for 1966 and an indicator variable for a district that fielded a candidate in the Little General Election outside Luo areas. The fourth regression examines shuffling rates. The main independent variable is whether a unit was majority Luo.

These regressions rely on the same dataset explained in Section 5.5.2 and include the same control variables. I use OLS for the first regression, a logit model with errors clustered at the unit level for the second and third regressions, and a Cox Proportional Hazard model for the fourth regression.

The results provide some support for the theory that misaligned areas should expect lower rates of bureaucratic embeddedness. Column 1 of Table 5.4 indicates that, across Kenyatta's entire presidency, Luo-majority jurisdictions were governed by a co-ethnic about one-quarter fewer years than other units, though this result is not significant at conventional levels ($p = 0.13$). Column 2 helps us understand why the results in Column 1 were not statistically significant. Non-co-ethnic postings to Luo-majority jurisdictions were statistically more likely after 1966, after Odinga formally defected, but similar to the rest of the country before 1966, when Odinga was still incorporated into Kenyatta's elite coalition. Simulating the predicted probabilities indicates that Luo-majority jurisdictions were 19.1 percentage points less likely to be assigned a co-ethnic after the KPU emerged than before (95% CI (Confidence Interval): $-28.4, -10.1$), which is in line with the hypothesis that management of Luo areas only changed after they were seen as misaligned.

Column 3 indicates that non-Luo districts that fielded KPU candidates did not experience different posting patterns than other districts in 1966, the year of the Little General Election. This null result may be explained by the timing of the election. Odinga and his faction defected from KANU in mid- to late April, and the Little General Election took place in June. It took a few weeks to transfer an administrator. Thus with only two months between the defections and the election, the center may have deemed it imprudent to change administrators and risk a temporary vacancy. Indeed, I count at least six jurisdictions that had their administrator transferred the day after the election; each had KPU candidates contest the Little General Election. Column 4, the result for shuffling, does not provide evidence in support of the hypothesis that administrators in Luo areas had shorter tenures than others. There are many potential reasons for this nonresult. One reason that seems plausible is that after 1966, the regime sought to lower embeddedness everywhere that a popular threat might launch or spread, and stopped differentiating between tenure lengths in misaligned Luo areas versus unaligned areas. Similar to Section 5.5.2, the control variables in Table 5.4 are not consistently significant.

TABLE 5.4 *Management of Administrators, Stopping the KPU*

	1 Co-ethnic OLS	2 Co-ethnic Logit	3 Co-ethnic Logit	4 Shuffle Cox
Luo Jurisdiction	−0.22	0.49		0.21
	(0.14)	(1.21)		(0.25)
After 1966		0.09		
		(0.29)		
Luo Jurisdiction * After 1966		−3.54*		
		(1.48)		
KPU Candidate, Outside Luo Jurisdictions			−0.14	
			(0.54)	
1966			0.32	
			(0.47)	
KPU Candidate, Outside Luo Jurisdictions * 1966			0.41	
			(0.65)	
Population (1969, logged)	0.04	0.26	0.22	−0.27***
	(0.05)	(0.36)	(0.32)	(0.08)
Area (sq. km., logged)	−0.46**	−0.48**	−0.43*	0.00
	(0.03)	(0.17)	(0.17)	(0.05)
1969 ELF	−0.21	−1.73†	−1.59	−0.16
	(0.15)	(1.01)	(0.97)	(0.25)
Minister	−0.03	−0.17	−0.24	0.12
	(0.11)	(0.61)	(0.61)	(0.18)
Intercept	0.20	−0.04	0.08	
	(0.65)	(4.88)	(4.42)	
Num. obs.	48	704	704	704

*** $p < 0.001$, ** $p < 0.01$, * $p < 0.05$, † $p < 0.1$. Regressions of the management of PCs and DCs from 1964 to 1978. The outcome in Columns 1–3 is the percentage of years that a jurisdiction was assigned a co-ethnic administrator. Column 4 displays shuffle rates. Column 1 reports results from an OLS regression. Columns 2 and 3 report results from logit regressions with errors clustered at the unit level. Column 4 reports results from a Cox Proportional Hazards model.

Evidence on specific postings supports the results. From the emergence of the KPU in 1966 until Kenyatta's death in 1978, only two Luo officers served in Luo-majority jurisdictions. While Luo-majority districts were only assigned co-ethnic administrators for 3 percent of jurisdiction-years after 1966, districts with a majority of one of Kenya's other four largest ethnic groups had co-ethnic administrators more than 25 percent of the time. For example, Daniel Owino – one of the two Luo officers mentioned previously – served as the PC of Luo-majority Nyanza Province from 1965 to 1967, beginning his career there when Odinga was still allied with Kenyatta. We might assume that Owino's shared ethnicity with Odinga predisposed him to align with the KPU after the party emerged, and thus allow the party to gain local strength. Yet Owino was a strong supporter of Kenyatta and "represented that minority group within the [Luo] who had for some years challenged Odinga's leadership" (Gertzel, 1970, 110). Owino was considered so loyal that he was installed as the KANU candidate of his home constituency in the 1966 snap elections. At the same time, he only stayed in his post as PC for two years. Kenyatta did not want to risk him becoming so attached to his co-ethnics that he was unwilling to coerce them.

5.5.4 The Provincial Administration and Other Concerns

The Provincial Administration's most infamous actions under Kenyatta's presidency were helping to resettle his co-ethnics across the country and stopping the KPU (and the dissent from Luo citizens that it sparked). However, Kenyatta used the Provincial Administration to carry out numerous other actions. Here I examine the agency's management in light of other popular threats or elite threats with popular elements.

First, I consider the management of bureaucrats in light of a popular insurgency in the country's arid north at the beginning of Kenyatta's presidency. The insurgency originated in the area of the former colonial Northern Frontier District (NFD), where ethnic Somalis comprise a majority of residents. The NFD comprised sparsely populated colonial districts that were administered as one during the colonial period. Tensions in the NFD heightened when neighboring Somalia gained independence in 1960 and expressed the goal to unite all Somali peoples and lands into one nation.[47] In the run-up to Kenya's independence, the colonial regime created the Northern Frontier District Commission to tour the NFD and hear the area's concerns. The commission recognized the overwhelming support for unification with Somalia, however it decided to keep the area within Kenya.[48] The area's inhabitants launched an insur-

---

47 The homeland of ethnic Somalis had been split into five areas during colonization – British Somaliland, Djibouti, Ethiopia, Italian Somaliland, and Kenya.

48 In a federal state, the colonial regime reasoned, Somali Kenyans would have substantial sub-national autonomy. And Kenyan leaders did not want part of the new country to secede (Lewis 1963).

gency against the state in 1963 (Anderson 2014). Somali perpetrators of the violence were called *shifta*, the Amharic word for 'bandit.' By the end of the insurgency in 1967, 3,000 (Mburu 2005; Hornsby 2011)–7,000 (TJRC) Kenyans had been killed. There were substantial losses on both sides, including the high-profile *shifta* assassination of a DC and a local chief.[49] There is evidence that Kenyatta managed bureaucrats in the Provincial Administration to stymie the *shifta* threat in Somali-majority districts after independence. These districts were 13.8 percentage points less likely to be assigned a co-ethnic DC in the years that *shifta* was active (95% CI: −35.8, −2.8), and 18.0 percentage points less likely to be assigned a co-ethnic DC than other parts of the country during Kenyatta's presidency as a whole (95% CI: −29.0, −9.0).[50]

Second, while none of the regression results indicate that units with ministers experienced different management procedures, the data provides some evidence that Kenyatta's management of administrators was motivated by other elite concerns. Nearly 40 percent of administrators were shuffled in 1973, the year before the national 1974 elections. Third, I rerun the main models after including other controls. Most notably, I control for the percentage of high-potential land in a unit as a measure of agricultural or economic importance.[51] These and other control variables do not affect the substantive interpretation of the results.

5.6 SUMMARY

This chapter examined the management of the Provincial Administration during the reign of Kenya's first president. I presented qualitative evidence about how President Kenyatta used the Provincial Administration to co-opt areas that were aligned with him and to coerce misaligned areas. He was fairly confident of the loyalty of high-ranking PCs and DCs, in part because he developed neopatrimonial relationships with them. But there was still a risk that these bureaucrats would refuse to carry out coercive orders or be unable to co-opt, depending on their local embeddedness in the jurisdiction in which they served. The quantitative results indicate

---

[49] The high death toll has led some scholars to consider coding this conflict a civil war (Sambanis 2004; Kimenyi and Ndung'u 2005).

[50] These predicted probabilities are estimated from a logit regression in which the dependent variable is a binary indicator for whether a district had a co-ethnic DC, and the independent variable is an interaction term between an indicator term denoting whether a district had a Somali majority and an indicator term for the years in which *shifta* was active.

[51] This data is from the same source as Table 5.1.

that an area's alignment towards the center affected the embeddedness of its bureaucrats: the center lowered the embeddedness of bureaucrats in misaligned areas while artificially increasing it in aligned areas. By strategically manipulating the embeddedness of bureaucrats, Kenyatta maintained an agency that proved able and willing to carry out his desired governance strategies across the country.

6

The Provincial Administration during President Moi's Autocratic Years

6.1 INTRODUCTION

Kenyatta's reliance on the Provincial Administration for social control served as a precedent for subsequent leaders. During the autocratic regime of President Daniel arap Moi (1978–1991), the agency continued its campaign of co-optation and coercion established under Kenyatta.

However, relying on this agency to protect against popular threats required securing bureaucratic compliance. And without perfect monitoring, Moi would not know if bureaucrats used their authority on behalf of another principal. This chapter examines how Moi's regime maximized compliance by accounting for the three relationships detailed in Chapter 2: the *alignment* of different areas towards Moi, bureaucrats' *loyalty* towards him, and the *embeddedness* of individual bureaucrats within the jurisdiction to which they were posted. By jointly considering these three relationships, managers can post and shuffle bureaucrats in a manner that maximizes compliance in strategically important areas.

This chapter analyzes alignment, loyalty, and embeddedness in turn. First, I describe the extent to which different parts of the country were aligned with Moi in order to define his popular threat landscape. I use archival and interview data to document how the Provincial Administration was used to co-opt aligned areas and coerce misaligned areas. Second, as in Chapter 5, I examine the loyalty of the Provincial Administration's top bureaucrats – Provincial Commissioners (PCs) and District Commissioners (DCs). These bureaucrats were loyal to Moi through patronage, and thus expected to benefit from his continued tenure in office regardless of their ethnicity. Third, I investigate embeddedness. Though the bureaucrats I examine were considered loyal to Moi, they were at risk of using their authority on behalf of the community in which they served. Qualitative evidence indicates that locally embedded bureaucrats tasked with coercion might fail to carry out orders to suppress because of their social bonds with residents. But embedded bureaucrats were in a better position to co-opt because of both their higher knowledge and their willingness to help local residents.

Since the data covers loyal bureaucrats, I examine the effect of an area's alignment on the manipulation of the embeddedness of bureaucrats posted there. The quantitative analyses thus examine annual data on the postings of all PCs and DCs from 1979–1991. The results show that aligned areas were assigned bureaucrats with higher levels of embeddedness or saw that embeddedness develop over time, whereas bureaucrats had particularly low levels of embeddedness in misaligned areas. I then assess archival data to estimate the effects of embeddedness on governance. I look at budgetary allocations and, as expected, find that areas governed by embedded bureaucrats could expect higher allocations than others.

This chapter's findings contribute to our understanding of ethnic favoritism. The analysis of budgetary allocations shows that Moi's co-ethnic areas received a larger share than their proportion of the population would suggest. This is in line with standard accounts of ethnic favoritism – a president's co-ethnic areas receive more resources.[1] But I also find that Moi's co-ethnic areas received *even higher* allocations when the bureaucrat in charge of finalizing the budgets was locally embedded. These findings suggest that co-ethnic areas of the president enjoy higher levels of public goods in part due to their management: presidents allow bureaucrats posted to an area to develop social attachments to local residents. While higher levels of embeddedness reduce a bureaucrat's willingness to coerce, a leader's aligned areas are not at risk of fomenting a popular threat. Elsewhere, however, bureaucrats are managed to stymie embeddedness – and in the process, development – precisely because misaligned and unaligned areas are at risk of launching or sustaining a popular threat.

The chapter also contributes to the literature on authoritarian regimes. While recent studies on autocracy have tended to focus on elite threats, this chapter shows that elite threats must be examined alongside popular threats. Indeed, the parts of the country that experienced significant

---

[1] For instance, see Bates (1989), Franck and Rainer (2012), Hodler and Raschky (2014), and Kramon and Posner (2016).

discontent were populated with the co-ethnics of Moi's most threatening elite rivals.

6.2 AREA ALIGNMENT AND THE PROVINCIAL ADMINISTRATION

I describe the alignment of different parts of the country toward President Moi during his autocratic regime. I then use qualitative archival and interview evidence to show that the Provincial Administration was used to co-opt aligned groups and coerce others.

6.2.1 Area Alignment toward Moi

Moi faced popular threats that were related to his challenges at the elite level (described in Chapter 4). He faced considerable popular unrest in areas inhabited by Kikuyu and Luo citizens. Further, and similar to Kenyatta, Moi needed to consolidate support among his base upon taking office.

Discontent among Kikuyu and Luo elites translated into unrest in their co-ethnic communities. Opposition in Luo-dominated areas of Nyanza Province was particularly strong in the immediate aftermath of the 1982 coup attempt. Before the regime regained control, some in the province tore down portraits of the president from public places and celebrated in the streets.[2] For several days after the attempted coup, there were spontaneous demonstrations in favor of the plotters in these areas (Currie and Ray 1986). Moreover, the regime planned pro-government "loyalty" rallies across the country to give the illusion of widespread popular support. But some Luo business owners subverted these rallies by firing employees who attended.[3] Popular discontent continued to simmer during Moi's autocratic regime. After the suspicious 1990 death of a prominent Luo politician, Robert Ouko, unrest in these parts rose again ("[s]tudents rioted and Luo farmers broke into open revolt"; "[f]or weeks, Kisumu [a Luo-majority city] was a scene of violence," Hornsby 2011, 472–473).

Moi also faced popular resistance in Nairobi, where the Kikuyu and Luo communities together comprise 50 percent of the population. Some of the protests against him were organized by university students.

---

[2] DC South Nyanza to Permanent Secretary Health, August 11, 1982, DA/1/151, Nyanza Provincial Archives, Kisumu, Kenya.
[3] Federation of Kenya Employers to DC Kisumu, August 20, 1982, DA/1/151, Nyanza Provincial Archives, Kisumu.

A Kikuyu student at the time who hailed from Central Province recalled that university protests "reflected the mood of the country. The students don't come from Nairobi. They come from all over ... we had enough."[4] Protests at the country's premiere university – the University of Nairobi – were so severe that Moi closed the campus down multiple times. In addition, Moi faced widespread strikes and work stoppages from the transport sector throughout the 1980s that threatened to bring Nairobi to a standstill (Widner 1992; Lynch 2011a).

The Provincial Administration severely repressed collective action against the regime (see Section 6.2.4), so opponents had to find less obvious ways to express their opposition. Dissatisfaction in Kikuyu and Luo areas, for instance, tended to be conveyed through antiregime rumors and subtle acts of resistance rather than protests or demonstrations. One interviewee who grew up in Central Province under Moi explained, "it was not very easy to protest under Moi because you would be shot. People did rebel [but] without showing it."[5] Nongovernmental organizations (NGOs) with foreign links, which were especially active in Central and Nyanza provinces,[6] disseminated pro-democracy political messages alongside their stated work (Ndegwa 1996; Brass 2016). Homegrown NGOs subverted Moi as well. For instance, Wangari Maathai, from Central Province and Africa's first female Nobel laureate, used her organization, the Greenbelt Movement, to combat deforestation and rally opposition to Moi's distribution of forest land, which had instigated the deforestation (see Section 6.2.3). Even art during these years was subversive: community theaters produced plays that espoused antiregime themes in the vernacular (Currie and Ray 1986).[7]

Separately, Moi need to win and later maintain support among his co-ethnic community. His position among the Kalenjin community was precarious from the start.[8] And Moi's position among his co-ethnics

---

4 Interview with former DC, June 29, 2017, Nairobi, Kenya.
5 Interview with former DO, October 10, 2015, Nairobi.
6 Interview with then DC, November 13, 2011, Nairobi.
7 These include works by the famous writer, Ngugi wa Thiong'o, who staged plays with strong antigovernment themes in his native Kikuyu language.
8 This was in part due to sub-ethnic politics. Moi hails from one of the smaller Kalenjin sub-tribes, the Tugen, which comprises less than 2 percent of Kenya's population. The Kipsigis subgroup is the largest Kalenjin subgroup. And the Nandi have long been considered the most educated and prominent of the Kalenjin subgroups (Lynch 2011a; Josse-Durand 2018). It would not have been unexpected for a Kalenjin from one of these more powerful subgroups to challenge him (Throup 1987).

was weakened by Kenyatta's settlement of perceived Kalenjin land while Moi was vice president – "a widely held view was that he had sold out Kalenjin land interests in return for personal preferment during the 1960s and 1970s" (Throup and Hornsby, 1998, 29). More generally, Kalenjin areas saw few improvements in development when Moi was vice president (Hornsby 2011).

Moi was able to gain the support of his co-ethnics soon after he took office, however, in part by distributing a large amount of resources to his base (described in more detail in Section 6.2.3). Above all else, many Kalenjins – and more broadly, pastoralists from Rift Valley – benefited from Moi's land policies, similar to how many Kikuyus benefited under Kenyatta. Moi formally settled many of his co-ethnics and allowed many others to illegally squat on government land.[9] In this way, the Kalenjin community came to trust Moi to look out for their best interests, or at least to do less harm than a president of another ethnicity. In turn, Moi could expect the support of his co-ethnics.

6.2.2 KANU Proved Insufficient to Solve Moi's Popular Threats

Moi made greater use of KANU than Kenyatta to develop ties with grass-roots supporters and forestall popular threats by attempting to create a "party-state" that fused the party with the state's administrative backbone (Widner 1992). But it is unclear if he strengthened the party enough to neutralize his political threats completely. Gabrielle Lynch (2011a) contends that Kenya never became a party-state under Moi, as ultimate control over grassroots affairs was never under the party, but always with the Office of the President and the Provincial Administration. Indeed, I find that bureaucrats in the Provincial Administration were critical to the operations of KANU. For instance, administrators sold KANU membership cards, KANU party manifestos, and invitation cards to special KANU events to their residents. They were expected to run *harambees* in honor of the party. Senior officers organized subsidized travel for residents in their jurisdiction to national KANU meetings in government cars.[10] One bureaucrat during these years recalls how, "you were being rated according to how many you have recruited to the party."[11] Another officer

---

[9] See the Report of the Commission of Inquiry into the Illegal/Irregular Allocation of Public Land (Ndung'u 2004).
[10] See XM/10/2, Kenya National Archives, Nairobi.
[11] Interview with then DC, November 21, 2011, Nairobi.

remarked, "during the single-party time there was a lot of politicization of PA. In that time there was no distinction between the party, the PA, and government. Everything was wrapped up together. I was expected to help Moi and we did. We had to support KANU [and] what they were doing on the ground."[12] In effect, KANU's strength in the later part of Moi's autocratic regime came from grafting itself onto the Provincial Administration.

Understanding Moi's ability to control the population and stave off popular threats during his autocratic regime therefore requires looking outside the party, to the Provincial Administration.

6.2.3 Co-Optation and Coercion to Address Land Demands from Moi's Base

Moi tried to co-opt his base through the state. Bureaucrats in the Provincial Administration distributed land and channeled resources to areas inhabited by his co-ethnic Kalenjin community.

Moi continued the spirit of Kenyatta's land allocation policies, privileging his own community at the expense of everyone else. Unlike Kenyatta, however, settlement schemes were not the main venue through which Moi distributed land during his autocratic regime. Moi allocated some 126,000 hectares of land from 1980–1991, a fraction of the 584,000 hectares that Kenyatta distributed as settlement scheme land. And in fact, the majority of Moi's allocations were not in Rift Valley, the home province of his co-ethnics.[13] Moi did not rely as heavily on settlement schemes to resettle his base, likely for two reasons. First, much of Rift Valley's fertile land that had been available for allocation through settlement schemes had been distributed under Kenyatta, as discussed in Chapter 5. Second, Moi was wary of using formal procedures to settle his co-ethnics. Opening up more land in Rift Valley to settlement schemes would legitimate the settlement scheme allocations that Kenyatta had made to Kikuyu settlers (Onoma 2010; Boone 2014; Klaus 2020).

Instead, Moi informally settled aligned pastoralist groups on government-owned land that was never intended for settlement, such as areas classified as Protected Land, Trust Land, or State Corporation Land. Many landless pastoralists perceived these protected areas as empty land

---

12 Interview with then DC, July 3, 2017, Nairobi.
13 Kikuyu-majority Nyandarua District in northern Central Province had the most allocations under Moi's autocratic regime.

to which they were entitled. For instance, one group of Kalenjin leaders from West Pokot claimed:

Land registration in Lelan Location has been suspened [sic] because the whole of the Location is still Gazetted [officially classified] as Forest. We are aware that part of Lelan is an important natural water catchment area. We request that Catchment areas already determined and surveyed be gazetted as Forest while the rest of the Location should be degazetted.[14]

Sometimes, pastoralists squatted on these public lands before asking Moi to change their official designation. Other times, squatters demanded the right to clear forests without eviction.

There are no formal records of the amount of land that Moi informally allocated. That was the point. Instead, I estimate the amount of informal allocations using Kenyan statistical abstracts that document the total amount of government land in districts across the country.[15] I analyze land categorization in 1977 and 1990, and find that in three of the four Kalenjin-majority districts with land data listed, the area of government-owned land reduced during this time.[16] The total amount of government land dropped from 550,000 to 487,000 hectares in Baringo (an 11 percent reduction), from 1,936,000 to 1,843,000 in Kericho (a 5 percent reduction), and from 3,440,000 to 3,259,000 in Uasin Gishu (a 5 percent reduction).[17] These percentages are substantively large. They suggest that Moi doled out 30 percent more land informally in Uasin Gishu alone than land through settlement schemes across the country as a whole.[18]

The Provincial Administration took a leading role in allocating land (formally and informally) to Kalenjin residents. Bureaucrats liaised between those who were clamoring for a spot in a newly opened scheme, elites in Nairobi who decided on when and where to degazette land, and other relevant state bureaucrats (e.g., District Forest Officer, District Development Officer) who oversaw this land. For example, consider the *Nyayo* Tea Zones, a parastatal launched in 1986 to settle and employ

[14] Leaders of Pokot District to President Moi, September 17, 1979, Unspecified Folio, Rift Valley Provincial Archives, Nakuru, Kenya.
[15] The statistical abstracts are published annually, but land was only categorized for some districts and only during a handful of years.
[16] Elgeyo-Marakwet and West Pokot districts are the two Kalenjin-majority districts without land data available in the statistical abstracts.
[17] Nandi District did not experience a decrease in total government land from 1977–1990.
[18] These numbers also track with the loss of Kenya's forest cover. From 1962–2004, the percent of Kenya's landmass under closed-canopy forests dropped from 3 percent to 1.7 percent (2004 Ndungu Commission). Also see Morjaria (2018).

thousands of Kalenjins on 1,300 hectares of forest reserve land.[19] District Forest Officers worked directly with DCs to discuss progress on tasks such as forest clearing and land demarcation. When Forest Officers resisted – they were tasked with preserving forest land, after all – provincial administrators undermined their authority by telling residents to disregard their commands. Further, bureaucrats in the Provincial Administration made these allocations even more valuable by providing new settlers with farm inputs.[20]

At the same time, these bureaucrats spearheaded the eviction of migrant groups in Rift Valley. Kenyatta-era forest squatters were kicked out to prepare land for Moi's own forest squatters. Catherine Boone (2014, 156) relays a conversation with a Kikuyu farmer in Nakuru: "most Kikuyu were expelled from the Mau [Forest] in the 1980s. Kalenjin moved in. Many were allowed to settle [in the Mau Forest area] south of Njoro. They clear-cut and started farming." Evictions also happened on privately owned land. For instance, aspiring farmers from various ethnic communities pooled together to buy Meteitei, a former white settler farm in Nandi District, in 1977. In 1983, non-Kalenjin members of the farm were chased off and local Kalenjin (nonmembers) illegally started squatting there. When asked why he did not take his complaint to the state after the eviction, the secretary of the farm responded, "How could I have done [that] when some provincial administrators were related to the invaders" (Klopp, 2001, 142)?[21,22]

6.2.4 Coercion to Clamp Down on Dissent

Moi relied on the Provincial Administration to neutralize popular dissent against him. Resistance to him was strongest in areas dominated by his misaligned ethnic groups, the Kikuyu and Luo. Qualitative evidence and secondary sources confirm that the Provincial Administration was most active in coercing dissidents in majority-Kikuyu and majority-Luo areas, both before and after the 1982 attempted coup attempt.

---

[19] Much of Rift Valley is well suited to growing tea.

[20] See ER/1/7, Rift Valley Provincial Archives, Nakuru.

[21] The eviction of migrants from this farm had repercussions almost a decade later: it became the first site of the preelection violence between armed Kalenjin and Maasai youths against Rift Valley's various migrant ethnic groups that left more than 1,500 dead and 300,000 displaced (Human Rights Watch 1993; Africa Watch 1993; Akiwumi 1999).

[22] The interviewee discusses the local chief, who by definition must be from the local community. But the sentiment is still valid, as archival documents suggest that some of the trained administrators in the area were Kalenjin.

The Provincial Administration directly restricted individuals' civil liberties in misaligned areas. For instance, administrators relied heavily on their intelligence networks to arrest dissidents as well as those who spoke out against the regime. One local councilor in Kirinyaga District in Central Province recalls restrictions on free speech: "the Provincial Administration represented the KANU government then. You could not even air your own words. You could not stand two or three people and talk about the ills of the government or you would be taken to the cells of the government. Your grievances were not heard."[23] One officer recalled how he was asked to spy on individuals in his jurisdiction who were not staunch KANU members:

[when] so-and-so isn't a true party stalwart, you cut down on his freedom of movement. When he is in a bar, you send your informers on him. Find out what he is planning to do. You are doing that for the party hierarchy. It depends on the interests of the party. We were all KANU members. You had to be a party member ... these were instructions from the party hierarchy and the party was the president himself. Everything was KANU.[24]

This coercion of the Kikuyu community extended to other groups affiliated with the Gikuyu, Embu, and Meru Association (GEMA). One councilor in Meru District complained about having his meeting permits rescinded after he was accused of "inciting people not to buy KANU stamps" and not to donate to *harambees* organized by regime elites.[25]

Provincial administrators were also at the front lines of censoring the press: *The Weekly Standard* reported that an administrator "threaten[ed] to arrest and cane [newspaper correspondents] if they ever file stories from his administrative domain without his permission ... [he] also ordered that stories written about [his jurisdiction] should be given to him for vetting before being filed by correspondents to their respective newspapers in Nairobi."[26] Similarly, a DC in Central Province that year demanded that he be allowed to vet newspaper articles by a local correspondent before publication.[27]

The Provincial Administration also clamped down on freedom of association. It was in charge of enforcing a new ban on ethnic societies, which

---

[23] Interview with former Councilor, November 16, 2011, Kerugoya, Kenya.
[24] Interview with former DO, November 7, 2011, Nairobi.
[25] Meru Councilor to Meru District Chairman, December 19, 1989, BB/1/130, Kenya National Archives, Nairobi.
[26] "Administration, Press Still Feuding," *The Weekly Standard*, August 19, 1988.
[27] Ibid.

was a clear attempt to weaken GEMA. Archival records indicate that this ban was indeed carried out against many ethnic societies, although pastoralist groups were often overlooked. In Siaya, a Luo-majority district in Nyanza Province, the Provincial Administration banned meetings of welfare organizations, claiming that they were political.[28] Officers also shut down non-ethnic civil society organizations founded by misaligned groups. The PC of Rift Valley, for instance, demanded the deregistration of a local Luo women's group two weeks after the coup attempt, explaining "through our investigations, it has been found that this group is not a welfare group but an under-ground political group which serves the interest of certain politicians."[29]

Members of the Luo community were physically coerced. Paramilitary officers, who are coordinated by the Provincial Administration, were called in numerous times to violently suppress protests in Luo-majority areas (Hornsby 2011). The Provincial Administration was accused of burning down the offices of civil society groups and carrying out "ruthless and unjustified beatings" in Siaya.[30] Archive folios document how administrators in Nyanza Province forced Luo residents to attend political *barazas* that praised the regime.[31] And even (non-Luo) areas that bordered Luo-majority areas complained about how local police officers – who are under the command of the Provincial Administration – violently clashed with innocent civilians on busy market days.[32]

The Provincial Administration also repressed foreign NGOs, which were perceived to be trying to undermine Moi's reign.[33] This is in part because, by the 1980s, NGOs began to attract individuals and recruit heavily from groups that were antagonistic towards Moi (Ng'ethe 1991; Kanyinga 1995; Ndegwa 1996; Brass 2016): "Leadership of the sector shifted from a missionary and voluntary orientation to a professional, educated middle class ... they saw NGO work as a welcome alternative

---

28 Chairman Kanyikwaya Gem Welfare Society to Chief Gem Location, January 26, 1981, DA/1/151, Kisumu Provincial Archives, Kisumu, Kenya.
29 PC Rift Valley to DC Nakuru, August 14, 1982, EC1/1/24, Rift Valley Provincial Archives, Nakuru, Kenya.
30 Private citizen to DC Siaya, September 16, 1981, DA/1/151, Nyanza Provincial Archives, Kisumu.
31 KANU Councilor to DC Siaya, November 24, 1982, DA/1/151, Nyanza Provincial Archives, Kisumu.
32 Permanent Secretary Provincial Administration to PC Nyanza, December 9, 1982, DA/1/151, Nyanza Provincial Archives, Kisumu.
33 "No Need for Meddling Missionaries," *The Weekly Standard*, July 22, 1988.

to restrictive government employment" (Brass, 2016, 68). This shift in leadership and organizational goals was especially felt in misaligned areas where international NGOs had more space than other arms of civil society. As one former administrator who worked in GEMA areas under Moi's autocracy noted:

NGOs were not only bringing development by the way. They were also involved in politics to some extent when it comes to civic education. Educating people concerning their rights, and so the assumption that possibly, especially during the KANU regime they were jittery about multiparty democracy. There were chances that these NGOs could be grooming their own people to take over leadership. You know, anything concerning development projects is connected to politics.[34]

Unsurprisingly, throughout the 1980s bureaucrats in the Provincial Administration closely monitored NGO activities.[35] NGOs were also frequently denied registration for no reason.[36] For instance, beginning in 1986, the Permanent Secretary of Provincial Administration required NGOs to get their local plans and budgets approved by the government, and in effect, their local provincial administrators (Brass 2016). To further prevent international NGOs from gaining local clout, many that were seen as too political were never invited to – or were explicitly forbidden to attend – District Development Committee (DDC) meetings.[37] By denying them the opportunity to engage with local elites and stakeholders, NGOs were hampered from carrying out the development work that gave them political clout among residents.

Administrators within the Provincial Administration were also instrumental in tempering urban unrest. They were involved in running union elections, helping to corporatize and subdue the union sector (LeBas 2011). Further, administrators in rural farming districts organized the delivery of maize to urban areas during the 1979–1980 and 1984–1985 droughts to prevent urban food riots (Bates 1989). After universities in Nairobi were shut down, Moi ordered students to return to their rural homes and report to their local administrative officer every Monday and Friday.[38] This measure lowered students' ability to cause civil unrest in Nairobi and was especially effective against Luo students, given the long travel times from Nyanza Province to Nairobi.

---

[34] Interview with then DC, November 13, 2011, Nairobi.
[35] "No Need for Meddling Missionaries," *The Weekly Review*, July 22, 1988.
[36] See, for instance, EC/1/24, Rift Valley Provincial Archives, Nakuru.
[37] Interview with then DC, November 13, 2011, Nairobi.
[38] "First-Year Students Back to Try Again," *The Weekly Standard*, October 28, 1988.

The Provincial Administration even limited collective action among secondary school students. A directive by the Permanent Secretary of Education in 1983 on unrest in secondary schools blamed principals: "To a large extent, the school administration is to blame. School strikes do not happen overnight."[39] But he asked principals to work with the Provincial Administration, given the inability of principals to keep students in check on their own: "when problems arise of whatever nature ... all those concerned must be consulted immediately, especially the Provincial or District administration." The directive continued, "others concerned with intelligence and security matters are aware of much of the local happenings within the environment of the schools. Heads should co-operate with the provincial and district Educational personnel and officers who are involved in intelligence matters in 'arresting' planned strikes."[40]

6.3 LOYALTY AND EMBEDDEDNESS

Section 6.2 described the alignment of different parts of the country towards Moi, and showed how they were governed differently by the Provincial Administration. This section provides evidence that one of the ways in which Moi ensured compliance with his orders was by cultivating loyalty from high-ranking bureaucrats. It then briefly discusses how even loyal bureaucrats were in danger of shirking from orders to coerce if they were locally embedded in their jurisdiction.

6.3.1 Loyalty through Neopatrimonialism

Moi perceived his co-ethnic officers – and those from pastoralist communities more broadly – as loyal. This perceived loyalty led to the recruitment and promotion of many officers from Rift Valley's ethnic groups, especially after the 1982 attempted coup. One administrator recounted the rise of a colleague who was appointed as a DC soon after the coup:

[F]or some, Moi didn't hide his favoritism. Like with [a particular Kalenjin DC]. He retired as a Senior DC but he did not understand administration ... . He was chosen because of tribalism. He advanced because he was a Kalenjin. This was not uncommon with Moi. Moi looked inwards after 1982.[41]

---

39 Permanent Secretary of Education to Education Officers and Provincial Administrators, June 24, 1983, HT/23/154, Nyanza Provincial Archives, Kisumu.
40 Ibid.
41 Interview with the DC, February 14, 2012, Kilifi, Kenya.

Similarly, another pastoralist recounts how he was brought in:

I came from the private sector. I was personnel manager for [a private company during the early 1980s]. How did I come to government? Because I was a Samburu. I was an educated Samburu … Moi was shaken after 1982. Moi was feeling insecure, uncertain. Looking for people who had gone to school from his small tribes. I came in early 1984 … to make sure of security.[42]

Though Moi may have preferred a Provincial Administration packed with his own co-ethnics and broader pastoralist community, he did not pack the state. Officers from Rift Valley's pastoralist ethnic groups never comprised more than 30 percent of all PCs and DCs, in part because Moi recognized the disadvantages of allocating these valuable positions solely to his aligned groups. Instead, as described in Chapter 4, Moi allowed bureaucrats from other ethnic groups to staff PC and DC positions as favors to elites whose support he needed. One of Moi's Permanent Secretaries for Internal Security explained that ethnic groups, "get resources and jobs depending on leadership … The guys at the top determine who will receive, who down the line will get what, and how much. When Moi became president, there were so many bottlenecks because the Kikuyu community were really dominating."[43] A former Deputy Permanent Secretary during the 1980s similarly explained how MPs from across Kenya's ethnic groups would ask Moi to appoint and promote within the Provincial Administration. Not all demands were equally successful, however: "the closer you are to power, the more effective your calls are."[44]

Figure 6.1 displays the ethnic composition of PCs and DCs for the country's five largest ethnic groups under Moi's autocratic regime. It shows that between 1978 and 1981, the number of Kalenjin officers actually decreased. But the starkest change in the Provincial Administration's ethnic composition during this time was the reduction in the number of Kikuyu officers. This is likely due, in part, to their overrepresentation under Kenyatta (46 percent of high-ranking officers were Kikuyu by the time of his death). By 1981, 27 percent of all presidentially appointed PCs and DCs were still Kikuyu. This was an overrepresentation given their share of the general population (21 percent) but on par with their 30 percent share in the cabinet at the time.[45] The ethnic composition

---

[42] Interview with former Assistant Minister, February 1, 2012, Nairobi.
[43] Interview with former Permanent Secretary, February 24, 2012, Nairobi.
[44] Interview with former Deputy Permanent Secretary, January 22, 2012, Mwea, Kenya.
[45] Further, and perhaps more practically, the predominance of Kikuyu administrators among Moi's initial PC and DC appointments may have been a consequence of the pool

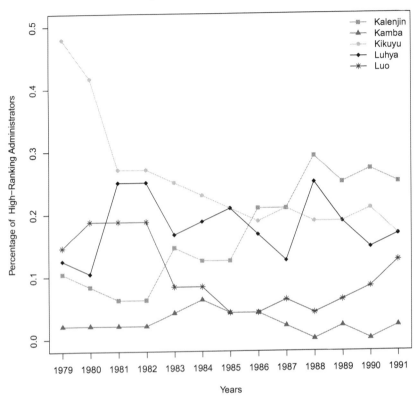

FIGURE 6.1 Percentage of Moi's high-ranking officers by ethnicity. Percentages plotted for the country's five largest ethnic groups by year, who were among the most well-represented within the Provincial Administration.

of the Provincial Administration changed after the attempted coup, following changes in Moi's elite coalition. The percentage of Kikuyu elites in the cabinet fell to 21 percent by 1983, and Luo representation remained low throughout the 1980s.[46]

Moi secured the loyalty of non-co-ethnic administrators by creating neopatrimonial relationships with high-ranking administrators. This was

of trained officers that Moi had to choose from and Kikuyu advantages in education. The length of time required to recruit and train new officers was too long for Moi *not* to rely heavily on Kikuyu officers in these early years.

46 The drop in numbers of officers from these groups was made up for by increases in the representation of smaller ethnic groups. Whereas the country's five largest ethnic groups comprised nearly 90 percent of all high-ranking Provincial Administration positions in 1979, they comprised 60–75 percent of high-ranking officers from 1983 to 1991, more in line with their collective 70-percent share of the population.

done, in part, through the initial selection of PCs and DCs. From 1978 to 1980, Moi replaced all of the country's PCs and the majority of DCs, who were all appointed by (and considered loyal to) Kenyatta. By personally selecting his own PCs and DCs from lower tiers of the Provincial Administration, Moi reinforced the idea that the agency's elite ranks are tied to the fate of the president.

These bonds were also solidified through money. High-ranking officers remained well compensated and were allowed to benefit materially from their office. Formal compensation continued to rise under Moi. He commissioned a follow-up to the 1971 Ndegwa Commission in 1979 to reevaluate compensation of PCs and DCs. The commission suggested, among other things, that some administrators be granted a higher job group (and thus a higher salary).[47] Informal compensation was high as well. Officers were rarely reprimanded by their superiors for predating on the local population through corruption. One former regime official claimed that Moi personally told elite officers to "eat [your] fill."[48] Moi would constantly distribute gifts of land to his PCs and DCs and term them "*zawadi ya mzee*" – an elder's token of appreciation.

These neopatrimonial bonds meant that even high-ranking officers from misaligned ethnic groups had aligned incentives with Moi. For instance, Hezekiah Oyugi was Moi's sole Luo PC at the time of the 1982 attempted coup. Though Oyugi was a co-ethnic of the coup plotters, he stood steadfastly by Moi. Oyugi called Moi as soon as he heard about the coup and pledged his loyalty even though "many thought Nairobi had been lost" (Hornsby, 2011, 380). Oyugi also arranged for Moi's evacuation from his Kabarak farm in Nakuru, where he had been during the coup attempt and which was considered a prime target for the coup plotters, and later helped arrange his armored return to Nairobi.[49]

During Moi's autocratic regime, high-ranking bureaucrats within the Provincial Administration were drawn from many of Kenya's ethnic groups, and he solidified neopatrimonial bonds with all of them. Even administrators from outside his aligned ethnic groups were considered loyal.

6.3.2 The Pitfalls of Local Embeddedness in Stopping Dissent

The ability and willingness of high-ranking bureaucrats to carry out Moi's orders depended not on loyalty alone, however. Compliance was

[47] Report of the Civil Service Review Committee.
[48] Interview with former Deputy Permanent Secretary, January 22, 2012, Mwea.
[49] "What Moi Did as Rebel Army Men Tried to Overthrow Government" Machua Koinange, *The Standard* August

also affected by their embeddedness in the jurisdiction in which they served. Most dangerous for Moi was that even loyal bureaucrats were liable to shirk if they were too embedded in their jurisdiction. A former administrator who was posted to Nyanza Province in the 1980s explained how he enjoyed serving there because he liked his local church and the Christian community; another officer serving in Nyanza Province recalled how much he and his family enjoyed that post, in part because the local children taught his own children how to properly eat fried fish (the Luo homeland is on Lake Victoria). One administrator serving in Central Province discussed how locals used to invite him over for dinner during the week, since his family was in Nairobi. Becoming integrated into these communities helped the administrators understand local residents' political motivations. But these officers were ready for a new post by the end of their short deployments, as they found it difficult to unequivocally carry out the coercive orders that were in the regime's best interests when they were so attached to the community.[50]

6.4 QUANTITATIVE ANALYSIS: BUREAUCRATIC MANAGEMENT UNDER MOI'S AUTOCRACY

I quantitatively assess the posting and shuffling patterns of PCs and DCs under Moi's autocratic regime. PCs and DCs were thought to be loyal to Moi because of their neopatrimonial relationships with him. But a bureaucrat's local embeddedness in a jurisdiction affected her ability and willingness to help locals. In this section, I recap area alignment toward Moi to lay out the observable implications of the theory during these years. I then use data on PCs and DCs to examine if they were managed with the goal of co-opting Moi's aligned base and coercing misaligned areas. I also examine the effects of these management practices on governance outcomes.

6.4.1 Recap: Alignment and Embeddedness under Moi's Autocratic Regime

Table 6.1 summarizes the country's regional alignment under Moi's autocratic regime and gives descriptive statistics about the posting and shuffling patterns of PCs and DCs. I define a jurisdiction as aligned if

---

[50] Interview with former PC, February 2, 2012, Nairobi; Interview with then DC, June 30, 2017, Nairobi.

TABLE 6.1 *Group and Area Alignment toward Moi during Autocratic Regime (1978–1991)*

Alignment	Group	Location	Time Period	Percentage of Co-ethnic Administrators	Average Tenure (Years)
Aligned	Kalenjin	Parts of Rift Valley Province	Throughout	37	3.2
Misaligned	Kikuyu Luo	Central and Nairobi Provinces Parts of Nyanza Province	After attempted coup (1982–1991)	4	2.2
Unaligned	Other ethnic groups	Various	Throughout	9	2.3
Total			1979–1991	13	2.2

the majority of its inhabitants are Kalenjin. I define majority Kikuyu jurisdictions outside of Rift Valley province and majority Luo jurisdictions as misaligned. I also code Nairobi as misaligned as the joint Kikuyu and Luo population is more than 50 percent. The table also provides information on the two measures of embeddedness I quantitatively evaluate – co-ethnicity between bureaucrats and the majority of area residents (Column 5) and length of tenure (Column 6). These descriptive statistics suggest that Moi increased embeddedness in aligned areas and that bureaucrats were less embedded in misaligned areas.

6.4.2 Bureaucratic Management and Moi's Base

I analyze the posting and shuffling patterns of PCs and DCs from 1979 to 1991 in light of Moi's objective to use the state to co-opt his aligned base. My theory, described in Chapter 2, would expect that Moi strategically managed bureaucrats in order to increase local embeddedness in aligned areas. Thus the data should reflect high levels of co-ethnic bureaucrats appointed to Kalenjin-majority jurisdictions. Co-ethnic (Kalenjin) bureaucrats would better carry out the center's directives to co-opt locals since the administrators would feel social pressure to help the population. We should also expect lower rates of shuffling in Kalenjin-majority jurisdictions. Moreover, jurisdictions in which Kalenjins comprise a substantial minority of the population should see more Kalenjin administrators appointed there: Since Kalenjin administrators in minority-Kalenjin units were not co-ethnics with the local majority but co-ethnics of the local Kalenjin minority, the center could expect administrators to co-opt the local minority at the expense of the majority. The theory is ambiguous about shuffling rates in Kalenjin-minority jurisdictions, because higher embeddedness through tenure might increase an administrator's embeddedness among the jurisdiction's entire population instead of only among the aligned Kalenjin.

I use the same datasets as in Chapter 5, but with a 1979–1991 sample period. I run two regressions on ethnic postings and two regressions on shuffling (Table 6.2).[51] The dependent variable in the first regression is the percentage of years that an administrative unit had an officer whose ethnicity matched the majority of residents. The main independent variable is whether the majority of a unit's residents are Kalenjin. The dependent

---

[51] These regressions parallel the regressions run for the Kenyatta co-optation analysis in Chapter 5.

TABLE 6.2 *Management of Administrators, Co-opting the Kalenjin*

	1 Co-ethnic OLS	2 Kalenjin OLS	3 Shuffle Cox	4 Shuffle Cox
Kalenjin District	0.29^{**}		-0.60^{**}	
	(0.09)		(0.19)	
20% Kalenjin District		0.18^{*}		-0.60^{***}
		(0.08)		(0.17)
Population (1979, logged)	0.04	0.05	-0.34^{***}	-0.33^{***}
	(0.04)	(0.04)	(0.07)	(0.07)
Area (sq. km., logged)	-0.01	-0.03	-0.04	-0.04
	(0.02)	(0.02)	(0.05)	(0.04)
1979 ELF	-0.08	-0.02	$-0.44^{\dagger}$	-0.35
	(0.13)	(0.13)	(0.24)	(0.24)
Minister	-0.11	-0.21^{*}	0.21	0.21
	(0.09)	(0.09)	(0.15)	(0.15)
Intercept	-0.27	-0.10		
	(0.49)	(0.51)		
Num. obs.	48	48	668	668

$^{***}p < 0.001$, $^{**}p < 0.01$, $^{*}p < 0.05$, $^{\dagger}p < 0.1$. Regressions of the management of PCs and DCs from 1979 to 1991. The dependent variable in Column 1 is the percentage of years that a jurisdiction had a co-ethnic administrator. The dependent variable in Column 2 is the percentage of years that a jurisdiction had a Kalenjin administrator. Columns 3 and 4 examine shuffling rates. Columns 1 and 2 report the results from ordinary least squares (OLS) regressions, and Columns 3 and 4 report results from Cox proportional hazards models.

variable in the second regression is the percentage of years that the unit was staffed by a Kalenjin bureaucrat and the independent variable is whether the unit had at least a 20 percent Kalenjin population by 1989.[52] The third and fourth regressions use Cox proportional hazard models to look at shuffling rates. The independent variable in Column 3 is whether a district was majority Kalenjin and 20 percent Kalenjin in Column 4. The regressions use the same controls as the Kenyatta analyses in Chapter 5.[53]

---

[52] This coding parallels Column 2 in Table 5.3, but it codes Bungoma – a district with a 9.9 percent Kalenjin population, and discussed in this chapter – as 0. Rerunning this model with Bungoma coded as 1 for the independent variable does not substantively change the results.

[53] Population and ethnolinguistic fractionalization (ELF) figures have been recalculated from the 1979 census.

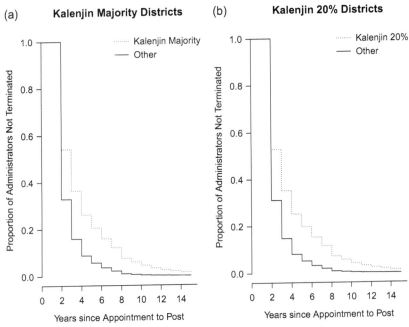

FIGURE 6.2 Hazard functions relating to Kalenjin co-optation from 1979 to 1991 during Moi's one-party autocratic regime. The figures graph the hazard function associated with Columns 3 and 4 of Table 6.2, respectively.

The results in Table 6.2 provide strong support that Provincial Administration bureaucrats were managed to better co-opt aligned Kalenjin areas during Moi's autocratic regime. Column 1 shows that Kalenjin-majority districts could expect an additional 3.7 years of being governed by a co-ethnic. Column 2 indicates that districts with at least a 20 percent Kalenjin population could expect an additional 2.3 years of having a Kalenjin administrator posted there. I graph the hazard ratios from Columns 3 and 4 in Figure 6.2. Districts with a Kalenjin majority (left) or at least a 20 percent Kalenjin population (right) experienced substantially lower shuffling rates than elsewhere. Figure 6.2a shows that more than 50 percent of administrators posted to a Kalenjin-majority district could expect to stay in their district for at least two years, and nearly 40 percent could expect to be posted for at least three years. Elsewhere, only about 35 percent of administrators could expect a tenure of at least two years, and less than 20 percent could expect a tenure of at least three years. Figure 6.2b shows similar results.

None of the control variables are consistently significant or signed in the same direction. This suggests that alternative explanations are not driving the results. Further, although not shown here, the results are robust to including other relevant controls, such as the percentage of high-potential land in a jurisdiction. Separately, I find evidence that administrators were used to co-opt the larger Rift Valley pastoralist community, not solely the Kalenjin ethnic group. I rerun Column 1 of Table 6.2 after substituting the indicator for a majority-Kalenjin jurisdiction with a majority-KAMATUSA (Kalenjin, Maasai, Turkana, Samburu) jurisdiction. Majority-KAMATUSA jurisdictions were 18 percentage points more likely to be assigned a co-ethnic administrator ($p < 0.05$). Substantively, this translates into an additional 2.2 years of having a co-ethnic administrator. I also rerun Column 3 after substituting the KAMATUSA-majority indicator for the Kalenjin-majority indicator. KAMATUSA-majority districts were also significantly less likely to have their administrators shuffled ($p < 0.001$).

The Benefits of Local Embeddedness in Co-opting Moi's Base
I find evidence that the management of administrators in aligned areas was associated with improved governance outcomes. While the Provincial Administration played an important role in doling out land, it was also instrumental in providing other important state resources, including monetary disbursements from the Rural Development Fund (RDF). Since at least the beginning of Moi's presidency, the central government allocated funds to each district through the RDF to spend on local development projects such as plant nurseries, cattle dips, and school electrification. Disbursements for projects were intended to serve specific administrative locations within a district (two administrative tiers below a district). While the DDC determined each district's project allocations, in practice the DC steered all project allocations and controlled which district elites even participated in meetings.

The archives contain RDF disbursements for Western Province from Moi's one-party years, with project allocations itemized to individual locations.[54] Western Province contained three districts at the time, all with a majority Luhya population. Two of the districts also had sizable local ethnic minority populations. Bungoma District was home to an

---

[54] Unfortunately, I could not find RDF disbursements for other provinces with sizable Kalenjin populations.

indigenous Sabaot population, a Kalenjin subgroup that comprised 10 percent of the district's population. Busia District was home to the Teso, who comprised about 30 percent of the district's population.[55]

DDC allocations tended to favor the district's majority ethnic group because elites from the majority group lobbied the DC for more allocations at the expense of the local minority ethnic group (Hassan 2016). This logic was echoed in my interviews with Teso respondents. One Teso villager said, "You see, Busia is Luhyas and Teso. And most of the leaders are Luhya so you find that most of the things used to go to those other areas like Nambale [in a Luhya-dominant area]."[56] Another explained:

When resources come to the district, it is the DDC [who allocates]. So you find that those who are a minority within the district never get anything. Those who are influential end up taking everything ... So normally, the instigation of recruitment for civil service – police, nurses, teachers – normally they decide on a number. How many are we recruiting this time? Maybe 1,000. Maybe each district is bringing in twelve. The Teso would argue that in the last selection of nurses, [Busia was] given twelve nurses and no Teso were taken because the Luhya took them all.[57]

As these quotes suggest, the DC is heavily influenced by local politicians when making allocation decisions. Local elites from the majority group are liable to have a stronger influence on the DC and push allocations to the majority's home areas.

This logic explains disbursements in Busia District. I use 1962 census information – at that time, the most recent census with ethnic information disaggregated at the sub-district level – to determine the majority ethnic group of each location. I then aggregate RDF allocations by the majority ethnic group of the receiving locations. These figures are presented by year in Figure 6.3 and aggregated in Table 6.3. Teso-majority locations received less than 20 percent of Busia's allocations from 1979 to 1988, much less than their 30 percent of the district population would suggest. In line with my interviews, elites from the majority Luhya population were able to ensure more than their fair share of RDF funds.[58]

However, Moi could counter this tyranny of the majority through his provincial administrators. We should expect that Moi advised all DCs

---

55 The ethnic breakdowns of these groups are consistent across the 1979 and 1989 censuses.
56 Interview with Teso resident, March 13, 2012, Amagoro, Kenya.
57 Interview with former Teso resident of Busia, December 3, 2011, Nairobi.
58 This situation was echoed across many other districts with local ethnic minorities and was the impetus for creating new administrative districts for local ethnic minorities throughout the 1990s (Kasara 2006; Hassan 2016).

TABLE 6.3 *Descriptive Statistics on RDF Allocations and Management of DCs*

District	Minority Group (Percent in District, 1979)	Percent of RDF Allocations 1979–1988	Percent of RDF Allocations years w/ co-ethnic DC
Bungoma	Kalenjin (10.0)	27.1	36.8
Busia	Teso (30.1)	19.7	–

posted to Bungoma (or other districts with a minority Kalenjin population) to privilege areas inhabited by his Kalenjin base. As expected, areas dominated by the minority Kalenjin population received 27 percent of the RDF's budgetary allocations for those years, significantly more than expected based on their 10-percent share of the population. These amounts can be partly explained by their aligned status.

But my theory suggests that Moi could better ensure the co-optation of Bungoma's Kalenjin population through active bureaucratic management. If the DC is a co-ethnic of the minority group, then she is liable to use her authority to divert resources to her own group due to her social attachments and embeddedness (as well as her loyalty to Moi). We should therefore expect that the center purposefully posted an administrator who shares an identity with the minority population when that minority is aligned, and that these aligned areas enjoy larger allocations. In line with the theory, Bungoma had a Kalenjin DC for six years during Moi's autocratic regime (most districts had a co-ethnic administrator for two years, as seen in Table 6.1). And indeed, the annual disbursements suggest that the total amount allocated to Kalenjin locations in the district was even higher during the years in which the district was governed by a co-ethnic administrator: RDF allocations during the years with a Kalenjin DC reached nearly 37 percent of the district's total allocation. The findings suggest that all DCs were willing to implement Moi's demands to co-opt his co-ethnics: Kalenjin-majority areas received more allocations than their numbers or minority status would suggest. However, Kalenjin DCs felt additional pressure from their co-ethnics to allocate even more resources to them. Kalenjin DCs in Bungoma were better able to resist demands from the majority Luhya population because of their social connections to the minority. We do not see similar patterns in next-door Busia District, because the Teso were not aligned with Moi (or at least, no more aligned than the majority-Luhya population).

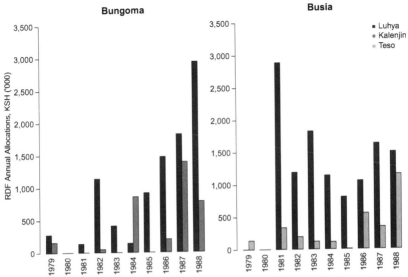

FIGURE 6.3 Rural Development Fund allocations for Western Province districts with substantial ethnic minority populations, from 1979 to 1988. The Luhya are the majority in both districts. The Sabaot are a Kalenjin subgroup with a 10-percent share of the population in Bungoma. The Teso comprise 30 percent of the Busia population.

6.4.3 Bureaucratic Management and Tempering Dissent

I now turn to evaluate the posting and shuffling patterns of PCs and DCs under Moi's autocratic regime in light of his popular threats from mis-aligned areas. PCs and DCs had strong neopatrimonial relationships with Moi and were seen as exceedingly loyal. They still posed a risk of shirking from their duty to coerce, however, if they were too locally embedded in their jurisdictions. The observable implications from Chapter 2 suggest that we should see lower levels of embeddedness in misaligned areas.

Using the same datasets as in Section 6.4.2, I run three regressions to examine ethnic postings in misaligned areas (see Table 6.4). Column 1 displays the results from an OLS regression in which the dependent variable is the percentage of years from 1979 to 1991 in which an administrative unit was staffed by an officer who was a co-ethnic of the majority of the unit's residents. Columns 2 and 3 report the results from logit regressions in which the dependent variable is an indicator variable for whether a unit was staffed by an administrator who was a co-ethnic of the majority of the unit's residents in a given year. The fourth regression uses a Cox proportional hazard model to assess rates of shuffling. The independent variable in Columns 1, 2, and 4 denotes whether the jurisdiction was a

TABLE 6.4 *Management of the Administrators, Coercing Kikuyu, and Luo Dissent*

	1 Co-ethnic OLS	2 Co-ethnic Logit	3 Co-ethnic Logit	4 Shuffle Cox
Kikuyu- or Luo-Majority Jurisdiction outside Rift Valley	−0.02	0.39		0.30
	(0.55)	(0.90)		(0.18)
After Coup Attempt		0.42	0.42	
		(0.51)	(0.51)	
Kikuyu-Majority Jurisdiction outside Rift Valley			1.69	
			(1.08)	
Nairobi Province			−15.86***	
			(1.49)	
Luo-Majority Jurisdiction			−15.82***	
			(0.85)	
Kikuyu or Luo-Majority Jurisdiction outside Rift Valley		−2.13*		
		(1.09)		
*Kikuyu-Majority Jurisdiction outside Rift Valley * After Coup*			−2.32*	
			(1.21)	
*Nairobi * After Coup*			−0.42	
			(0.51)	
*Luo-Majority Jurisdiction * After Coup*			−0.47	
			(0.62)	
Population (1979, logged)	0.04	0.23	0.23	−0.31**
	(0.04)	(0.34)	(0.34)	(0.07)
Area (sq. km., logged)	−0.02	−0.20	−0.20	−0.00
	(0.03)	(0.18)	(0.18)	(0.05)
1979 ELF	−0.12	−0.94	−0.58	−0.20
	(0.15)	(1.08)	(1.25)	(0.44)
Minister	−0.07	−0.29	−0.16	0.16
	(0.09)	(0.68)	(0.71)	(0.15)
Intercept	−0.02	−2.67	−2.94	
	(0.55)	(4.26)	(4.20)	
Num. obs.	48	668	668	668

*** $p < 0.001$, ** $p < 0.01$, * $p < 0.05$. Regressions of the management of PCs and DCs from 1979 to 1991. Column 1 gives the results from an OLS regression, Columns 2 and 3 from logit models with results clustered at the jurisdiction level, and Column 4 from a Cox proportional hazard model.

majority Kikuyu or Luo district outside of Rift Valley. Column 2 interacts this variable with an indicator variable for observations that occurred after the attempted coup (1983–1991). I break up this interaction term in the third regression.

These results provide some evidence that threatening misaligned areas were governed to increase bureaucrats' compliance with orders to coerce. The results in Column 1 are not statistically significant. Misaligned jurisdictions did not have significantly different rates of being assigned a co-ethnic administrator than the rest of the country. Columns 2 and 3 help explain this insignificant result. The substantive interpretation of Column 2 is that misaligned jurisdictions were 15.0 percentage points less likely to be assigned a co-ethnic administrator than other jurisdictions *after* the coup than before (95% CI: −0.42, 0.01). Column 3 investigates the findings in Column 2 by separating jurisdictions that are Kikuyu-majority from those that are Luo-majority. The results indicate that Kikuyu-majority jurisdictions outside Rift Valley could expect fewer co-ethnics after the coup, whereas Luo-majority jurisdictions were less likely to be assigned a co-ethnic administrator throughout the sample period. This result fits with the elite politics of Moi's autocratic regime as described in Chapter 4: Whereas Kikuyu elites were incorporated until the coup, Luo elites were mostly excluded throughout Moi's presidency. Separately, the strong negative results for Nairobi on the lower-order term, alongside the insignficant results for the interaction term, may be a consequence of latent urban unrest – since the potential for popular mobilization is higher in urban areas, they are often treated differently than the rest of the country. Whereas most work has focused on urban bias and co-optation through material goods,[59] these results suggest that urban areas are simultaneously governed by bureaucrats who are more willing to suppress should co-optation fail.

Column 4 indicates that misaligned areas were more likely to have their administrators shuffled. I simulate shuffling rates after holding control variables at their means and find that only 25 percent of administrators posted to misaligned jurisdictions could expect to stay on for more than two years; outside of misaligned areas, 38 percent of administrators could expect to stay in their post for more than two years.

---

[59] See, for instance, Bates (1981), Wallace (2014), Ballard-Rosa (2016), and Thomson (2019).

6.5 SUMMARY

This chapter examined the management of the Provincial Administration during the first thirteen years of Moi's presidency. It began by demonstrating his reliance on the agency to co-opt aligned areas and coerce misaligned areas. I then showed that Moi attempted to ensure compliance from high-ranking PCs and DCs, in part, by developing neopatrimonial relationships with them. But these bureaucrats were still at risk of shirking from orders to coerce the local population, depending on their degree of embeddedness in the jurisdiction in which they served. Since embedded bureaucrats' incentives were aligned with the residents in their jurisdiction, locally embedded bureaucrats might be unwilling to coerce them when necessary. Instead, I show that Moi decreased the embeddedness of bureaucrats in misaligned areas and artificially increased it in aligned areas. By strategically manipulating the embeddedness of bureaucrats, Moi had an agency that proved able and willing to carry out his desired management practices on the ground across the country.

7

Moi, the Provincial Administration, and Multiparty Elections

7.1 INTRODUCTION

Chapters 5 and 6 examined the numerous popular threats that Presidents Kenyatta and Moi (1978–1991) faced during the country's autocratic era. Each president used the state to maintain control in the parts of the country that mattered most for his political stability. Popular threats largely emanated from misaligned groups – co-ethnics of elites who were not incorporated into the regime. Unincorporated elites had the resources and ill will to mobilize their followers against both presidents, sowing underlying discontent that could coalesce into collective action. Each president also needed the strong backing of his aligned co-ethnics to maintain some level of popular support and legitimacy.

This chapter examines Moi's reliance on the Provincial Administration after the country transitioned to an electoral regime. The change in regime type reshaped the nature of the popular threats that he, and Kenyan leaders after him, faced. After the transition, the most serious popular threat to his rule was through the ballot box, as unincorporated elites were spearheading the electoral campaign to unseat him. Moi was therefore forced to reevaluate the importance of different groups, and the areas they inhabit. To win reelection, he had to maintain the strong support of his aligned groups, but their numbers were too few to sustain a winning electoral coalition on their own. And misaligned groups were unlikely to support him over their own co-ethnic elites vying for the presidency. Moi's continued tenure in office thus hinged on garnering the support of some unaligned groups. In line with the argument in Chapter 2, the main focus of the Provincial Administration's coercion thus shifted from misaligned to unaligned groups.

The Provincial Administration had the tools to help Moi create and sustain a winning electoral coalition, yet he could not ensure compliance from all of this agency's bureaucrats. The center could not monitor all bureaucrats and sanction noncompliance; the agency was not comprised solely of loyal bureaucrats who would comply absent monitoring as Moi did not pack the state with his co-ethnics; the state lacked sufficient cash to distribute patronage to lower-level bureaucrats to buy loyalty; and even loyal bureaucrats were liable to shirk if they had strong social connections to the area in which they served.

The center was able to alleviate its principal-agent problem and rely on the Provincial Administration to help Moi win reelection (twice), however, by strategically managing bureaucrats based on three relationships: an area's *alignment* towards the leader, a bureaucrat's *loyalty* towards the leader, and a bureaucrat's *local embeddedness* within her posted jurisdiction. By considering all three relationships together, we observe that the center posted and shuffled bureaucrats to best ensure compliance where it mattered the most for regime security. In line with the theory developed in Chapter 2, I show that areas could expect variation in the *loyalty* of the administrator posted in their jurisdiction and in the bureaucrat's *embeddedness* within the community depending on the area's political *alignment* towards Moi.

This chapter explores the management of all trained bureaucrats in the Provincial Administration from 1992–2002. As in Chapters 5 and 6, I examine the agency's highest-ranking officials – Provincial Commissioners (PCs) and District Commissioners (DCs) – who were all considered loyal to Moi. I also analyze the management of District Officers (DOs), the lower-level rank that comprised about 90 percent of trained administrators by 1992. DOs have played an especially important role in Kenyan politics since 1992 as they oversee grassroots political campaigns. Variation in DO loyalty helps me explore different facets of the theory. Unlike at higher levels, there are too many DOs to buy off through patronage. Instead, an individual DO's loyalty depends largely on her co-ethnicity with political elites, and expectation of promotion to cushy PC and DC positions. I present evidence that Kalenjin DOs, co-ethnics of President Moi, were perceived as the most loyal. Kikuyu DOs, who were co-ethnics of Moi's most viable opposition candidates, were perceived as the most disloyal.

The quantitative analyses presented in this chapter show that the center took into account an individual bureaucrat's relationships with Moi and the relationship with the area in which they served when deciding where to post and how often to shuffle them. First, I show that Moi managed bureaucrats with the goal of co-opting his aligned base. Kalenjin bureaucrats were disproportionately sent to aligned areas both because Kalenjin administrators were considered loyal, and thus likely to comply with orders, and because they were locally embedded through co-ethnicity with locals, and thus felt social pressure to improve the livelihoods of their co-ethnics. The management of bureaucrats in aligned areas thus allowed the state to redistribute resources in the run-up to Moi's reelection campaigns and organize a campaign of ethnic violence designed to evict migrant groups from the ancestral Kalenjin homeland.

Second, I show that the center managed bureaucrats in order to coerce unaligned areas. Such areas were disproportionately administered by loyal bureaucrats who could be expected to comply with orders from the center. Further, bureaucrats posted to unaligned areas tended to be less embedded in the local area, which reduced their incentives for shirking from orders to coerce. Misaligned areas mattered less to the overall election outcome, as Moi could win without their votes. Misaligned areas were therefore disproportionately likely to be governed by disloyal bureaucrats. In other words, disloyal bureaucrats were relegated to areas where their expected noncompliance would do little harm to the election outcome.

The empirical focus in this chapter – a former autocrat who contested in multiparty elections – forms the basis of an alternative explanation for Africa's stalled democratization. Many other countries in sub-Saharan Africa transitioned from an autocratic to electoral regime after the end of the Cold War. Yet only nine former autocrats were voted out in founding elections. And from 1990–2015, sitting incumbents lost reelection in only twenty-one elections on the subcontinent (Bleck and van de Walle 2018), a reelection rate that is significantly higher than other world regions (Arriola 2012).[1] The ability of many African leaders to stay in office is seen as especially puzzling since incumbents often rely on their seemingly weak states to tilt elections in their favor. This chapter addressees this puzzle by suggesting that a state's capacity can be temporarily rerouted to fulfil important political tasks. In Kenya, the state's capacity to help Moi varied across jurisdictions depending on the bureaucrat stationed there. The finite number of loyal bureaucrats were selectively posted to places where compliance was the most necessary.

---

[1] Also see Baker (1998), van de Walle (2007), Lynch and Crawford (2011), Bleck and van de Walle (2018), and Cheeseman (2010).

7.2 AREA ALIGNMENT AND VARIATION IN THE PROVINCIAL ADMINISTRATION'S ACTIONS

I first lay out Moi's political landscape during his last decade in office to define the alignment of different ethnic groups. I then describe how officials in the Provincial Administration used their authority to co-opt Moi's aligned areas both by distributing agricultural land and allegedly organizing ethnic clashes that evicted migrants from in and around Rift Valley. I then provide evidence regarding the role of the Provincial Administration in coercing the opposition in the run-up to Moi's 1992 and 1997 elections.

7.2.1 Area Alignment toward Moi

Moi needed to build and sustain a minimum-winning coalition at the polls to stay in office under the new electoral regime. As under autocracy, this popular challenge was a consequence of elite-level incorporation (see Chapter 4): Moi's ability to win votes from different ethnic groups was a function of whether a group had a co-ethnic elite who was a viable contender for the presidency.

Moi's co-ethnic Kalenjin ethnic group remained his core, aligned group. Kalenjin-majority constituencies voted for him at rates of more than 90 percent. Yet this ethnic group comprised only 11 percent of the country's population. Moi's broader language group also supported him at high rates (80 percent plus), but they comprised only an additional 4 percent of the country's population. Ensuring their overwhelming support and high turnout would form the foundation of any reelection strategy, but Moi also needed to win votes among some unaligned groups, or at least prevent them from voting for the opposition.

I analyze secondary sources and archival newspaper material from 1992, coding Moi's viable opposition candidates in that election as the Kikuyu elites Kenneth Matiba of the Forum for the Restoration of Democracy-Asili (FORD-A) and Mwai Kibaki of the Democratic Party (DP). They each won about 25 percent of the vote in 1992 and had strong support in multiple parts of the country. Their showings are especially strong given that they split the Kikuyu vote.[2] In 1997, Moi's only viable

---

[2] Since coding viability in the run-up to the 1992 election using the 1992 election results introduces posttreatment bias, I instead include these figures to give a sense of their support across the country. The quantitative analyses that examine elections focus on bureaucratic

opponent was Kibaki (DP). I thus consider Kikuyu-majority areas as misaligned.

I classify all other ethnic groups as unaligned since they did not have a co-ethnic elite who was a viable presidential candidate, even though they varied in their support of Moi. This classification is perhaps most contentious for the Luo ethnic group; Oginga Odinga (FORD-K) won 16 percent of the vote in 1992, and his son Raila Odinga (National Development Party) 11 percent in 1997. I believe my narrow classification is justified, however, because neither candidate had much appeal among other ethnic groups. Moreover, the younger Odinga was not even able to consolidate support among his co-ethnics in 1997.[3]

7.2.2 KANU Was Unable to Solve Moi's Popular Threats

As before, Moi had to look beyond the Kenya African National Union (KANU) to garner sufficient popular support. KANU's strength was based on its strong connection to the Provincial Administration throughout the 1980s. But the reintroduction of multiparty elections and the need for the appearance of an apolitical state required the state to separate itself from day-to-day party operations. To be sure, the connection between the Provincial Administration and KANU persisted. But it was much weaker than in the 1980s. Unsurprisingly, the party fell into a period of decay beginning around 1992; KANU party branches declined in strength, and party donations and recruitment, even in aligned areas, decreased. As KANU grew weaker, the Provincial Administration remained strong and proved to be crucial for Moi's reelection campaigns: "the Provincial Administration, in fact, played a key role in KANU's campaign, one far more important than ... the local party apparatus" (Throup and Hornsby, 1998, 372).

7.2.3 Addressing Kalenjin Land Demands: Co-optation and Coercion in the Rift

Bureaucrats serving in the Provincial Administration during Moi's electoral regime continued pursuing many of the same resource distribution

---

management *after* the 1992 race, thereby allowing me to use the 1992 election results to more systematically code viability in the run-up to the 1997 race.

3 That said, I consider more expansive definitions of aligned and misaligned groups in additional quantitative analyses and the results remain unchanged.

strategies, including of agricultural land, that they had carried out during his autocratic regime.

Throughout the 1990s, the Provincial Administration allowed Kalenjin farmers to continue squatting on government land. For example, in 1992 a group of Ndorobo farmers (close kin of the Kalenjin)[4] in Nakuru District were squatting in the Mau Forest, home of the country's largest water reservoir. The government had planned to allocate land to these squatters in conjunction with a British Government initiative designed to preserve other areas of canopy land. This decision prompted landless Kalenjin residents to settle in the area in the hopes of getting a title deed during the Ndorobo registration process. A local forest officer noted that several new houses were built in the forest during this period: "they were told that if they have no house they cannot be registered."[5] The British initiative eventually fell through. Forest rangers demanded that the Provincial Administration evict Ndorobo and Kalenjin squatters. Instead, the Nakuru DC undermined the forestry department: some Ndorobo and Kalenjin residents in Nakuru were "given authority to farm [in protected forest land] by the DC's office" and the DC "also incited the people to resist any information originating from forest dept."[6]

Similarly, the Provincial Administration oversaw the creation of dozens of settlement schemes that spanned almost 300,000 hectares during Moi's final decade in elected office, more than twice as much land as was formally allocated under his autocratic years. Many of the settlement schemes that officially launched in the 1990s were only possible after the Provincial Administration helped the government reclassify land initially set aside for preservation.[7] After the schemes were created, Moi relied on administrators to determine the beneficiaries. For instance, in early 1997, the Kalenjin DO for Nakuru's Olengurone Division – the district's sole Kalenjin-majority division – was "told *by the president* to prepare a list of the landless and arrange for the surveyors to come and demacate [sic] the earmarked pace."[8] This is in line with recent findings on forest

---

[4] See Lynch (2006b) and Lynch (2011b).

[5] Provincial Forest Officer to Permanent Secretary Environment and Natural Resources, February 18, 1994, EA1/4/49, Rift Valley Provincial Archives, Nakuru, Kenya.

[6] Forester to District Forester, January 11, 1994, EA1/4/49, Rift Valley Provincial Archives, Nakuru.

[7] For instance, more than 60,000 square hectares of closed canopy forest land, which was concentrated in Kalenjin areas, was reclassified from 1993 to 2002; 83 percent of this land was distributed for private use (e.g., individual plot allotments) (Morjaria 2018).

[8] Emphasis added. DO Olengurone to DC Nakuru, February 17, 1997, EA/7/76, Rift Valley Provincial Archives, Nakuru.

excisions during the 1990s, in which districts like Nakuru saw public land converted to private farms (Morjaria 2018).

As before, co-optation of the aligned Kalenjin ethnic group also required administrators to coerce other groups. The Provincial Administration was used to evict Kikuyu squatters from land they had worked on but never formally owned.[9] And there were numerous reports on the role of administrators in evicting squatters from misaligned groups living in forest land during the 1990s.[10]

But during these years, the actions of the Provincial Administration were much more coercive than before. This agency allegedly organized a violent campaign to evict nonindigenous groups from Rift Valley during the ethnic violence (or "clashes") of the 1990s. With the return to multiparty elections, pastoralist ethnic groups considered indigenous to the Rift feared the consequences of another Kikuyu presidency and the possible loss of their land at the hands of the state. And many pastoralist elites feared losing their parliamentary seats under (free and fair) multiparty competition. This was especially true for Members of Parliament (MPs) in constituencies on the periphery of Rift Valley which had experienced the highest levels of in-migration by nonindigenous groups throughout Kenya's postindependence history.

Pastoralist MPs in the early 1990s revived the debate about a return to *majimboism*, the federal state structure negotiated at independence, to address land fears among their constituents and increase their chances of reelection. As described in earlier chapters, *majimboism* introduced institutional safeguards and ethnicity-based land policies to prevent nonnative groups from encroaching into Rift Valley. Independence-era elites also expected *majimboism* to secure parliamentary seats in the Rift for pastoralists by preventing further in-migration by migrant groups, or even encouraging out-migration.[11]

Majimboism was not formally reintroduced during the 1990s. But many pastoralist elites incited their followers to implement its underlying tenet – that ethnic groups should only reside in their home province – and to do so violently. A wave of election-related ethnic violence erupted during this period, largely in and around Rift Valley Province. The clashes

9 See EA/7/76, Rift Valley Provincial Archives, Nakuru.
10 "Vacate Forest Settlers Told," *The Daily Nation*, October 3, 1997, p. 4.
11 In the run-up to independence, Rift Valley's indigenous groups were in the Kenya African Democratic Union (KADU), while its most populous nonindigenous groups – the Kikuyu, Luhya, and Luo – were in KANU or wavered between KANU and KADU.

were instigated by young Kalenjin and Maasai men, with significant organization and funding provided by the state. The violence was most intense in the run-up to the 1992 election; an estimated 1,500 were killed and 300,000 displaced by 1993 (Africa Watch 1993; Boone 2011). The main targets were members of the province's largest migrant groups – the Kikuyu, Luhya, and Luo.[12]

Some members of the Provincial Administration allegedly organized and facilitated many of these attacks in order to help Moi maintain support among his pastoralist base. The Akiwumi Report, written by the Judicial Commission of Inquiry set up to investigate the clashes, concluded that the violence was "encouraged and supported by Provincial Administrators."[13] For instance, "since all meetings require licenses and, hence, government approval, it is impossible to avoid the conclusion that [planning] meetings were sanctioned, if not coordinated, by local authorities" (Klopp, 2001, 146). One MP remarked, "It is difficult for even a layman to believe that about 100 people from a location or constituency can be armed with arrows to attack their neighbours without assistant chiefs, chiefs, informers and district officers being aware of what is happening."[14] Africa Watch (1993, 34) documented that the DC of Uasin Gishu, a Rift Valley district that was 53 percent Kalenjin and 17 percent Kikuyu in 1989, incited Kalenjin residents in his jurisdiction to violence: "A week before the fighting, the Uasin Gishu district commissioner had reportedly said at a public meeting that 'in Kenyatta's days, if a Luhya had said something against the Kikuyu he would be killed, so now why should Kikuyus say things against the Kalenjin.'"

Even when administrators did not organize the violence, they often knew about attacks that were set to take place in their jurisdiction and worked to make them more effective. For instance, the Akiwumi Report found that some bureaucrats called community meetings to distract local migrant community members while perpetrators torched homes.[15] Human Rights Watch details incidents in which provincial administrators used their authority over other coercive organs to order police officers to stand down (effectively, obstructing other bodies from maintaining

---

[12] Some Kalenjins and other pastoralists were also affected by retaliatory attacks, but these attacks were less frequent and less intense than those on migrant groups. By 1989, Rift Valley was 19 percent Kikuyu, 10 percent Luhya, and 4 percent Luo.

[13] Government of Kenya (2002, 4).

[14] As seen in Klopp (2001, 146).

[15] Government of Kenya (2002, 56).

order) in clash sites, seemingly in an attempt to allow violent flare-ups in the future.[16] When perpetrators were caught, provincial administrators often got them released.[17] Overall, the Akiwumi Report summarizes that the Provincial Administration had "a general reluctance ... to take any pre-emptive action."[18] And while most of the historical record suggests that the Provincial Administration facilitated the violence, there is also evidence that some officers played a direct role in evicting migrants within their jurisdiction.[19]

After the violence abated, the Provincial Administration was reluctant to help with relief efforts for members of unaligned or misaligned groups. Its officers harassed church officials who housed clash victims or distributed food.[20] Both the Akiwumi Report and Africa Watch document how officers were unsympathetic to victims of these attacks, at times telling them to return to their homes even though administrators were aware that local perpetrators were still active. One Rift Valley DC said that evicted clash victims "were expected to return where they originally came from."[21] Africa Watch gives an example of this behavior from Bungoma District in Western Province:

Africa Watch visited Kapkateny and Namwela camps where approximately a hundred clash victims were being housed in make-shift housing or abandoned buildings. Yet, when asked about the situation, a Bungoma district officer denied the existence of the camps and told Africa Watch that the clashes 'were a problem a year ago, but now we don't have that problem anymore'.[22]

A group of Kikuyu victims from Enoosupukia in Maasai-majority Narok District described their experience more than a decade after their displacement:

[A]fter demolition of Maela Camp for Enoosupukia Victims, by the KANU government in 1994, a section of Enoosupukia Victims left Maela and have scattered all over the country ... Remember December 24th 1994 when the KANU government pretended that it was settling us (victims), people were put in Lorries at night and were dumped in various places in central province. Dumped just like garbage.

---

[16] Human Rights Watch (1993, 57).
[17] Government of Kenya (2002, 36).
[18] Government of Kenya (2002, 56).
[19] See, for instance, Akiwumi (1999, 28).
[20] Human Rights Watch (1993, 90).
[21] Government of Kenya (2002, 4).
[22] Human Rights Watch (1993, 92).

The letter also describes another group of victims from Enoosupukia that had been resettled:

> Remember the two hundred victims settled at Moi-Ndabi [in Nakuru]. They were said to have been settled but were they really settled in good faith? ... they were also dumped into somewhere they would be evicted by floods. They were warned not to associate with the remaining colleagues, they were forced to make statements labeling the remaining victims as thaggeries [sic] brought by the opposition for free land. Today they are as good as non-settled persons.[23]

This same group of internally displaced persons had written a complaint letter about the deliberate unhelpfulness of the DO leading the registration of clash victims in 1994: "there was a big omission of victims names in each section [village]. The fate of those victims is still unknown." Provincial Administration bureaucrats made the ethnic clashes more effective by coordinating the perpetrators while failing to adequately address the plight of victims, and preventing their resettlement in the Rift after the violence abated. Doing so helped Moi: much of the land left by evictees went to Kalenjin recipients, further binding this group to Moi.

7.2.4 Coercion during Moi's Reelection Campaigns

The Provincial Administration coerced opposition candidates, as well as unaligned and misaligned groups that were liable to support the opposition, in the run-up to Moi's 1992 and 1997 election campaigns.[24]

The Provincial Administration's interference in the country's multi-party elections began with collecting intelligence. As they did during the autocratic era, provincial administrators in the field continued to send reports about political dynamics in their jurisdictions. But the Permanent Secretary of Provincial Administration expected reports with increased urgency in the run-up to the 1992 election. He wrote the following to his PCs:

> As you are well aware the political climate in the country has reached a new and critical crescendo, a situation which is unprecedented ... I have found it necessary that I should get weekly reports from you on popularity rating of various political

---

[23] Private citizen to DC Nakuru, December 15, 2005, EA1/4/49, Rift Valley National Archives, Nakuru.

[24] Much has been written about these flawed elections. For instance, see Barkan (1993), Ajulu (1998), Ng'ethe and Barkan (1998), Throup and Hornsby (1998), Kagwanja (2001), Kanyinga (2000a), Ombongi (2000), Brown (2006), and Howard and Roessler (2006).

parties and Parliamentary aspirants. This information will be very important for strategic planning and provision of remedial measures where necessary. As this will be very sensitive information, you are requested to send hand-written reports only.[25]

Officers complied.[26] Reports from PCs and DCs documented KANU's estimated popular support in the jurisdiction, at times broken down by administrative location. Officers explained the reasons for instances of lower-than-expected support, such as a slowdown in recruitment drives by KANU branch officers, negligence by local elected KANU leaders, and area residents' hostility to the ruling party. Their reports also provided information on specific opposition organizers and candidates, such as how candidates funded their campaigns. Bureaucrats made sure to point out when the candidate had a close associate or family member working in the state, because the regime could drain an opposition candidate's political coffers, or at least prevent the opposition from benefitting from state money, by firing the opponent's relative. Administrators also detailed how much opposition candidates had recently contributed to *harambees* and other local development projects as a measure of their grassroots support. The reports also assessed the oratory skills of local opposition organizers.[27] Officers spied on other bureaucrats and local community members. For instance, one DO explained the "easy penetration and influence" of Kibaki's DP through the actions of a local bureaucrat who was prone to taking bribes and organizing local boycotts of KANU events.[28] DOs even forwarded local gossip about vote-buying efforts in their jurisdiction to superiors.[29]

Administrators restricted the organizing power of opposition parties and candidates. Although the Provincial Administration could no longer legally prevent opposition parties from forming or registering branches after 1992, they often did so in practice.[30] In a move that resembled the Provincial Administration's treatment of the Kenya People's Union under Kenyatta, the agency relied on outdated ordinances, some of which dated back to the colonial era, to legally restrict the activities of opposition

[25] Permanent Secretary Provincial Administration to all PCs, November 20, 1992, DN/20/20, Nyanza Provincial Archives, Kisumu.

[26] See DN/20/20, Nyanza Provincial Archives, Kisumu.

[27] Ibid.

[28] DO Mbogoini to DC Nakuru, October 16, 2000, EA1/11/9, Rift Valley Provincial Archives, Nakuru.

[29] Ibid.

[30] See EC1/1/27.

parties. The Provincial Administration also implemented new administrative, legal, or judicial mandates to stall the opposition. For instance, the High Court issued an edict against one opposition party, stating that it was "hereby restrained from holding, attending, advertising, organizing or otherwise howsoever conducting [its] affairs."[31] Field officers routinely used similar rulings or other ordinances to deny opposition candidates licenses to hold meetings. For example, 1997 opposition candidate Raila Odinga claimed that, "the PA was interfering directly ... If I wanted to hold a campaign rally I had to get a permit in writing from the DC where I would be compelled to answer questions before him. Many times, I was stopped from holding rallies on false grounds."[32] One MP running on the DP ticket in Eastern Province recalls:

[I]t was quite difficult even to hold public rallies [in the 1990s]. [Administrators] used to follow us there. They would even put stones on the road so you don't get in, they just blocked it [even if] you have [managed to get] your meetings licensed. At the last minute you are told the rally is cancelled on security grounds. And you ask them who has told you, they say instructions from above.[33]

Some opposition candidates tried to subvert the need for a permit by conducting "walkabouts" or "meet-the-people" tours where they would simply walk around a jurisdiction to meet residents. Officers tried to subvert these too by calling them what they were – unlicensed meetings – and shutting them down with the help of armed police.[34]

When administrators did allow opposition candidates to meet the public, they closely supervised the events. Speakers were instructed not to criticize KANU or President Moi. Administrators stopped rallies when they did, sometimes violently, by throwing teargas into the crowd (Throup and Hornsby 1998). In some instances, officers refused to provide adequate security for opposition candidates' rallies. There were even accusations that some officers mobilized KANU supporters to attack opposition voters at rallies where security was not provided.[35]

The Provincial Administration created administrative hurdles for opposition supporters as well, for example, by making it difficult for

---

[31] Kisumu Branch FORD-K Secretary to Sub-Branch Chairmen, January 4, 1996, HT/23/151, Nyanza Provincial Archives, Kisumu.
[32] Interview with Raila Odinga, May 22, 2014, Boston, MA.
[33] Interview with former MP, July 3, 2012, Nairobi.
[34] "DO's attempt to stop Michuki campaign fails," *The Daily Nation*, November 9, 1992.
[35] "Odinga Blames DC," *The Daily Nation*, November 26, 1992.

them to obtain proper identification or register to vote.[36] Officers were accused of withholding relief food from presumed misaligned voters in drought-stricken areas. Provincial administrators also made it costly for citizens to support the opposition by imprisoning them for fictional transgressions or threatening their safety. In addition, they also failed to prosecute the crimes of KANU "youth wingers" who engaged in antiopposition activity (Throup and Hornsby 1998).

The Provincial Administration also used its authority to give KANU officials special access to the public. Provincial administrators were the only state officials with the ability to call *barazas*, community meetings, to disseminate government information. Administrators infused these *barazas* with "politically loaded statements," reiterating the regime's development record or promising future resources while denigrating opposition parties as "anti-development."[37] In addition, administrators restricted which politicians they allowed to speak at *barazas*. During the autocratic era, it was customary for the KANU district chairman to attend relevant *barazas* within the district. Yet during the electoral era opposition parties and opposition party chairman were barred from speaking at *barazas* due to claims that their attendance would inject too much politics into governing affairs. KANU representatives were still allowed to attend, however. Officers were also expected to turn state-sponsored Moi Day and *Jamhuri* (Independence) Day events, which fell two months and two weeks before each election, respectively, into rallies for KANU.[38]

7.3 BUREAUCRATIC LOYALTY TOWARD MOI

Moi relied heavily on the Provincial Administration to carry out the tasks that were necessary to maintain support among his base and to prevent the opposition from winning. But officers had varying levels of loyalty to Moi – which corresponded to variation in their predisposition to comply with orders from the top. I investigate this loyalty relationship among three groups of bureaucrats: (1) high-ranking administrators of all ethnicities, as studied in Chapter 6, (2) lower-level Kalenjin administrators, and (3) lower-level Kikuyu administrators.

---

[36] "Will This Election Be Free and Fair?" *The Daily Nation*, November 16, 1997, p. 16.

[37] "A Curious Directive," *The Weekly Review*, January 12, 1996, pp. 14–15.

[38] "Occasion turned into KANU Campaign," *The Daily Nation*, October 21, 1992, p. 2. "Poll Officials Fail to Uphold Impartiality, Opposition Says," Gitau Warigi, *The East African*, December 23, 1997.

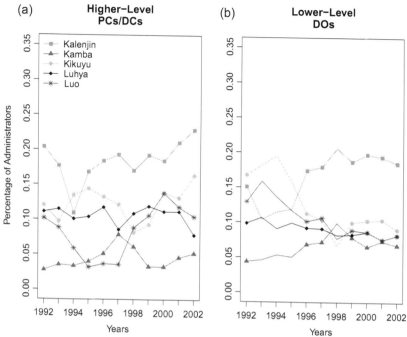

FIGURE 7.1 Percentage of administrators by ethnicity for the country's five largest ethnic groups during Moi's electoral regime. Figure 7.1a plots the ethnic breakdown by year for presidentially appointed PCs and DCs. Figure 7.1b plots the ethnic breakdown by year for lower-level DOs. I represent years with missing DO (1993–1995, 1998) by omitting points for those years.

7.3.1 High-Ranking Officers: Loyalty to Moi

As in the past, the top ranks of the Provincial Administration – PCs and DCs – were diverse during Moi's multiparty years. Moi recognized the political value of these positions for elite incorporation, and balanced the agency's ethnic diversity. He even reduced the number of Kalenjin DCs by nearly 5 percent in the run-up to the 1992 election in response to complaints about Kalenjin overrepresentation in these highly visible positions (Throup and Hornsby 1998). Figure 7.1a illustrates that Kalenjin officers made up less than 25 percent of all PCs and DCs in any given year during Moi's electoral years.

Patronage helped cement high-ranking provincial administrators' loyalty toward Moi. These bureaucrats had strong incentives to support his reelection campaigns because they were likely to lose their jobs under a new leader. Each president appoints his own PCs and DCs, precisely to create a neopatrimonial relationship with them. One of Moi's (non-Kalenjin) PCs who served during the 1990s, but was pushed out by Moi's successor in 2003, explained, "After NARC government came in, quite a number of us were [forced to retire]. It was political .... We were seen to be strong supporters of Moi, so that was another regime."[39]

Throup and Hornsby (1998) assessed the actions of PCs and DCs in the months leading up to the 1992 election and found that nearly all of them used their authority to help Moi or his party; only one of eight PCs and three of forty-six DCs were neutral.[40] They report that only one DC was thought to support the opposition (though this coding is questionable, as Moi later promoted the officer to serve as a PC).

7.3.2 Low-Ranking Kalenjin Officers: Loyalty to Moi

Unlike the more senior ranks of the Provincial Administration, officer loyalty toward Moi varied among lower-level DOs. As I described in Chapter 4, DOs were not prone to the same levels of predation as their superiors. And the pyramid structure of the bureaucracy meant that only a fraction of DOs would ever reach the ranks of DCs, let alone PCs.

Kalenjin DOs' incentives were most closely aligned with Moi's for two reasons. The first follows from the logic of elite incorporation. Lower-level Kalenjin bureaucrats believed their best chances for advancement to a coveted DC position (or another high position within the state) would come under a co-ethnic president, not necessarily because they had a neopatrimonial bond with Moi, but because the Kalenjin elites that DOs were clients of made up the plurality of Moi's cabinet and informal advisers. Elites advocated for their preferred clients and favored them for promotions or other top jobs in the state outside the Provincial Administration. For instance, one officer attributed his rise through the ranks to his strong performances during promotional interviews. He described his good rapport with elites in the Ministry of Provincial Administration during the interviews, many of whom were also Kalenjins who he had known from before he entered the agency.[41] The incorporation of Kalenjin elites

39 Interview with former PC, February 2, 2012, Nairobi.
40 Throup & Hornsby (1998).
41 Interview with former DO, March 2, 2012, Nairobi.

only grew after 1992 as Moi changed his strategy from incorporating powerful elite rivals to incorporating KANU stalwarts. Kalenjin MPs were more secure in their incorporation and were less likely to be rotated out of the cabinet because of the staunch alignment of Kalenjin voters. The security of Kalenjin elites meant that Kalenjin DOs could expect more benefits from their incorporated patrons than DOs whose incorporated elites were from another ethnic group.

The second reason is that the Provincial Administration had preferential practices toward Kalenjin DOs, which helped them forge a direct neopatrimonial relationship with Moi. To begin, the 1992 and 1997 elections were highly ethnicized and cemented loyalty to KANU as an integral component of Kalenjin identity (Ndegwa 1997). Many Kalenjins – not simply bureaucrats – feared the consequences of a Moi loss: "there was a fear that Kalenjin would be marginalized and persecuted in the event of KANU losing power … [T]hese fears were strengthened by a general and indiscriminate critique of … KANU as Kalenjin which inevitably pushed Kalenjin further into the KANU fold" (Lynch 2011a).

The perceived loyalty of Kalenjin DOs created a self-fulfilling cycle in which they were given special treatment precisely because of their perceived loyalty. One DO explained, "you would find many Kalenjins getting promoted at the cost of others. In most cases, Kalenjins were favored against others."[42] This favoritism was not wholly unwarranted, as Kalenjin DOs were expected to comply with orders. For instance, one administrator recalled how his Kalenjin DO colleagues had their salaries topped up under the table during the 1990s for completing political tasks.[43] Some Kalenjin officers were even promised the land of evicted migrants during the ethnic clashes (Klopp 2002). One officer discussed his rise throughout the 1990s due to his qualifications: he had been posted to "difficult" stations (i.e., those that needed to be coerced) and performed well.[44] Since Kalenjin officers could be trusted, they were more likely to be sent to these difficult stations where they could prove themselves. Even without connections to incorporated political elites who would lobby on their behalf, Kalenjin DOs could expect to benefit under a continued Moi presidency.

---

[42] Interview with former DO, October 13, 2011, Nairobi.
[43] Interview with former DO, June 29, 2017, Nairobi.
[44] Interview with former DO, January 17, 2012, Nyeri, Kenya.

7.3.3 Low-Ranking Kikuyu Officers: Disloyalty to Moi

The lower ranks of the Provincial Administration were diverse, as seen in Figure 7.1b.[45] Most troubling for the center were Kikuyu DOs, who were the second most numerous officers for much of the 1990s.

For the same reasons that Kalenjin DOs were considered loyal, Kikuyu DOs were considered the most disloyal. These bureaucrats had strong incentives to see Moi go and had the weakest incentives to use their authority on his behalf. Moi had kicked most Kikuyu elites out of the cabinet after the return to electoral competition; they held fewer than 6 percent of cabinet posts during his final decade in office. As a result, Kikuyu DOs could not expect to rise through elite connections. Consider the exception that proves the rule. One of Moi's most ardent elite supporters throughout the multiparty era was Joseph Kamotho, a Kikuyu who served in several Cabinet positions.[46] By 2001, there had been no Kikuyu DCs promoted in four years.[47] In response, Kamotho led a group of MPs to successfully petition Moi for the advancement of his favored (Kikuyu) DO to a DC.[48]

Further, and unlike DOs of other ethnicities who did not have a viable co-ethnic presidential candidate, Kikuyu bureaucrats could expect favoritism should Moi lose the election. One officer explained "how tribalism works" in the Provincial Administration: "I was restricted under Moi's time because I was a Kikuyu. I could not move up. But I was promoted when Kibaki came in."[49] Another Kikuyu DO put it succinctly: "I was always being overlooked for promotions, but there were many less qualified Kalenjins who advanced instead of me."[50] The administrator then described his fairly quick advancement within DO grades after 2003. Kikuyu DOs could expect to be promoted in part because they would have political elites around a Kikuyu president who would advocate on

---

45 The DO graph is missing data points in 1993–1995 and 1998 because the archival data that I used to create the DO dataset were missing returns from at least one province for these years. I average the number of administrators from a specific ethnic group across the remaining provinces to estimate the total number of administrators from that group, though I realize doing so introduces bias because administrators of different ethnicities were unevenly distributed across different provinces.

46 Kamotho lost his reelection bids but was one of Moi's twelve nominated MPs.

47 We see a slight increase in the percentage of Kikuyu DCs in 2000 in Figure 7.1 because a Kikuyu officer who was working in a ministry was redeployed as a DC.

48 Interview with then DC, July 3, 2017, Nairobi.

49 Interview with then DC, October 5, 2015, Nairobi.

50 Interview with former DO, December 1, 2011, Nairobi.

their behalf. And to the extent that a Kikuyu president would try to create a direct neopatrimonial relationship with co-ethnic DOs, as Moi did with Kalenjin DOs, Kikuyu DOs could expect career benefits regardless of their elite connections.

As expected, qualitative evidence suggests that numerous Kikuyu DOs failed to obey their politicized orders because they did not want Moi to win reelection. One Kikuyu DO recalled how he did not carry out orders such as rejecting the permits of opposition parties or harassing their supporters because, "when I implement a policy, I am supporting the government of the day and their political party – the policies that are being implemented always favor a political party. And I did not support that political party."[51] Another Kikuyu DO during these years recounted, "when you are a civil servant you are directly involved in politics. I was assisting the people ... When you are assisting Moi's enemy [the people] then he sees this as a threat to him."[52] Yet another Kikuyu officer who was a DO in the 1990s explained how he attempted to give local opposition organizers the opportunity to campaign to voters. He tried to be neutral in the run-up to each of Moi's reelections because it was "time to overcome our tyranny. How can [only] one party rule Kenya?"[53]

The following example of noncompliance was recorded in the national archives. KANU leaders in early 1992 complained to Nairobi about their Kikuyu DO when they tried to carry out a KANU recruitment drive:

we expected the Provincial Administration in particular to give us a helping hand, but to the contrary, the Provincial Administration in Isiolo didn't give us any assistance ... We carried some security personnel throughout our visits, but to our surprise some of these [police] officers were instructed to abandon us on the way by the DO, before we could even finish the exercise ... [we] didn't get any assistance from the District Officer but to the contrary the officer incited wananchi [the people] against KANU by telling them not to pay [registration fees].[54]

While this administrator's actions were not egregious – if anything, he seems to have demonstrated impartiality in the new multiparty environment – the type of behavior that the center demanded was what was needed to win the election. Archival records suggest that the officer was rotated to a desk job in Nairobi soon after this letter was received.

---

[51] Interview with former DO, November 9, 2011, Nairobi.
[52] Interview with former DC, June 29, 2017, Nairobi.
[53] Interview with former DO, July 3, 2017, Nairobi.
[54] Isiolo leaders to Permanent Secretary of Provincial Administration, February 24, 1992, BB/1/250, Kenya National Archives, Nairobi.

Non-Kalenjin and non-Kikuyu DOs varied in their loyalty to Moi and their subsequent willingness to carry out politicized orders. DOs outside these two groups did not have a viable co-ethnic in the race, but their chances of rising through the ranks still depended on the election. Officers had a sense of their co-ethnic elites' likely incorporation based on their elites' standing with candidates. Some lower-level officers thus believed that they might fare better under a new Kikuyu-led administration, while others perceived that they would be better positioned under a continued Moi presidency. But overall, the incentives of lower-level non-Kalenjin and non-Kikuyu DOs were not as strong.

7.4 QUALITATIVE EVIDENCE OF STRATEGIC MANAGEMENT

Before turning to the regression analyses, I present qualitative evidence to show that bureaucrats within the Provincial Administration were indeed strategically managed: those in charge of posting and shuffling them explicitly considered expected compliance stemming from loyalty and embeddedness when making these decisions. I highlight evidence that showcases the role of bureaucratic loyalty in management decisions, since Chapters 5 and 6 held loyalty fixed and focused solely on variation in embeddedness.

7.4.1 Strategic Management in and around Rift Valley

Interviews with administrators and former ministry elites revealed that careful attention was paid to postings to Rift Valley, both because of the center's attempt to co-opt Moi's aligned voters and because of the ethnic clashes in the area. The center appointed Kalenjin administrators to Rift Valley because they were thought to be the best able to co-opt Moi's aligned voters. One DO explained, "some politicians prefer to have certain people. If you had worked in Baringo – that is the district of the president – you cannot just come from nowhere and work in Baringo."[55] Kalenjin administrators in Kalenjin jurisdictions were expected to loyally comply with central directives *and* to have a strong connection to residents that would encourage them to go beyond their mandate to help residents. Further, bureaucratic embeddedness was a two-way street: not

---

55 Interview with former DO, November 10, 2011, Nairobi.

only would Kalenjin administrators feel a stronger bond with Kalenjin citizens, but the residents would feel more comfortable with a co-ethnic administrator. The Permanent Secretary of Provincial Administration in the early 1990s explained that he sent Kalenjin administrators to Kalenjin strongholds within Rift Valley because residents were unwilling to work with non-Kalenjin administrators – especially those affiliated with the opposition: "Some Kikuyu served in Rift Valley ... But there are certain areas where you would get complaints .... People protesting. Maybe they perceive him to be in another political party. Supporting another political party. Maybe undermining central government."[56]

The interviews conducted for this study also indicate that bureaucratic postings in and around the Rift were made after taking into account the ongoing ethnic clashes. One Kikuyu DO described his posting patterns in the early 1990s. He was initially stationed in Eastern Nyanza, on the border with Rift Valley, when the ethnic clashes were active. He was then suddenly transferred clear across the country after he carried out the formal duties of his position: maintaining law and order. In explaining this transfer, the officer said:

I learned [from my subsequent DC] that I was removed because I was trying to stop the ethnic clashes which were starting between Nyanza and Rift Valley. But they were planned, so when they saw that I was stopping the plan, I was transferred. I could not be stationed to a place where I could not perform loyally. I was an enemy at the beginning of multiparty elections. However good you are as a civil servant [the question is] "good towards what?" Policy was political.[57]

The Akiwumi Report details a similar incident in Nakuru District. When the clashes first broke out, the two DOs in the area – one Luo, one Kikuyu – "acted swiftly, and we think, decisively ... [they] mobilised the security men under their command, moved to the scene of the clashes and arrested over one hundred and forty suspects for various offences including murderer and arson. Their action stopped the clashes in the Kamwaura area within two to three days." But the officers were "transferred immediately thereafter." One officer was transferred "even before he completed his report on the clashes." The report concludes, "we have a feeling that whoever effected the transfers must have wanted

---

[56] Interview with former Permanent Secretary of Provincial Administration, February 24, 2012, Nairobi.
[57] Interview with former DO, November 9, 2011, Nairobi.

those officers out of the way so that realisation of the purpose of the clashes should no longer be obstructed or hindered" (Government of Kenya 2002, 55).

However, there was a marked difference in the purported logic of the postings of Kalenjin administrators during the clashes. One Kalenjin DO who worked in notably contentious areas throughout Nyanza and Rift Valley told me that his superiors deployed him with a mission to "supervise opposition activity" given his "low tolerance for non-KANU stations."[58] A colleague, another former Kalenjin DO from the 1990s, recalled how his superiors had praised his ability to follow orders during the 1990s when he was posted to a jurisdiction that experienced intense violence during his deployment. Unwilling to discuss the perpetuation of violence in the area, he simply discussed his role in resettling many Kalenjin residents after the violence abated.[59] Even the Akiwumi Report noted patterns of strategic postings. In Miteitei Farm in Nandi District, where the clashes first broke out, "Apart from [one officer], the other officers of the Provincial Administration below the District Commissioner were all Kalenjin."[60]

Figure 7.2 plots the assignments of Kalenjin administrators in 1992, alongside divisions affected by the violence.[61] The map zooms in on the provinces where the preelection violence was most intense: Nyanza, Rift Valley, and Western with Rift Valley outlined in bold. Figure 7.2a plots districts with a Kalenjin DC. Figure 7.2b plots divisions in which more than 50 percent of DOs were Kalenjin in 1992. Layered over each map, I hatch divisions that saw violence in 1992 using data from Boone (2011). Figure 7.2a shows that the farming districts that were perceived to be historic Kalenjin land had Kalenjin DCs. Similarly, many divisions in these districts had Kalenjin DOs (Figure 7.2b). The posting patterns of Kalenjin

---

[58] Interview with former DO, November 23, 2011, Nairobi.
[59] Interview with former DO, January 17, 2012, Nyeri.
[60] Government of Kenya (2002, 14).
[61] The outbreak of highly-visible political violence suggests that there are instances in which monitoring bureaucrats is possible, even in states perceived as weak. In these rare instances, the center can use bureaucratic behavior to evaluate *actual* loyalty (Hassan and O'Mealia 2018). Promotions in these cases, then, are not only affected by elite incorporation, but by a bureaucrat's actions. Unfortunately, the data on bureaucrats' promotions in the 1990s is not detailed enough to evaluate the relationship between the occurrence of political violence in a jurisdiction and the promotion of DOs. Chapter 8, however, shows that bureaucrats whose jurisdictions saw violence that benefited the incumbent after the 2007 election, regardless of ethnicity, were more likely to be promoted.

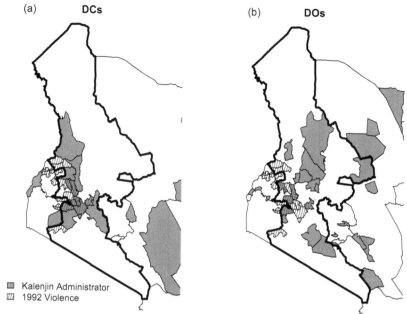

FIGURE 7.2 Posting of Kalenjin DCs and DOs in 1992. Figure 7.2a graphs districts with Kalenjin DCs in 1992. Figure 7.2b depicts divisions in which the majority of DOs in 1992 were Kalenjin. Overlaid on both maps are divisions affected by violence in the run-up to the 1992 election.

DCs and DOs show some overlap with the preelection violence, a relationship I explore quantitatively in Section 7.5.

7.4.2 Strategic Management to Win Reelection

Though the Provincial Administration as a whole was crucial to helping Moi win his reelection campaigns, not all officers could be expected to comply with orders to coerce the opposition and its supporters. The qualitative evidence suggests that a bureaucrat's perceived loyalty and expected compliance informed decisions about how she was posted and shuffled. These management decisions were made in an effort to ensure compliance where it mattered most for Moi's reelection campaign.

Elites within the Ministry of Provincial Administration strategically posted Kikuyu DOs where they could do the least damage if they shirked from orders to coerce. The country's Permanent Secretary of Provincial Administration during these years discussed the idea of "preventative deployments." He gave a measured answer when asked to discuss his management of officers: 'You need to rotate so that you don't have administrators who have the opportunity to sell their political ideology."[62] One Kikuyu DO during these years was more open:

What was the vision, what was the policy of the regime? To survive! The issue for OP [the Office of the President] was who will help them survive, versus who is the enemy. If they sent somebody like me [a Kikuyu] to where I come from, that is where the opposition was. These places were not a danger to the regime – I could only be posted to divisions where it was safe because, there, what could I do?[63]

Ministry elites, according to this officer, kept him away from electorally valuable areas. Instead, they sent him to Central Province, where Moi did not expect to win many votes. Though the officer would be embedded, given co-ethnicity with locals in his new post, this was where his disloyalty could do the least damage to Moi's reelection campaign.

Whereas Kikuyu DOs were liable to shirk because they were disloyal to Moi, there was a risk that high-ranking PCs and DCs – whose loyalty was cemented through patronage – might do so if they were too locally embedded in their jurisdiction. The strong social bonds that embedded officers had or developed over time with local residents might make them unwilling to carry out orders to coerce. The country's sole Kikuyu PC by the 1997 election described how it would have been difficult to be posted among his co-ethnics, "You have your orders, but how can you arrest your brother?"[64] Since he would be most liable to shirk in Kikuyu-majority places, as opposed to the Kikuyu DO who was liable to shirk anywhere, the center posted him to Nyanza Province throughout much of this period. That province had a Kikuyu population of 0.2 percent: very few of his "brothers" lived there. During his post, the *The Weekly Review* described him as:

clearly the most powerful and politically active PC in the country, [he] always has his way with the president on major issues and controversies, especially when he is pitted against politicians from the province ... He goes about his business and conducts affairs of his office knowing that as long as he has the confidence of his superiors, it does not matter what public opinion was saying."[65]

Several other PCs and DCs from unaligned and misaligned ethnic groups during this period discussed their reticence to govern their own co-ethnics

---

[62] Interview with former Permanent Secretary of Provincial Administration, February 24, 2012, Nairobi.
[63] Interview with former DO, November 9, 2011, Nairobi.
[64] Interview with former PC, July 3, 2017, Nairobi.
[65] "Commissar," *The Weekly Review*, May 9, 1997, p. 5.

because of what they were expected to do on Moi's behalf. One Luhya DC during these years explained the difficulty of working in a district with a substantial Luhya population. Though he claimed that he would have a better grip on the dynamics in the district, he would not have been able to do his job. He would have been expected to police his "brothers" and castigate them if they started "making noise." The problem with reprimanding your own co-ethnics, he continued, is that people in the community hear about your actions and judge you on a personal level.[66]

7.5 QUANTITATIVE ANALYSIS: BUREAUCRATIC MANAGEMENT UNDER MOI'S ELECTORAL REGIME

I now quantitatively assess the posting and shuffling of administrators during Moi's electoral regime. I begin by reviewing the alignment of different parts of the country. Next, I examine management with regards to the center's attempt to co-opt aligned areas. I then evaluate management in unaligned areas. As in the last two chapters, I examine posting and shuffling patterns of high-ranking PCs and DCs who were considered loyal to Moi through patronage. This chapter also examines the posting patterns of lower-level DOs whose loyalty varied, and largely mapped onto co-ethnicity with Moi or rival opposition elites. The data on DOs is not precise enough to analyze their shuffling patterns.

7.5.1 Recap: Area Alignment under Moi's Electoral Regime

I recap the country's alignment in the run-up to Moi's 1992 and 1997 elections in Table 7.1. Kalenjin-majority areas were considered aligned for the entirety of Moi's electoral regime. Moi was term limited and could not run again after 1997. I therefore define misalignment and unalignment as lasting from the lead-up to the 1992 election until the lead-up to the 1997 election. Moi of course continued to face discontent after the 1997 election, but by then he had overcome the last serious popular threat to his personal rule. The table also gives descriptive statistics on the posting of officers. The first number is the percentage of co-ethnic high-ranking officials in areas with different alignments: aligned (unaligned) areas had the highest (lowest) levels of co-ethnic PCs and DCs. The second number

---

[66] Interview with former DC, January 19, 2012, Nairobi.

TABLE 7.1 *Group and Area Alignment toward Moi during Electoral Regime (1992–2002)*

Alignment	Group	Location	Time Period	Percentage of Co-ethnic Administrators	Average Tenure (Years)
Aligned	Kalenjin	Parts of Rift Valley Province	1992–2002	25 / 26	4.9
Misaligned	Kikuyu	Central Province Parts of Coast, Nairobi, Rift Valley Provinces	1992–1997	14 / 18	3.7
Unaligned	Other ethnic groups	Various	1992–1997	5 / 5	3.5

gives the percentage of co-ethnic lower-level DOs: aligned areas also had the highest level of co-ethnic DOs. Unfortunately, the dataset on DOs is not refined enough to measure DO tenure.

7.5.2 Quantitative Analysis: Bureaucratic Management among the Aligned Kalenjin

Applying the theory in Chapter 2 to Moi's electoral years suggests that Kalenjin-majority areas should have been disproportionately governed by co-ethnic Kalenjin administrators for two reasons. First, Kalenjin administrators could more easily develop social connections with Kalenjin communities and would feel the strongest social pressure to help local Kalenjin residents with land allocations, and at the extreme, perpetuate violence against local out-groups. Second, and specifically among lower-level DOs where loyalty was variable, Kalenjin administrators were more likely to comply with politicized directives than DOs of other ethnicities. And since Kikuyu DOs were seen as the most disloyal, we should expect that they were disproportionately kept away from Kalenjin communities. With regard to shuffling, we should expect longer tenures for all administrators in Kalenjin-majority jurisdictions. Bureaucrats with longer tenures can become socially embedded, which makes them more willing and better able to use their authority on behalf of Kalenjin residents.

I begin by analyzing high-ranking PCs and DCs employing similar datasets as those used in Chapters 5 and 6. I run two analyses on the posting of these high-ranking administrators that correspond with Columns 1 and 2 of Table 7.2. The dependent variable in each is whether an administrator was a co-ethnic of the majority of the population in the unit for a particular half-year.[67] The key main independent variable in Column 1 is whether the unit was majority Kalenjin. The independent variable in

---

[67] President Moi created thirty new districts between 1992 and 2002, which complicates the creation of the dataset and the construction of control variables. New "split" districts were often drawn around ethnic groups that were a local minority in the original "parent" district (Kasara 2006; Hassan 2016). For example, consider the two ethnic minority groups of Western Province discussed in Chapter 6. Mount Elgon district was created for the Sabaot in 1993, and Teso district was created for the Teso in 1995. Many of the variables included in the regressions are therefore not uniform across a parent and split district (Grossman and Lewis 2014). To address this issue, I determine the boundaries and creation date of each new district. I then recreate all control variables after each new district was created. The analyses for PCs and DCs are therefore based on a time-series dataset at the half-year, unit level with new districts added in the time period after which they were created.

TABLE 7.2 *Management of Administrators in and around Rift Valley during Moi's Electoral Regime*

	PCs/DCs				DOs			
	1 Logit Co-ethnic	2 Logit Co-ethnic	3 Cox Shuffle	4 Cox Shuffle	5 OLS Co-ethnic	6 OLS Kalenjin	7 OLS Kikuyu	8 OLS Kalenjin
Kalenjin Majority	2.12*** (0.56)				0.19*** (0.03)			
Rift Valley Province		1.42* (0.60)	-0.27 (0.17)	-0.25† (0.14)		0.11*** (0.02)	-0.08*** (0.02)	0.09† (0.05)
Kikuyu or Luhya Majority		0.67 (0.66)		-0.27† (0.15)				
Rift Valley Province * Kikuyu or Luhya Majority		-2.89* (1.26)		0.74* (0.29)				
Pre-1992 Election Violence								0.35** (0.11)
1989 Population, logged	0.64* (0.32)	0.29 (0.24)	-0.01 (0.06)	0.04 (0.07)	0.03 (0.03)	0.02 (0.02)	-0.02 (0.03)	-0.14 (0.13)
Area, sq. km., logged	-0.09 (0.14)	-0.22 (0.16)	0.03 (0.04)	0.03 (0.04)	-0.04* (0.02)	0.00 (0.01)	0.02 (0.02)	0.13** (0.04)
1989 ELF	1.15 (1.05)	1.89* (0.95)	-0.09 (0.22)	-0.25 (0.23)	0.03 (0.03)	0.04 (0.03)	0.00 (0.03)	0.21 (0.14)
Minister	-1.12† (0.60)	-0.68 (0.51)	-0.16 (0.12)	-0.20 (0.13)	-0.07** (0.02)	0.08* (0.04)	0.00 (0.04)	0.25*** (0.07)
Experience	-0.06 (0.04)	-0.07* (0.04)	0.01 (0.01)	0.01 (0.01)				
Woman	0.31 (1.11)	0.24 (1.03)	-0.42 (0.37)	-0.43 (0.37)				
Intercept	-6.93* (2.75)	-2.88 (2.07)			0.01 (0.21)	0.03 (0.14)	0.17 (0.14)	0.30 (0.71)
Num. obs.	1,484	1,484	1,484	1,484	251	251	251	84

*** $p < 0.001$, ** $p < 0.01$, * $p < 0.05$, † $p < 0.1$. Regressions of the management of provincial administrators from 1992–2002 in and around Rift Valley Province. The outcome in Columns 1 and 2 is a binary indicatory for whether a jurisdiction was assigned a co-ethnic administrator. Columns 3 and 4 examine shuffling rates. The outcome in Columns 5–8 is the percentage of observations from 1992–2002 that a unit had a co-ethnic (Column 5), Kalenjin (Column 6, 8), or Kikuyu (Column 7) administrator. Columns 1 and 2 report results from logit regressions with errors clustered at the district level, Columns 3 and 4 report results from Cox-Proportional Hazards models, and Columns 5–8 report results from OLS regressions with errors clustered at the district level (ELF = ethnolinguistic fractionalization).

202

Column 2 is an interaction term between whether a district was in Rift Valley and whether the district's ethnic majority was considered a migrant group. Columns 3 and 4 examine the shuffling patterns of PCs and DCs. The independent variable in Column 3 is an indicator variable for whether the unit was majority Kalenjin. The independent variable in Column 4 is the same interaction term as in Column 2.

The second half of Table 7.2 examines the posting patterns of lower-level DOs. These regressions rely on the datasets of DO postings described in Chapter 4. The dependent variable in Columns 5–7 is the percentage of DOs from 1992–2002 who were co-ethnics of the division majority (Column 5), Kalenjins (Column 6), or Kikuyus (Column 7).[68] The main explanatory variables are an indicator for a Kalenjin-majority division in Column 5 and an indicator for divisions in Rift Valley Province in Columns 6 and 7.

Column 8 examines DO postings with regard to the ethnic clashes in Rift Valley. The ethnic clashes began in the run-up to the 1992 election but continued far into the 1990s. It becomes difficult to disentangle whether different types of bureaucrats were sent to clash sites *in response to* the violence or *to perpetuate* the violence after it began. I try to bypass this endogeneity issue by looking only at DO postings in Rift Valley in the run-up to the 1992 election, when and where the clashes initially broke out. Many parts of Rift Valley had the preconditions for violence, yet violence only broke out in some locations. Column 8 therefore evaluates if similar divisions were more likely to experience violence if they were governed by a Kalenjin DO. The dependent variable in Column 8 is the percentage of DOs that were Kalenjin in 1992 and the independent

---

[68] Hundreds of lower-level divisions were also created in the 1990s. I cannot trace the boundaries and creation date of each new division to recreate the control variables as I did for new districts (see Footnote 67), because systematic information on division creation was not kept and cannot be inferred from other available records. I therefore determine which 1989 division each DO was stationed in as new divisions were created. I then calculate the average ethnic make-up of DOs for that division for each half-year. The unit of analysis for the DO dataset is therefore the division level, as seen in the 1989 census for every half-year. This method of dealing with the creation of new divisions is practical, but some may be concerned about pooling parent and split divisions together, in part for the reasons described previously regarding district creation. However, I am less concerned about pooling parent and split divisions together given the logic for creating divisions in the 1990s. For the most part, new lower-level units were not created around local ethnic minorities or because amenities were lacking in one part of the unit. Unlike new split districts, most new split lower-level units (i.e., divisions) had similar ethnic breakdowns and amenities as their parent unit.

variable indicates whether a division experienced violence in the run-up to the 1992 election.[69] I include the same controls as in Chapter 6. I also add controls for gender and experience, measured as the number of years since the bureaucrat entered the Provincial Administration, for the analyses on high-ranking bureaucrats.[70]

The results in Table 7.2 provide strong support for the theory – that administrators were strategically managed to ensure compliance with politicized orders in Rift Valley. Kalenjin-majority jurisdictions were more likely to be governed by a co-ethnic. Column 1 indicates that Kalenjin-majority administrative units were 25 percentage points more likely to be assigned a co-ethnic PC or DC (95% CI: 0.11, 0.39), and Column 5 indicates that, between 1992 and 1997, Kalenjin-majority divisions could expect a Kalenjin DO for a year longer than other divisions ($p < 0.001$). Postings across Rift Valley are different from the rest of the country. Columns 6 and 7 show that a division in Rift Valley could expect about seven more months of a Kalenjin administrator and five fewer months of a Kikuyu DO from 1992–1997 (both, $p < 0.001$). Further, the center strategically managed postings within the Rift to increase embeddedness among Moi's aligned base and reduce embeddedness elsewhere. Column 2 finds that Kikuyu- or Luhya-majority districts in Rift Valley were 15 percentage points less likely to be assigned a co-ethnic DC than other Rift Valley districts (95% CI: 0.29,−0.01).

Column 8 also provides evidence that the outbreak of violence in Rift Valley Province in the run-up to the 1992 election was correlated with postings of Kalenjin DOs. Divisions that experienced violence were 35 percentage points more likely to have been governed by a Kalenjin DO earlier that year ($p < 0.01$). The data on posting patterns and violence are not precise enough to conduct a more detailed analysis in the preelection period. And the endogeneity concerns discussed above dissuade me from analyzing violence in later years. But the results are in line with accounts of the role Kalenjin administrators played in perpetuating the violence (e.g., the Akiwumi Report).

---

[69] Data on which divisions experienced ethnic violence is from Boone (2011). I also cross-checked the data against the Akiwumi Report and data on violence listed in Kimenyi and Ndung'u (2005).

[70] Including these two personal characteristics requires me to use logit regressions on time-series data instead of ordinary least squares (OLS) regressions on collapsed data, as I did in Chapters 5 and 6. The results are robust to rerunning Columns 1 and 2 as OLS regressions in which observations for each district are averaged from 1992–2002 and after the person-specific controls are dropped.

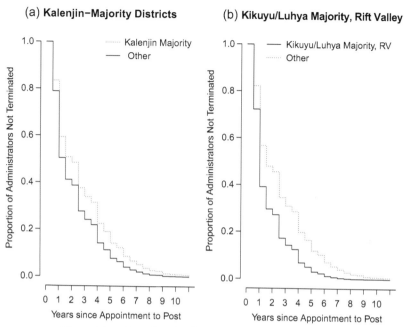

FIGURE 7.3 Hazard functions for shuffling patterns in Rift Valley during Moi's electoral regime. The figures graph the hazard function associated with Columns 3 and 4 of Table 7.2, respectively.

Figure 7.3 plots the hazard graphs associated with Columns 3 and 4. DCs stationed in Kalenjin-majority districts could expect longer tenures ($p = 0.1$): Whereas 60 percent of DCs in Kalenjin-majority districts could expect to remain in a post for more than one year, only 50 percent of DCs elsewhere could expect to do so. Approximately 35 percent of DCs in Kalenjin-majority districts could expect a tenure of at least three years, compared with about 25 percent for other districts. Figure 7.3b shows that DCs in Kikuyu- or Luhya-majority districts in Rift Valley could expect shorter tenures than DCs elsewhere. Whereas DCs posted to migrant-majority districts in Rift Valley had a 40 percent chance of staying on another year, those sent elsewhere had a nearly a 70 percent of staying an additional year.

In other analyses, I consider the management of administrators after redefining an area's alignment toward Moi. I rerun the analyses from Table 7.2 after substituting out the indicator variable for a Kalenjin-majority jurisdiction with an indictor variable for a jurisdiction whose majority ethnic group was one of the ethnic groups considered indigenous to Rift Valley (KAMATUSA). The results for postings of PCs and DCs indicate that KAMATUSA-majority districts were 16.6 percentage points more likely to be governed by a co-ethnic than non-KAMATUSA districts (95% CI: 0.06, 0.28). KAMATUSA-majority divisions could expect a co-ethnic DO for about eleven more months than other divisions from 1992–1997 ($p < 0.001$). In other specifications, I consider postings to districts with substantial Kalenjin minority communities. I find that divisions with at least a 20 percent Kalenjin population could expect more than an additional thirteen months of a Kalenjin DO than other divisions from 1992–1997 ($p < 0.001$).

7.5.3 Quantitative Analysis: Bureaucratic Management and Winning Reelection

I now analyze the management of administrators in the run-up to Moi's 1992 and 1997 reelection campaigns. I begin by evaluating whether areas of different alignments were sent bureaucrats with different loyalties. Given that Moi's Kalenjin co-ethnics were not numerous enough to create a winning electoral coalition, he sought to win votes in unaligned areas. Misaligned areas had the most to gain from his electoral loss and therefore would be too costly to win over. We should therefore expect to find that loyal bureaucrats were sent to (and disloyal bureaucrats were kept away from) unaligned jurisdictions. I evaluate these claims by examining postings of DOs. Whereas high-ranking PCs and DCs were considered loyal, there was variation in loyalty among DOs. I define an unaligned jurisdiction as one in which the majority ethnic group was not Kalenjin or Kikuyu. The regressions are reported in Table 7.3. The dependent variables are the percentage of DOs in a division from 1992–1997 that were Kalenjin or Kikuyu, respectively. The regressions include similar controls as in Table 7.2.

Table 7.3 indicates that the center sent loyal bureaucrats to electorally valuable areas. Unaligned jurisdictions could expect 6 percentage points more Kalenjin DOs and 8 percentage points fewer Kikuyu DOs. Substantively, the results indicate that unaligned jurisdictions were likely to have a Kalenjin administrator for five more months than other jurisdictions, and were likely to have a Kikuyu administrator for six less months. These numbers are especially large, given that Kalenjins comprised only 17 percent of DOs during these years and Kikuyus represented 13 percent of DOs.

I run other alternative specifications to validate these results. First, I rerun the models after removing observations in Rift Valley, given

TABLE 7.3 *Management of Administrators, Moi's Reelection Campaigns*

	1 OLS Kalenjin	2 OLS Kikuyu
Unaligned Jurisdiction	0.06*	−0.08**
	(0.03)	(0.03)
Rift Valley Province	0.18***	−0.15***
	(0.03)	(0.03)
1989 Population, logged	−0.04	−0.02
	(0.03)	(0.03)
Area, sq. km., logged	−0.02	0.02
	(0.02)	(0.02)
ELF	0.03	−0.02
	(0.04)	(0.04)
Minister	0.04	0.05
	(0.05)	(0.06)
Intercept	0.29	0.29†
	(0.19)	(0.15)
Num. obs.	251	251

*** $p < 0.001$, ** $p < 0.01$, * $p < 0.05$, † $p < 0.1$. Regressions of the management of provincial administrators from 1992–1997 to unaligned jurisdictions. The outcome is the percentage of observations that a unit had a Kalenjin (Column 1) or Kikuyu (Column 2) administrator. The table reports the results from OLS regressions with errors clustered at the district level.

the findings in Table 7.2. The results from this specification are even starker than what was presented in Table 7.3; unaligned jurisdictions could expect 7 percentage points more Kalenjin DOs ($p < 0.05$) and 12 percentage points fewer Kikuyu DOs ($p < 0.001$). Second, I rerun the models after reclassifying Luo-majority divisions as misaligned given that each election included a strong, though not necessarily viable, Luo candidate: to the extent that Moi believed he could not win votes in Luo areas, we should expect similar results as in Table 7.3. Indeed, the results for Kikuyu DOs are substantively similar. The results for Kalenjin DOs, however, lose their significance. This suggests that the center posted Kalenjin DOs to Luo areas in hopes of winning votes. Third, I rerun the analyses after redefining unaligned areas based on Kenya's electoral rules. During these years, a successful presidential candidate had to win the plurality of the vote and at least 25 percent of the votes in five of eight provinces. I define unaligned provinces as those in which Moi *could* meet the 25-percent threshold but was not assured of it and find substantively similar results.[71] Fourth, I also consider the posting patterns of DOs of other ethnicities. I run regressions parallel to those in Column 7 for Kamba, Luhya, and Luo DOs – the other three ethnic groups in Figure 7.1 – and I find no statistically significant patterns.

The results in Table 7.3 indicate that the center posted loyal bureaucrats to unaligned areas. This makes sense: given the importance of unaligned areas to winning the election, the center wanted those areas governed by loyal bureaucrats who were willing to comply with orders that helped Moi. But it is still unclear whether the regime attempted to win votes in unaligned areas through co-optation or coercion. The theory in Chapter 2, and the qualitative evidence throughout this chapter, suggests that bureaucrats are liable to coerce unaligned voters, partly because Provincial Administration bureaucrats have a comparative advantage in coercion. We should therefore expect unaligned areas to be governed by loyal, unembedded bureaucrats who have fewer social connections with locals that may inhibit them from using their authority to coerce.

I examine these claims in Table 7.4. The dependent variable in Column 1 is whether a DO was a co-ethnic with the majority in the division. Columns 2 and 3 give an additional test of coercion and loyalty by including two more variables in the analyses of DO postings from 1993–1997. I include an interaction term between a division's lagged vote share for Moi from the 1992 election with an indicator variable for whether the division was considered unaligned. Support for Moi differed drastically within unaligned areas – in some unaligned jurisdictions, over 80 percent voted for Moi, while in others less than 20 percent did so. Thus, we should expect coercion to be more effective in unaligned areas with low levels of expected support for Moi. In these areas, coercion from DOs would be the most useful for two reasons. First, and mechanically, the same level of effort to limit opposition campaigns would have a greater impact in an opposition-leaning area than in an area where support for Moi was close to its natural maximum. Second, if DOs were rotated frequently (i.e., unembedded) to ensure their willingness to coerce, then they were unlikely to have deep relationships with area residents. Unembedded DOs were therefore likely to apply coercion widely and indiscriminately, because

---

[71] See Hassan (2017).

TABLE 7.4 *Management of DOs, Optimizing Coercion during Reelection Campaigns*

	1 OLS Co-ethnic	2 Logit Kalenjin	3 Logit Kikuyu	4 Logit Kalenjin	5 Logit Kikuyu
Unaligned Division	-0.19^{***}	1.28^{***}	-0.79^{**}	1.49^{***}	-0.83^{***}
	(0.03)	(0.32)	(0.25)	(0.45)	(0.25)
Lagged Vote Share		1.34^{**}	-0.39	3.07^{***}	-0.65
		(0.44)	(0.40)	(0.53)	(0.46)
Rift Valley Province		0.59^{*}	-1.32^{***}		
		(0.29)	(0.28)		
*Unaligned Division * Lagged Vote Share*		-2.02^{**}	0.58	-3.97^{***}	0.88
		(0.66)	(0.49)	(0.71)	(0.57)
1997		0.06	-0.32^{**}	0.05	-0.37^{**}
		(0.13)	(0.12)	(0.18)	(0.12)
1989 Population, logged	0.02	-0.25	0.29	-0.52^{**}	$0.45^{\dagger}$
	(0.04)	(0.20)	(0.24)	(0.16)	(0.25)
Area, sq. km., logged	-0.03	$-0.28^{\dagger}$	0.18	-0.36^{**}	$0.23^{\dagger}$
	(0.02)	(0.15)	(0.14)	(0.13)	(0.13)
ELF	0.02	-0.07	-0.06	-0.49	0.02
	(0.04)	(0.30)	(0.26)	(0.33)	(0.27)
Minister	0.00	0.37	0.12	$0.59^{\dagger}$	-0.04
	(0.03)	(0.29)	(0.41)	(0.33)	(0.46)
Intercept	0.20	-0.47	-2.89^{*}	0.94	-3.80^{**}
	(0.20)	(1.11)	(1.40)	(0.93)	(1.47)
Num. obs.	251	$3,558$	$3,558$	$2,878$	$2,878$

$^{***}p < 0.001$, $^{**}p < 0.01$, $^{*}p < 0.05$, $^{\dagger}p < 0.1$. Regressions of the management of provincial administrators from 1993–1997 to unaligned jurisdictions with varying levels of electoral support for President Moi in the 1992 election. The outcome is the percentage of observations that a unit had a co-ethnic DO (Column 1), Kalenjin DO (Columns 2 and 4), or Kikuyu DO (Columns 3 and 5). Column 1 reports the results of an OLS regression; the other columns report results from logit regressions. Standard errors across the models are clustered at the district level.

they could not distinguish Moi's supporters from supporters of the opposition. Indiscriminate coercion is thus most useful in unaligned areas with low levels of support for Moi: Not only will a DO's victims more likely be opposition supporters, but there is a lower chance that the officer will mistakenly coerce a supporter of the incumbent.[72] Second, I include an indicator variable for whether a posting occurred in 1997. Though coercion would be useful in the long run-up to the 1997 election to reduce latent support for the opposition, it would prove most effective in the immediate run-up to the election. Columns 4 and 5 replicate Columns 2 and 3 after excluding divisions in Rift Valley, precisely because of the strong results found in Table 7.3.

The results in Table 7.4 provide evidence to support my theory. Column 1 indicates that jurisdictions with a majority ethnic group coded as unaligned with President Moi were 19.6 percentage points less likely to be assigned a co-ethnic administrator. I simulate predicted probabilities from Columns 2 and 3 in Table 7.4 to interpret the results in Figure 7.4. We see that whereas Kalenjin DOs were substantially more likely than DOs of other ethnicities to be sent to unaligned jurisdictions with a low vote share for Moi in 1992 (and thus a low expected vote share for Moi in 1997), Kikuyu DOs were substantially less likely to be sent to these areas. However, Kalenjin and Kikuyu DOs were posted to unaligned divisions with high past support for Moi at similar rates. This finding is in line with the assertion that DOs were more effective at coercing unaligned jurisdictions. Table 7.4 also finds that Kikuyu DOs were less likely to be posted to the field in 1997 than in 1993–1996. This suggests that not only were Kikuyu DOs strategically posted around the country, but their assignment to the field versus within a ministry in Nairobi was done with an eye towards ensuring necessary compliance when it mattered most.

I perform two additional robustness tests. First, I reconsider the analyses using different definitions of alignment, as I did with the results in Table 7.3. I again rerun the regressions in Table 7.4 with a more expansive definition of area alignment. The results are substantively similar if we redefine KAMATUSA-majority jurisdictions as aligned (instead of unaligned). I also rerun the analyses after redefining Luo areas as misaligned. The results are substantively similar. The results are also similar if I substitute an indicator variable for divisions in unaligned provinces into the interaction term from Columns 2–5. Second, I evaluate whether there is evidence that postings of a DC and DOs in that division were coordinated. I find that DCs and DOs were more likely to be co-ethnics of each other in Kalenjin-majority districts, since Kalenjin DCs and Kalenjin DOs were more likely to be sent to those jurisdictions.

---

[72] For other implications of indiscriminate violence, see Zhukov and Talibova (2018) and Rozenas and Zhukov (2019).

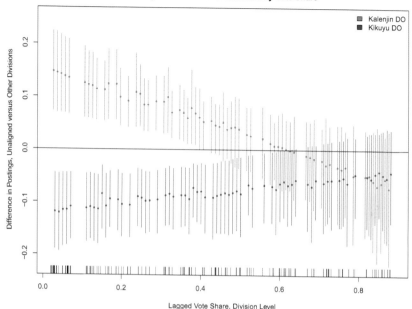

FIGURE 7.4 Simulated probabilities of postings of Kalenjin and Kikuyu DOs to divisions of different vote shares for Moi from the 1992 election. Simulated from Column 2 (light gray) and Column 3 (dark gray) of Table 7.4.

7.6 SUMMARY

This chapter examined the Provincial Administration under President Moi's electoral regime. Moi's greatest popular threat during these years was a loss at the polls. But he avoided this fate, in part, by having Provincial Administration bureaucrats misuse their authority to help co-opt groups he needed support from and coerce those most likely to challenge him. Compliance from these officers was not guaranteed, however, since the central government could not fully monitor their behavior; nor could the center align the incentives of all officers with Moi through patronage or packing. Further, even presumably loyal officers were liable to shirk orders to coerce the population if they had strong bonds with local residents in the jurisdiction in which they served. Yet the center was able to ensure the behavior that it needed from bureaucrats in the aggregate by strategically managing their placements to maximize compliance where it mattered most.

8

Kibaki and the Provincial Administration

This chapter assesses the Provincial Administration under Kenya's third president, Mwai Kibaki. The agency had proven itself capable of helping the country's previous two presidents overcome popular threats, across both autocratic and electoral regimes. Yet two factors made it difficult for Kibaki to use this bureaucracy in a similar way as his predecessors. First, Kibaki initiated numerous formal reforms to depoliticize the Provincial Administration. As a victim of the agency's misuse of authority for over a decade, he campaigned on a platform to rein in its role as the arm of the president at the grassroots level.[1] When Kibaki took office, he implemented reforms to revamp what those officers would be allowed to do. Second, given Moi's efforts to post and shuffle bureaucrats to maximize his hold on power, when Kibaki took office the Provincial Administration was still informally optimized to support Moi. Kibaki viewed different parts of the country as strategic for reelection, and would need to change where administrators would co-opt and coerce.

Despite these constraints, this chapter finds that Kibaki was still able to rely on the Provincial Administration to help him win reelection. He used the agency to co-opt aligned, co-ethnic areas and coerce areas inhabited by unaligned and misaligned groups. And since his government could not guarantee compliance from all officers, it maximized bureaucrats' compliance in electorally important areas by sending the limited pool of loyal officers to those places. In this way, the management patterns of

---

[1] 2002 NARC Party Manifesto.

bureaucrats under Kibaki are in line with the predictions from Chapter 2 and parallel to those under Moi's electoral regime after we account for differences in area alignment and bureaucratic loyalty towards each leader.

As in Chapter 7, I examine all of the Provincial Administration's trained field bureaucrats. This includes Kibaki's high-ranking Provincial Commissioners (PCs) and District Commissioners (DCs), who were all thought to be loyal to him through neopatrimonial bonds of money. I also evaluate the management of lower-level District Officers (DOs), whose loyalty was thought to be dependent on co-ethnicity between the officer and political elites who could influence promotion decisions. I provide evidence that Kibaki's co-ethnic, aligned areas were managed in a way that increased co-optation in the run-up to his 2007 reelection. And as in Chapter 7, I find that the center posted bureaucrats to increase compliance with orders to coerce strategically valuable unaligned areas. Further, the most disloyal officers during these years – low-ranking Luo DOs who were co-ethnics of the main 2007 opposition candidate, Raila Odinga – were posted to areas where their potential noncompliance would have little impact on the election outcome.

The results of this chapter echo the findings of Chapters 5, 6, and 7. A leader can solve the principal-agent problem inherent in relying on bureaucrats to carry out the dirty work that prevents popular threats by taking into account their perceived loyalties, and thus perceived willingness to comply. Subsequent Kenyan presidents have considered bureaucrats with whom they have a neopatrimonial relationship – either through patronage or co-ethnicity – to have aligned incentives. Even absent monitoring, these bureaucrats are expected to comply because they benefit from the leader staying in office.

The second half of the chapter shifts gears to evaluate promotion decisions, including cases in which the center can observe compliance. The usual actions that the Provincial Administration is expected to perform are difficult to observe and measure, making it difficult to reward (punish) those who (do not) follow orders. This difficulty in monitoring is what creates a principal-agent problem in the first place. But Kenya experienced a wave of postelection violence in 2007–2008 that some provincial administrators allegedly helped inflame. Actions taken by administrators during this bout of large-scale violence represented a rare moment in which officers' politicized actions were highly visible. I leverage the location of violence to examine future promotions in the Provincial Administration. I find evidence that bureaucrats whose jurisdictions saw violence in support of Kibaki, regardless of ethnicity, were more likely to be promoted in the years after the violence.

Taken together, this chapter's analysis of the hiring, posting, shuffling, and promotion of bureaucrats presents a fuller picture of the politicization of the civil service, even in an electoral regime with regular turnover at the top. While some research has argued that electoral competition can reign in neopatrimonial hiring (Geddes 1994; Besley 2006) or the growth of public sector employment (O'Dwyer 2006; Grzymała-Busse 2007), my findings lend support to the idea that electoral competition has different, but still politicized, effects on the public sector (van de Walle 2001; Sigman 2017; Brierley Forthcoming; Pierskalla and Sacks 2016). The fact that I show this result under President Kibaki, whose reign is considered the most open of Kenya's first three leaders, demonstrates the ability of informal norms to undermine formal laws and helps explain how unconsolidated electoral regimes can continue despite robust electoral competition.

In addition, the analysis of promotions after political violence contributes to our understanding of how a principal can reward and sanction agents to perpetuate neopatrimonialism in the state (Policzer 2009; Hassan and O'Mealia 2018). In countries with histories of political violence, some of the bureaucrats who populate higher levels of a bureaucracy likely earned their position after proving their willingness to carry out violence on behalf of the incumbent. And their incentives to help keep the current administration in office will be even higher because the opposition is more likely to reprimand agents who carried out violence them should they come to power. Moreover, new recruits are initiated into a bureaucratic culture that rewards loyalty over competence, thereby strengthening incentives for compliance with politicized orders in the future.

8.2 AREA ALIGNMENT, THE PROVINCIAL ADMINISTRATION, AND THE 2007 ELECTION

Determining whether Kibaki strategically managed bureaucrats in the same way as his predecessors requires assessing which areas of the country were aligned with him and which were not. In this section I first recap the political landscape in the run-up to Kibaki's 2007 reelection campaign to define the alignment of different ethnic groups. Second, I provide evidence of the actions that the Provincial Administration carried out in areas with different alignments.

8.2.1   Area Alignment toward Kibaki

Kibaki began his presidency with strong cross-cutting support. But this support splintered along ethnic lines in the run-up to the 2005 referendum and especially before the 2007 election.[2] By then, the country's area alignment was largely a function of the ethnicity of the main presidential candidates. Kibaki's Kikuyu co-ethnics were considered aligned with him and his Party of National Unity (PNU). His only viable opponent was Raila Odinga, a Luo (Orange Democratic Movement, ODM). Luo-majority areas are considered misaligned because they expected to be co-opted, instead of coerced, should Kibaki lose office. I consider the Kamba ethnic group as unaligned even though they had a co-ethnic presidential contestant, Kalonzo Musyoka (ODM-Kenya), because he was not a viable candidate: pre-election polls estimate that his support was around 15 percent, and concentrated among areas inhabited by his co-ethnics.[3]

Recent scholarship on the run-up to the 2007 election supports my classification of area alignment. Using newspaper reports of presidential campaign rallies, Horowitz (2016) finds that the vast majority of rallies occurred outside Kibaki's aligned (Kikuyu) and misaligned (Luo) areas. Kibaki held no rallies in Luo supermajority constituencies, and only 8 percent of his rallies were in Kikuyu supermajority constituencies. Similarly, Odinga held only 1 percent of his rallies in Kikuyu supermajority constituencies and 5 percent in Luo supermajority constituencies. In line with the theory, the voters in these areas were unlikely to support a non-co-ethnic candidate. However, Horowitz (2016) finds that Musyoka was less viable and that Kamba areas were considered unaligned: 12 percent of Kibaki's rallies were in Kamba supermajority areas, proportional to their 11 percent of the population. Odinga held no rallies in Kamba areas, likely due to lingering animosity from the Kamba towards Odinga after

---

[2] For a discussion of ethnic cleavages in the 2005 referendum, see Murunga and Nasong'o (2006), Lynch (2006a), and Kimenyi and Shughart (2010). For a discussion of ethnic cleavages in the 2007 election, see Gibson and Long (2009) and Kanyinga (2009). Also see Bratton and Kimenyi (2008) and Kimenyi and Romero (2008).

[3] For instance, *The Daily Nation* on October 7, 2007 released the results of three national polls that showed that 35–41 percent of voters intended to vote for Kibaki, 46–50 percent of voters intended to vote for Odinga, and 11–15 percent intended to vote for Musyoka ("Raila Maintains Lead in New Opinion Polls"). On December 8, 2007, *The Daily Nation* reported that 39–42 percent of voters intended to vote for Kibaki, 43–47 percent intended to vote for Odinga, and 10–17 percent intended to vote for Musyoka ("Raila Tips Scale but Kibaki Stays Close").

the ODM split.[4] And while Kibaki and Odinga spent little time in their co-ethnic areas, 29 percent of Musyoka's rallies were in Kamba superma-jority areas, seemingly in an attempt to solidify support from his supposed base.[5] In other words, while votes were largely set in Kibaki and Odinga's co-ethnic areas, votes in areas inhabited by Musyoka's co-ethnics were very much up for grabs.

8.2.2 Provincial Administration Co-optation and Coercion Based on Area Alignment

Kibaki relied on the Provincial Administration to deliver central gov-ernment resources to his base. The evidence suggests that the Provincial Administration was especially attentive to aligned Kikuyu communities in Rift Valley where they were a substantial minority, simultaneously co-opting Kibaki's co-ethnics while withholding support from their neigh-bors. One Member of Parliament (MP) from a pastoralist area in Rift Val-ley whose constituency bordered a Kikuyu farming community described the agency's role in forgiving loans of his Kikuyu neighbors in the wake of a drought while refusing to do so for his constituents:

> When a famine like what we've had, when [the local Kikuyu community] experi-ence a severe drought to the extent that they lose their crop, then the government writes off [their crop losses], it waives loans … The government is writing off several billions. The government through Provincial Administration also provides these Kikuyu communities when they are about to start ploughing their lands they provide them with farm inputs, seeds, and fertilizers … why doesn't the government re-stock just like the way they assist the farming communities by providing us with farm inputs or even writing off loans [for our losses]? So this is where the government has failed and most specifically Provincial Administration.[6]

In addition, and as under Kenyatta, the Provincial Administration played an important role in allocating land to Kikuyus. Kibaki oversaw the cre-ation of thirty settlement schemes from 2003 until his 2007 reelection campaign, representing a total of about 72,000 hectares of land – more than 31,000 hectares of which was allocated in Kikuyu-majority districts in Rift Valley. The Provincial Administration also helped settle Kikuyu citizens on Rift Valley land that was already settled by others. Just as

---

4 Chapter 4 recounts how Musyoka and Odinga initially came together to form ODM in 2005, but split in the run-up to the 2007 because each wanted to stand for the presidency.
5 Also see Elischer (2013).
6 Interview with then MP, March 1, 2012, Nairobi, Kenya.

Moi had used the agency to evict Kenyatta's Kikuyu squatters who were living on forest land to make room for Kalenjin squatters, under Kibaki it evicted Moi's Kalenjin squatters to make room for Kikuyu squatters.

For instance, a DO in Nakuru District in 2004 wrote to his superiors about a group of squatters on government land in his jurisdiction. He noted that "one sensitive thinf [sic] is that all of them are Kalenjin while the area is predominantly kikuyu [sic]. The Kikuyus have been reported to be waiting to see what shall be done." In a follow-up letter, the DO noted that the squatters "have now started accusing some kikuyus [sic] of plotting to have them kicked form [sic] these shambas [farms]." The DC, in a handwritten note, responded: "Govt. instructions and policy are very clear and the DO should take appropriate action."[7]

Separately, provincial administrators used their authority over normal administrative tasks to carry out low-intensity coercion against Odinga supporters. DOs were accused of demanding voter cards before administering government services, or refusing to provide state services if an individual came from an unaligned or misaligned group.[8] At other times, PCs, DCs, and DOs used the chain of command to drum up support for Kibaki's 2007 party, the PNU. A former DC who served in two districts that I code as unaligned during Kibaki's first term explained:

Maybe you didn't like Raila and Raila's [expected] government. So you campaigned for the better person. Both at the individual level but also you used your office and the muscle of your office to campaign for the president. Whip [bureaucrats under you] and make sure they make the people understand why we should not vote for Raila.[9]

This sentiment echoes a formal complaint that Musyoka lodged against his DC, who he claimed had summoned civil servants working in his district to support Kibaki.[10] The Provincial Administration was also expected to help PNU legislative candidates, especially in unaligned areas, where they could not expect to win by riding on Kibaki's coattails. One DO explained that his colleagues, "could be prevailed upon to play a role in [a] political meeting ... So, if [the local MP] is a government MP,

---

[7] DO Mbogoni to DC Nakuru, October 6, 2004, EA1/4/49, Rift Valley Provincial Archives, Nakuru, Kenya.
[8] *The Daily Nation*, "Kalonzo Warns On Poll Rigging." December 3, 2007. http://allafrica.com/stories/200712030019.html
[9] Interview with former DC, June 9, 2018, Nairobi.
[10] *The Daily Nation*, "Kalonzo Asks Team to Monitor PNU," November 27, 2007. http://allafrica.com/stories/200711262196.html.

the party of that MP is the same party that runs the government, and that MP is not even a Minister, or whatever, but the MP is going to support party issues. The DO would be told to support that MP."[11]

One tactic that bureaucrats sometimes used to justify curtailing the movement of opposition candidates in unaligned areas was to cite the need to maintain law and order. Odinga explained:

Under the guise of trying to create order, the DC would determine the order of rallies [among candidates] so that there are no parallel rallies as supporters [of different candidates] are likely to clash. But there was bias. They would pick convenient dates for the government. In rural areas there are market days where people come to markets and everyone is in town so people don't have to come [to town] because of your rally. Since they are there already, they can come and listen. To hold a rally on other days in remote areas, people have to travel 20, 30, 40 kms which they will not do on non-market days. So you get less turnout.[12]

Musyoka was barred from attending rallies because provincial administrators claimed that he would incite the audience to violence.[13] One opposition MP discussed how an administrator in his jurisdiction used a program intended to promote peace between cattle rustling communities to instead fund cattle-rustling against ODM candidates and supporters:

She is PNU party. She goes around rubbishing me ... They [the Provincial Administration] run something called peace caravan .... She is given resources. They go around talking about 'peace, peace, peace' but sometimes there is a lot of cattle rustling going on. And sometimes you wonder if this thing is no longer business. And you wonder if these resources are not for their pockets [but for someone who instigates] fights between communities. Why would you set up an illegal arrangement?

When I asked the MP why he thought he was targeted, he responded: "ODM. ODM. ODM. You never know how many other things are going on to make it difficult for ODM to grow. Maybe there are a number of other provincial administrators who are promoted to suppress the growth of ODM."[14] Another opposition MP from a pastoralist community similarly noted:

---

[11] Interview with then DO, January 18, 2012, Nairobi.
[12] Interview with Raila Odinga, May 22, 2014, Boston, USA.
[13] *The Daily Nation*, "Kalonzo Barred from His Rallies," June 5, 2007.
[14] Interview with then MP, February 27, 2012, Nairobi.

The problem is the institution because this institution of Provincial Administration has been misused by the Office of the President. Is it not enough reason when residents request for [a service], you are approached there on the ground, [but] nothing happens? And then as a result probably people sometimes clash and then the government takes sides ... . They carried out security operation, they rounded up cattle from water points, 4,115 herds of cattle were seized from my constituency and were distributed to neighboring communities ... why, because [the recipients] they're in PNU.[15]

The Provincial Administration also played a crucial role during the election. Odinga accused the agency of facilitating vote rigging:

The PA was used very extensively by my opponent to support his campaign, most importantly in the recruitment of polling agents. PA officers were the ones who were tasked with identifying "honest men of integrity" [in air quotes] to act as polling agents, polling clerks. The electoral commission recruited returning officers, the presiding officers and the polling clerks through the PA because the PA are the ones who supposedly know the terrain. But this facilitated in the rigging because these were men they knew they could buy and would act decisively.[16]

Since provincial administrators recruited returning officers, they could hire poll workers on whom the government could rely during the vote count.

While the Provincial Administration was able to misuse its authority to help Kibaki stay in office, the agency was much less politicized during his administration than during Moi's electoral regime. The opposition under Kibaki was formally granted freedoms considered necessary for free and fair competition that they were denied under Moi. For instance, while Raila Odinga noted that administrators scheduled his 2007 rallies on non-market days, his rallies during his 1997 bid were rarely approved (and those that were approved were often canceled on the day). While provincial administrators used their position to push residents in their jurisdiction to vote for Kibaki in 2007, top administrators actively campaigned with Moi in the 1990s. At the same time, the Provincial Administration still acted impartially in a systematic way in 2007. Just as the Kibaki administration was able to informally undermine formal reforms intended to depoliticize recruitment and promotion (see Section 8.3), the Provincial Administration was able to informally co-opt aligned Kikuyu areas while coercing the opposition despite formal reforms intended to depoliticize this agency.

---

[15] Interview with then MP, March 1, 2012, Nairobi.
[16] Interview with Raila Odinga, May 22, 2014, Boston.

8.3 BUREAUCRATIC LOYALTY TOWARD KIBAKI

Kibaki relied on the Provincial Administration to treat areas of different alignments differently. One might assume that bureaucrats refused to comply with Kibaki's political demands as a result of the depoliticization of the state that he promised in his 2002 election campaign. And indeed, I find that Kibaki did implement many of the public sector reforms that he proposed. But the Provincial Administration remained politicized in part because the Kibaki government undermined the spirit of some of these reforms in an attempt to sustain neopatrimonial relationships with some officers.

In this section, I first review the reforms that the Kibaki administration carried out in 2003–2004. I then examine the expected benefits of Kibaki remaining in office, which affected the loyalty of, three categories of officers – high-ranking PCs and DCs, lower-level DOs, and lower-level Luo DOs – toward Kibaki. I show that loyalty, and thus compliance, was affected by a bureaucrat's expected benefits from a continued Kibaki presidency versus an Odinga presidency.

8.3.1 Reforming the Provincial Administration?

One of the most prominent policy platforms of Kibaki and his National Rainbow Coalition - Kenya (NARC) in the run-up to the 2002 election was to reform the Provincial Administration. His goal was to overturn the status quo of "the many cases of harassment ... by politically correct provincial administrators" (NARC 2002 Party Manifesto, pp. 3–4). The NARC party manifesto proposed four strategies to reform the state; the last three related directly to abuses by the Provincial Administration:

1) ensure a complete separation of powers between the three arms of government, 2) put in place a mechanism that enables Parliament to vet all appointments to nationally critical positions in the public service, 3) ensure that departments that need more independence in order to guarantee individual freedoms and justice to all are removed from the Office of the President and given the necessary autonomy, and 4) commit ourselves to retrain, equip and remunerate police and other security services to make sure that they are user-friendly, carry out their work efficiently, effectively and fairly.

Despite these promises, the Kibaki government did not introduce legislative confirmation for provincial administrators (point 2) or distance the agency from the Office of the President (point 3). However, Kibaki led a concerted – and visible – effort to fire the most political administrators and retrain those who remained (point 4). In total, four of eight PCs and more than twenty DCs were fired less than one year after he took office. By 2005, only one of Moi's eight PCs and twenty-seven of seventy-one DCs remained. Further, it is estimated that the government spent more than $15 million by 2007 on training to give administrators a more democratic and apolitical understanding of their role.[17] Kibaki also introduced performance evaluations for administrators and made it a point to standardize promotions by requiring administrators to complete certain training and courses before advancing to higher positions. These reforms were based on ideas about New Public Management (Hood 1995; Ferlie, Fitzgerald, and Pettigrew 1996), and took root across government agencies during Kibaki's presidency (Obong'o 2009; Hope 2012).

In addition, the center formally diminished the authority of provincial administrators in the field. To begin, other central government ministries were given more latitude to carry out their functions with less oversight from the Provincial Administration. For example, DCs no longer had to approve expenditures for every project funded by central government disbursements within the district. Further, Kibaki inaugurated the Constituency Development Fund (CDF) in 2003, which gave each MP a pot of money to spend on development projects in her constituency. Though the DC sat on the CDF committee, allocations were largely driven by MPs (Harris 2016; Harris and Posner 2019). And after the 2007 election, Provincial Administration bureaucrats played a much smaller role in administering elections. Yet as I discuss in the rest of this chapter, the formal rules and procedures designed to depoliticize this agency were undermined informally.

8.3.2 High-Ranking Officers: Loyalty to Kibaki

Kibaki's co-ethnic Kikuyu comprised less than 30 percent of high-ranking PCs and DCs in 2007 (see Figure 8.1). But this category of officers was considered loyal to Kibaki regardless of their ethnicity. Kibaki began to cultivate this loyalty at the top by pushing out many of Moi's PCs and DCs – ostensibly to make the Provincial Administration apolitical, in line with NARC's manifesto. But one DC appointed by Kibaki explained that the true goal was to oust administrators who were considered loyal to

---

[17] *The Daily Nation* "Sh1 Billion Used for Training Officers," 25 June 2007.

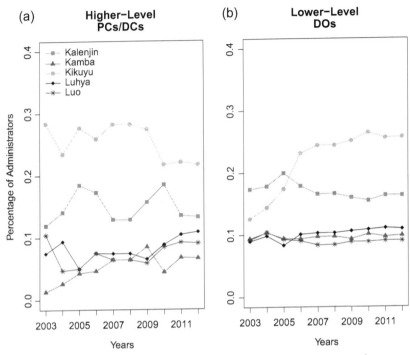

FIGURE 8.1 Percentage of administrators by ethnicity for Kibaki's presidency. Figure 8.1a plots the ethnic breakdown by year for presidentially appointed PCs and DCs. Figure 8.1b plots the ethnic breakdown by year for lower-level DOs. I include percentages for the country's five largest ethnic groups, who were also among the most well-represented ethnic groups within the Provincial Administration.

Moi.[18] One of Moi's former PCs confirmed that the goal of the early retirements used to push him and his colleagues out was to replace them with administrators who would owe their position to Kibaki and therefore prove loyal to the new government.[19]

While most of Moi's appointed administrators were pushed out, those who stayed were thought to be willing to shift their loyalties to Kibaki. Perhaps most tellingly, the few DCs from the Kikuyu and broader Gikuyu, Embu, and Meru Association (GEMA) communities in office in 2002 retained their position for at least a year under Kibaki, if not until the 2007 election. Kibaki cultivated loyalties among other ethnicities too.

---

18 Interview with then DC, July 2, 2012, Nairobi.
19 Interview with former PC, February 2, 2012, Nairobi.

For instance, of the twenty-seven DCs initially appointed by Moi who remained by 2005, thirteen had been appointed a year or less before Kibaki's inauguration. These administrators had only begun to reap the rewards of their office under Moi, despite having worked up through the ranks of the Provincial Administration for an average of twenty-five years. They were likely amenable to serving a new president so long as they were able to use their office to predate.

In sum, Kibaki reemphasized the neopatrimonial linkages to his appointees by pushing out the high-ranking administrators seen as closest to Moi and "retraining" those perceived to be willing to serve a new government. These administrators, and the new ones he appointed, owed their position to Kibaki. They were motivated to help keep him in office, since they were likely to lose their positions if Odinga became president.

8.3.3 Low-Ranking Kikuyu Officers: Loyalty to Kibaki

There was variation in the loyalty of lower-level DOs, however, as they did not have the same bonds of patronage as higher-level PCs and DCs. My theory would suggest that Kikuyu DOs would be considered the most loyal because they had the best chances of advancing to a presidentially appointed position should Kibaki stay in office (as I empirically show in Section 8.5). By 2006, Kikuyu DOs had become the plurality, as seen in Figure 8.1b. They comprised about 25 percent of DOs before the 2007 election.

During my interviews, Kikuyu DOs under Kibaki attributed their expectations for advancement to formal criteria. In line with the reforms that he initiated early in his presidency, these administrators argued that Kibaki tried to move past ethnicity and sought to appoint the best people for the job. A standard line I heard was that Kibaki was a technocrat and he only promoted officers due to merit. In line with the reforms that he initiated early in his presidency, these administrators argued that Kibaki tried to move past ethnicity and sought to appoint the best people for the job. Many Kikuyu DOs who were promoted to DCs by Kibaki attributed their advancement to their qualifications. They had completed the requisite trainings, had learned what they could as a DO, and had served for decades. It was simply their time to advance.

While in theory advancement could be an apolitical process based purely on merit and qualifications, in practice Kikuyu administrators were favored for enrollment in the requisite courses for advancement. Due to the shortage of available slots in these courses, the center could invite its preferred candidates and delay the invitation of others. At the same time, the large number of Kikuyu political elites in the cabinet and in Kibaki's informal "kitchen cabinet" meant that Kikuyu DOs were more likely to have the necessary political connections to secure an (early) invitation. A senior officer in Harambee House who helped oversee supplemental coursework for administrators under Kibaki noted that political elites often manipulated his officer training timetables in favor of Kikuyu officers. Another Harambee House administrator explained that prominent Kikuyu elites would call him and demand the promotion of their favored administrators.[20] Both officials noted that favoritism of the president's co-ethnics was less blatant than when they initially joined the Provincial Administration under Moi. Instead, the center was able to shroud favoritism for some officers through formal procedures and criteria such as the completion of trainings, (subjective) performance evaluations, and preference in stations.[21]

8.3.4 Low-Ranking Luo Officers: Disloyalty to Kibaki

Many Luo administrators believed their careers would advance if Kibaki lost his reelection bid and Odinga became president. This perception was not unwarranted. The percentage of DCs, the position that DOs hoped to advance to, was less than 7 percent Luo by 2007 – substantially less than their percentage in the population (12 percent by 1989). One Luo DO who began his career before the 2007 election explained why his career had stalled:

> Within the scheme of service there are certain requirements for you to move from one job group to the next. Now you find some of these requirements which are critical for your career progression are at the mercy of the government. I'll give you an example, I was employed in 2007. We had a scheme of service where you enter at Job Group J and after two years you are [supposed to be] confirmed and you are moved to Job Group K. But before you move to Job Group K you must have undergone a paramilitary course. Now, we had people employed in 2008, 2009, 2010. Now sometimes, someone is employed in 2008 or 2010 – behind you – is taken for the paramilitary course. He comes back. But now he qualifies to move to Job Group K because he has completed the paramilitary course which you haven't been called for. Are you getting me? So because this 2009 person comes from the correct community he has taken the course and he is now being promoted. And you have stalled.[22]

[20] Interview with then DC, June 29, 2017, Nairobi.
[21] Interview with then DC, August 2, 2017, Nairobi.
[22] Interview with then DO, July 17, 2017, Machakos, Kenya.

This officer recognized that he was not qualified to be promoted to serve as a DC in the scheme of service, or even advance to the next job group within the rank of DO. Yet he attributed his failure to be invited to the requisite training course to the fact that he did not have prominent co-ethnic elites close to the president who could advocate for him.

Instead, Luo DOs could have expected a substantial increase in their likelihood of getting promoted if Odinga won the 2007 election. When I asked this Luo DO what an Odinga presidency would mean for his career, he replied "If your tribe is perched up there then you can find your way up. And you find us supportive of the system if it is supportive of our tribe. Tribalism is real."[23] An Odinga presidency would allow the DO to call on his co-ethnic political elites to help him undertake the necessary requirements for advancement.

There is some evidence that Luo DOs were unwilling to comply with politicized orders, and instead used their authority to benefit the opposition. One Luo administrator explained that he has always attempted to be fair during election seasons (he served during the 2007, 2013, and 2017 elections – each of which represented a contest between a Kikuyu incumbent or protegé and Odinga as the most viable opposition candidate). Raila Odinga confirmed that Luo DOs tended to be the most impartial towards him and often allowed him to hold rallies unencumbered.[24]

Non-Luo DOs also felt that they were disadvantaged compared to Kikuyu DOs in being selected for the required training courses. One Kalenjin DO who had begun under Moi lamented that he and his co-ethnics had been consistently overlooked for promotions since 2002, saying that "it was better then, under President Moi." Even though this DO was from a different district than Moi, and a different Kalenjin sub-tribe, his MP had the "ear of the president" during the 1990s.[25] But the election outcome would have less clear-cut effects on the likelihood of promotions for non-Kikuyu and non-Luo administrators. Both Kibaki and Odinga were expected to incorporate political elites of different ethnicities. Yet elites outside the president's ethnic group were unlikely to have the same pull in advocating for their favored DOs.

---

[23] This interview took place in the run-up to the 2017 election, which was similar to the 2007 election in that it featured Raila Odinga contesting a Kikuyu incumbent.
[24] Interview with Raila Odinga, May 14, 2014, Boston.
[25] Interview with then DO, February 13, 2012, Mombasa, Kenya.

8.4 QUALITATIVE EVIDENCE OF STRATEGIC MANAGEMENT

In this section, I analyze the posting and shuffling of PCs, DCs, and DOs during Kibaki's presidency and find that areas of different alignment were governed differently. Before discussing the quantitative results, I present interview evidence on the central government's preemptive management of bureaucrats: bureaucratic elites made decisions about the management of individual provincial administrators, and posted and shuffled officers in order to maximize compliance in strategic areas.

Some interviewees explicitly connected posting patterns to the expectation that Luo DOs could not be trusted to comply with politicized orders. For instance, a former administrator who was working in Harambee House before the 2007 election explained that the center was, "looking around and seeing, 'that is [so and so], she can never campaign for [Kibaki]. She is campaigning for Raila. So let us post her there. Let us not involve her in some of our discreet decision making.' Do you get?"[26] Kibaki could limit the amount of damage that presumably disloyal Luo DOs could inflict on his chances of reelection by posting them strategically.

However, I found evidence that Kikuyu administrators were posted to increase co-optation in Kikuyu-majority areas through local embeddedness. While all Kikuyu areas are considered aligned, the presence of Kikuyu officials was arguably most effective in parts of Rift Valley that had sizable Kikuyu communities but where they were viewed with hostility by indigenous groups. In these areas, Kikuyu administrators could simultaneously co-opt local Kikuyu residents and coerce others who were vying for the same resources (and land). A former PC of Rift Valley under Kibaki noted his inclination to send Kikuyu administrators to parts of the Rift with sizable Kikuyu communities. He explained that Kikuyu communities in Rift Valley still feel apprehensive being outside their home province, and that a Kikuyu administrator puts them at ease.[27] His logic in posting Kikuyus to Kikuyu-majority areas was not nefarious – indeed, at the time of the interview, the memory of the 2007–2008 postelection violence was still fresh. But others explained that Kikuyu administrators were posted explicitly to help settle Kikuyus on historically pastoralist land. One Kalenjin MP whose constituency contained part of the

---

26 Interview with former Deputy Secretary of Provincial Administration, June 9, 2018, Nairobi.
27 Interview with then PC, October 16, 2015, Nakuru, Kenya.

fertile Mau Reserve discussed the perception of provincial administrators among his constituency:

> We have seen a surge in the Kikuyu administrators [in my constituency] and that is part of the reason why we see mischief with the Provincial Administration ... because it will reach a time you know a president can just decide to put his cronies to interfere with the activities of my constituents and claiming they are appointees of the president.[28]

8.5 QUANTITATIVE ANALYSIS: BUREAUCRATIC MANAGEMENT UNDER KIBAKI

In this section I first recap the alignment of different parts of the country towards Kibaki. With this in mind, I then quantitatively assess the loyalty and embeddedness of bureaucrats sent to different areas.

8.5.1 Recap: Alignment and Embeddedness under Kibaki

Table 8.1 gives descriptive statistics of the posting and shuffling patterns of administrators in the run-up to Kibaki's 2007 reelection campaign. Columns 1–4 indicate group and area alignment towards Kibaki. Columns 5–7 display information on posting and shuffling patterns across differently aligned areas; the first number in each column corresponds to high-ranking PCs and DCs and the second to DOs. Column 5 gives the percentage of loyal administrators sent to a jurisdiction (the statistic for high-ranking officials is left blank, as all PCs and DCs are considered loyal). Column 6 gives the percentage of co-ethnic administrators posted to areas with different alignments. Column 7 displays the average tenure length of PCs and DCs in jurisdictions with different alignments (I do not have this data for DOs).

The descriptive statistics are in line with the theory. Areas that were considered strategically valuable were administered by the limited number of loyal officers: aligned areas had the highest level of loyal DOs, and a large percentage of loyal DOs were also sent to unaligned areas. The center increased embeddedness in aligned areas to help co-opt Kibaki's co-ethnic Kikuyu community by posting more co-ethnic administrators and lengthening their tenure. The central government also decreased embed-

---

TABLE 8.1 *Group and Area Alignment toward Kibaki; Run-up to 2007 Election*

Alignment	Group	Location	Time Period	Percentage of Loyal Administrators (%)	Percentage of Co-ethnic Administrators (%)	Average Tenure (Years)
Aligned	Kikuyu	Central Province Parts of Coast, Nairobi, Rift Valley Provinces	2003–2007	– / 28	43 / 28	2.4 / –
Misaligned	Luo	Parts of Nyanza Province	2006–2007	– / 16	4 / 4	1.4 / –
Unaligned	Other ethnic groups	Various	2006–2007	– / 19	3 / 7	1.5 / –

dedness in misaligned and unaligned areas to facilitate coercion by posting more out-group administrators and shortening their tenure.

8.5.2 Bureaucratic Postings in the Run-up to the 2007 Election

This section quantitatively evaluates whether administrators were strategically posted and shuffled as outlined in the theory. I begin with the posting and shuffling of high-ranking PCs and DCs, who all had financial motivations to help Kibaki stay in office. These administrators were considered loyal because they could expect to be fired from their lucrative position if Kibaki lost office, just as so many of their predecessors had lost their jobs when he became president. I also examine the posting patterns of lower-ranking DOs. Loyalty among these officers varied based on co-ethnicity with Kibaki or Odinga; Kikuyu (Luo) administrators expected to advance more easily through the ranks should Kibaki (Odinga) win.

The theory expects aligned areas to be co-opted through higher levels of local embeddedness. The goal was for administrators to develop social connections with area residents that made them more willing and better able to serve the interests of the local community. Therefore we should find that Kikuyu-majority areas had more co-ethnic administrators with longer tenures. Misaligned and unaligned areas should instead have had administrators with low levels of embeddedness: by posting non-co-ethnic administrators and shuffling them frequently, the center sought to prevent them from developing strong social bonds with local residents that might cause them to shirk from orders to coerce. The theory has separate predictions for officers with varying degrees of loyalty to the president. We should expect loyal Kikuyu DOs, who were presumed to be the most loyal under Kibaki, to be sent to aligned and unaligned areas, as these were strategically valuable for the election. However, disloyal Luo DOs, presumed to be the most disloyal, should be kept away from unaligned areas in particular, as these determine the election outcome.

I begin with analyses of PCs and DCs from 2003–2007.[29] Given that all of these administrators were considered loyal, I examine whether the center was willing to allow embeddedness in aligned areas throughout

---

[29] Kibaki created around eighty new districts, and therefore appointed eighty DCs, in the run-up to the 2007 election. Yet I only include the districts, and DCs, that existed in 2003 because the vast majority of new districts were not operational before the election. Indeed, the administrative officer returns I collected do not list administrators in many of these new districts until 2008.

Kibaki's first term. Column 1 of Table 8.2 presents the results of a logit model with results clustered at the jurisdiction level.[30] The dependent variable is whether an administrator was a co-ethnic of the majority of residents in a jurisdiction, and the independent variable is whether a jurisdiction was majority Kikuyu. Column 2 examines the tenure lengths of PCs and DCs. The independent variable is an indicator variable for whether the unit was majority Kikuyu.

The remaining columns in Table 8.2 examine the posting patterns of DOs. I focus on 2006–2007, during Kibaki's first term after the opposition emerged and it became clear where his misaligned and unaligned areas were located. Columns 3 and 4 examine postings to aligned jurisdictions. The dependent variable in Column 3 is the percentage of years in which a jurisdiction was governed by an administrator who was a co-ethnic of a majority of residents. The independent variable in Column 3 is an indicator for Kikuyu-majority jurisdictions. The dependent variable for Column 4 is the percentage of years in which a jurisdiction was governed by a Kikuyu DO. The independent variable in Column 4 is an indicator variable for Kikuyu-majority jurisdictions interacted with jurisdictions in Rift Valley. Columns 5 and 6 examine postings to unaligned jurisdictions. The dependent variable for Column 5 is the same as in Column 4, the percentage of years in which a jurisdiction was governed by a Kikuyu DO, but the independent variable is an indicator for an unaligned division. Column 6 replicates Column 5 after substituting in the percentage of years in which a jurisdiction was governed by a Luo DO for the dependent variable.

The results are largely in line with the theory's predictions. Substantively, Column 1 indicates that Kikuyu-majority jurisdictions were 42.2 percentage points more likely to have a co-ethnic PC or DC than the rest of the country from 2003–2007 (95% CI: 0.22, 0.62). I simulate hazard ratios from Column 2, which can be substantively interpreted as the likelihood that an administrator will stay in a station for a particular length of time. The hazard ratio for administrators in aligned, Kikuyu-majority jurisdictions after one year was 0.78, but only 0.70 for other jurisdictions. After two years, the hazard ratio was 0.71 in Kikuyu-majority jurisdictions but only 0.58 elsewhere. Taken together, the results indicate that the center was most willing to allow local embeddedness –

---

[30] I run a logit model in order to include administrator-level characteristics. The results are substantively similar if I omit the administrator-level characteristics and instead run an ordinary least squares (OLS) regression parallel to Column 3.

TABLE 8.2 *Management of Administrators Before Kibaki's Reelection*

	PCs/DCs		DOs			
	1 Logit Co-ethnic	2 Cox Shuffle	3 OLS Co-ethnic	4 OLS Kikuyu	5 OLS Kikuyu	6 OLS Luo
Kikuyu Jurisdiction	3.22***	−0.68*	0.20***	−0.12***		
	(0.67)	(0.28)	(0.04)	(0.03)		
Rift Valley				−0.09**		
				(0.05)		
Kikuyu Jurisdiction * *Rift Valley*				0.21†		
				(0.11)		
Unaligned Jurisdiction					0.07**	−0.04
					(0.03)	(0.03)
1989 Population, logged	0.05	−0.19*	0.04*	0.02	0.04	−0.01
	(0.38)	(0.09)	(0.03)	(0.03)	(0.03)	(0.03)
Area, sq. km., logged	−0.26	0.04	0.00	0.01	0.01	0.03
	(0.21)	(0.05)	(0.02)	(0.02)	(0.02)	(0.02)
1989 ELF	0.97	0.09	−0.01	0.07	0.10*	−0.05
	(1.08)	(0.30)	(0.04)	(0.05)	(0.05)	(0.05)
Minister	−0.11	0.20	−0.07**	−0.06	−0.06	−0.02
	(0.71)	(0.16)	(0.03)	(0.04)	(0.04)	(0.03)
Experience	−0.02	0.00				
	(0.06)	(0.01)				
Woman	−1.00	0.09				
	(1.59)	(0.40)				
Intercept	−1.45		−0.13	0.03	−0.14	0.14
	(3.66)		(0.16)	(0.21)	(0.20)	(0.20)
Num. obs.	757	757	243	243	243	243

***$p < 0.01$, **$p < 0.05$, *$p < 0.1$. Regressions of the management of provincial administrators during Kibaki's first term. The outcome in Column 1 is a binary indicator for whether a jurisdiction was assigned a co-ethnic administrator. Column 2 examines shuffling rates. The outcome in Columns 3–6 is the percentage of observations in which a unit had a co-ethnic (Column 3), Kikuyu (Columns 4 and 5), or Luo (Column 6) administrator. Column 1 reports results from a logit regression with errors clustered at the district level, Column 2 reports results from a Cox Proportional Hazards model, and Columns 3–6 report results from an OLS regression with errors clustered at the district level.

through co-ethnicity or tenure – in aligned areas where the government wanted officers to co-opt the local community.

The results for DOs also support the theory. Substantively, Column 3 indicates that Kikuyu-majority divisions could expect to be governed by a co-ethnic for five more months from 2006–2007 than the rest of the country. The interaction term in Column 4 suggests that the results in Column 3 are driven by Kikuyu-majority divisions in Rift Valley, where land and other state resources between indigenous groups and Kikuyu residents was the most disputed. This result suggests that the center intentionally sent a disproportionate amount of Kikuyu administrators to these areas to ensure that they sided with Kikuyu residents over other residents in local claims. Column 5 finds that unaligned jurisdictions could expect 7 percentage points more Kikuyu DOs than the rest of the country, equivalent to an additional two months of being governed by Kikuyu DOs from 2006–2007. Column 6 displays the postings of Luo administrators. Luo administrators were not posted to unaligned areas at different rates than other administrators at conventional levels of significance, though the main independent variable is signed in the correct direction. No control variables are consistently significant across the models.

I run additional analyses and alternative specifications of the results listed in Table 8.2. First, the results are substantively unchanged after introducing other control variables, including the percentage of high-potential farming land or the share of the jurisdiction that voted in favor of the 2005 constitutional referendum. Second, due to the inconclusive results from Column 6 about Luo DOs, I examine where Luo DOs were posted. I rerun a similar model to Column 6, substituting unaligned areas with majority-Kamba areas. Though I classify the Kamba ethnic group as unaligned, many Kambas were unlikely to vote for either Kibaki or Odinga since they had a co-ethnic candidate in the race. Actions intended to undermine Kibaki in these areas would have less of an effect on the election outcome than in other unaligned areas, as many Kamba voters were unlikely to have voted for Kibaki anyways. I find that Luo DOs were 11 percentage points more likely to be sent to Kamba-majority areas than elsewhere ($p < 0.01$). In line with my theory, this suggests that Luo DOs were posted away from strategically valuable areas.

Third, I rerun some of the analyses after redefining area alignment. I rerun Columns 1–3 after coding GEMA-majority areas as aligned and find similar, though weaker, results. GEMA-majority districts were 28.0 percentage points more likely to be governed by a co-ethnic PC or DC than other jurisdictions (95% CI: 0.11, 0.48), and 19.7 percentage points more likely to be governed by a co-ethnic DO ($p < 0.001$). The haz-ard ratio for administrators in GEMA-majority districts was 0.75 (ver-sus 0.68 for other jurisdictions after one year), and 0.67 (versus 0.58 for other jurisdictions after two years). I also rerun Column 5 after reclas-sifying Kalenjin areas from unaligned to misaligned, given that Odinga's vice presidential nominee was a Kalenjin. The results are substantively unchanged: unaligned areas could still expect 7.2 percentage points more Kikuyu DOs (substantively, this is equivalent to an additional two months of Kikuyu DOs over a two-year period) than the rest of the country ($p < 0.05$).

One interesting result, which I examine in more detail in Section 8.6, regards postings to the headquarters of a district or province. In each province and each district, some bureaucrats are assigned not to run their own division, but are instead expected to help their PC or DC carry out administrative tasks such as type up reports to send to Nairobi, send out invitations for province- or district-wide meetings, or manage the PC or DC's schedule. Many have described the duties of DOs in headquarters as "paperwork-esque." Bureaucrats posted to provincial or district head-quarters thus have much less effect on citizen livelihoods. Following a similar logic as keeping Luo DOs away from strategically valuable areas, Kikuyu DOs were 5.8 percentage points less likely to be posted to head-quarters during these years ($p = 0.06$).

8.6 PROMOTIONS

In Section 8.5 I presented evidence that the Kibaki administration strate-gically managed the posting and shuffling of administrators in the run-up to the 2007 election. Aligned areas experienced higher levels of local embeddedness to better co-opt local residents, while other areas had lower levels of officer embeddedness to better coerce their populations. And since officers' willingness to comply with orders varied, the center sent those perceived to be the most loyal to strategically valuable aligned and unaligned areas.

In this section, I first examine promotions based on perceived loyalty. Compared with higher-level PCs and DCs, lower-level DOs did not ben-efit monetarily from their position. But Kikuyu DOs were thought to be loyal because they expected to advance more quickly under a co-ethnic president. I thus first evaluate this claim.

Second, I evaluate promotions based on *revealed* compliance. Even though Kikuyu DOs may have been perceived to be the most loyal, DOs of other ethnicities were willing to comply with politicized orders too. Indeed, the very fact that the top ranks of the Provincial Administration were not packed gave bureaucrats, of any ethnicity, some chance of advancing. Though the odds of advancing were lower than among the president's co-ethnic DOs, some lower-level DOs from misaligned or unaligned groups may have been willing to use their authority on behalf of the incumbent on the chance of advancing.

However, the center cannot observe the routine, everyday actions of administrators, and thus cannot reward based on actual compliance. But bureaucratic actions during periods of political violence are visible (Hassan and O'Mealia 2018). I therefore leverage the 2007–2008 postelection violence to examine bureaucratic promotions after the violence abated. The presence or absence of violence, and the direction of the violence if it broke out, provide evidence of compliance, and more broadly, indicate a bureaucrat's willingness and ability to use her authority to benefit the government in the future.

8.6.1 Promotions Based on Perceived Loyalty: Kikuyu Advancements

I use annual personnel data on all provincial administrators from 2005–2012 to track the promotions through the ranks. I examine only these years, as this type of data was not available before 2005. The data lists an officer's "job group" in a given year. The scheme of service for trained officers was divided into ten job groups during these years, running from J (lowest) to T (highest), as seen in Table 8.3.[31] The table also gives the number of officers in that position as of 2005 and their average start date. I note that the scheme of service changed in March 2007 to make fresh recruits, "District Officer Cadets," the new job group J and shift administrators below job group Q up one grade.

I use these annual returns to create a dataset in which the unit of observation is an individual administrator. I count how many job groups a bureaucrat rose. Unlike the other personnel datasets used throughout this book, the data here includes both officers in the field and those posted to other ministries in Nairobi. I therefore restrict the sample to administrators who spent at least some time in the field.

---

[31] Each job designation for field officers has a parallel in the ministries (e.g., a District Officer III is equivalent to an Assistant Secretary III). The scheme of service also includes job groups S, U, and V, but those are reserved solely for administrators in Harambee House.

TABLE 8.3 *Scheme of Service and Descriptive Statistics for Administrators as of 2005*

Job Group	Job Designation	# of Officers	Average Start Date
J	District Officer III	236	2001
K	District Officer II	68	1995
L	District Officer I	207	1993
M	Senior District Officer	101	1989
N	District Commissioner II	29	1987
P	District Commissioner I	56	1985
Q	Senior District Commissioner II	23	1980
R	Senior District Commissioner I	3	1978
T	Provincial Commissioner	8	1979

Scheme of service and descriptive statistics for field officers as of 2005. There is no job group O.

Table 8.4 presents regressions that evaluate promotions. The independent variable for both columns is whether an administrator is Kikuyu, and the dependent variable is the number of job groups that an officer progressed. Column 1 examines all officers who served at least one year from 2005–2012. Column 2 restricts the analysis to administrators whose first job in the sample period was within the DO ranks. I control for factors that may confound the analysis: the number of years the administrator served between 2005 and 2012, the officer's initial job group when they entered the dataset, gender, and whether they began before 2007 (and thus before the across-the-board increase in job groups for the majority of officers).

The regression results indicate that Kikuyu administrators were indeed more likely to advance than their colleagues. Kikuyu administrators, across all ranks, could expect to progress 0.12 more job groups than administrators of other ethnicities ($p < 0.01$). Kikuyu DOs could expect to progress 0.09 job groups more than DOs of other ethnicities ($p < 0.05$).[32] These advantages are substantial: the mean advancements for DOs was 0.78.

Administrators of other ethnicities could not expect this same boost under Kibaki. I rerun the regressions after sequentially substituting the

[32] Re-running the analysis after limiting the sample to administrators who began before the change in the scheme of service does not substantively alter the results.

TABLE 8.4 *General Promotion Trends*

	1 All	2 DOs
Kikuyu	0.12**	0.09*
	(0.05)	(0.05)
Woman	0.04	0.04
	(0.05)	(0.05)
First Job Group	0.05***	0.02
	(0.01)	(0.02)
Tenure Length	0.17***	0.16***
	(0.01)	(0.01)
Began before 2007	0.49***	0.53***
	(0.05)	(0.05)
Intercept	−0.78***	−0.68***
	(0.06)	(0.07)
Num. obs.	1,348	1,249

***$p < 0.001$, **$p < 0.01$, *$p < 0.05$, †$p < 0.1$. OLS regressions in which the dependent variable is the number of job groups that an officer rose from 2005–2012.

Kikuyu indicator variable for each of the country's other largest ethnic groups. Only the indicator for *Kalenjin* bureaucrats is significant, but negative. This stalling out of Kalenjin administrators likely helped reinforce Kikuyu loyalty toward Kibaki. Kikuyu DOs not only expected to advance under Kibaki; they also assumed they would be penalized if Odinga took office as Moi's co-ethnics were under Kibaki.

8.6.2 2007–2008 Postelection Violence

The 2007 election was marred by postelection violence that left some 1,500 Kenyans dead and 750,000 displaced (Human Rights Watch 2008).[33] The violence occurred in both directions: there was opposition-instigated violence against groups aligned with Kibaki (and the Kikuyu in particular), and incumbent-instigated violence against groups aligned with Odinga. The Provincial Administration is alleged to have played

---

33 There are reports of sporadic violence before the announcement of the results on December 30, but the vast majority of violence took place after the election.

a role in facilitating some cases of incumbent-instigated violence, and in letting some opposition-instigated violence happen. Taken together, the 2007–2008 violence presents an opportunity to observe the – very visible – revealed loyalties and compliance of bureaucrats in their jurisdictions.

The initial wave of violence was what I term "opposition-instigated." It was concentrated in Rift Valley, but later spread to parts of Nyanza and Western provinces, and had similar dynamics to the violence during the 1990s: perpetrators aimed to evict Kikuyu residents. The violence was perpetrated by youths from groups seen as supportive of Odinga, including pastoralist ethnic groups considered indigenous to Rift Valley.[34]

But unlike the 1990s, a second wave of incumbent-instigated violence broke out in support of Kibaki, perpetuated by young Kikuyus. This violence was centered around Nakuru district. Though Nakuru is in Rift Valley, it has been a majority-Kikuyu district since independence. This revenge violence targeted Kalenjin and Luo residents and began around January 24, 2008. According to the Waki Report, written by the Commission of Inquiry into Post-Election Violence, the second wave of violence in Nakuru was organized and financed by Kibaki's inner circle. The Waki Report recounts that in Naivasha, in Nakuru District:

> The Commission received credible evidence to the effect that the violence in Naivasha between the 27th and the 30th January 2008 was pre-planned and executed by [Kikuyu gang] members who received the support of Naivasha political and business leaders. The Commission has also evidence that government and political leaders in Nairobi, including key office holders at the highest level of government may have directly participated in the preparation of the attacks. Central to that planning were two meetings held in State House and Nairobi Safari Club in the run up to the election with the involvement senior members of the Government and other prominent Kikuyu personalities.[35]

The Waki Commission did not allege that the trained ranks of the Provincial Administration organized the violence. However, the actions of administrators had the potential to either facilitate or stop the second wave of violence. For example, the Waki Commission suggests that one

---

[34] There were also attempts to violently evict Kikuyus outside Rift Valley, including in Kisumu, Kenya's third-largest city. Violence in Kisumu was perpetuated by Luo youths, who targeted Kikuyu urban residents and other ethnic groups not seen as aligned with Odinga. Archival records indicate that 580 families (2,671 people in total) were internally displaced from Kisumu to Nakuru District, the closest Kikuyu-majority district to Kisumu (HT/1/90, Nyanza Provincial Archives, Kisumu, Kenya).

[35] Waki Report, pp. 121–122.

administrator in Naivasha made it easier for Kikuyu youth to inflict violence by lifting the curfew ban on January 27 (Waki Report, 127).

Some of my interviewees hinted that administrators who helped facilitate incumbent-instigated violence were later promoted as a reward for complying with regime directives. One MP described the sudden promotion of an administrator in her constituency in 2008:

[the administrator] is a person I've known since before he rose through the ranks. And when he came on [in my district] he was a good friend. A family friend so to speak. But there was a time when I took great exception to what he was doing on behalf of the government – failing to stop the mayhem that was there. And it looks like he was doing it on somebody's behalf because the leaders promoted him. If you had been in a place where security is not being curbed and you are head of security, it shouldn't be a plus for you. It ought to be a minus. I will not focus on [him] alone because its a system that is breeding that. Because if it were not [him] it would be somebody else being pressured in the same way. It is not necessarily that he himself is a bad administrator, but it is that he had instructions to do a job.[36]

One administrator discussed the promotion patterns he saw among his colleagues in the wake of the postelection violence:

Under all the regimes some people go [through the ranks] faster than others. Especially if you are amenable in use in dirty games. Yes Kikuyus had the advantage [under Kibaki], but not just co-ethnic. Even the others especially the people who are willing to do things that are extra-judicial like. You see, we used to oversee elections then [in 2007] and more.[37]

These interviews indicate that promotions in the wake of the postelection violence were based on observed loyalty rather than presumed loyalty as proxied through ethnicity. I evaluate these claims in the following analyses.

8.6.3 Management in the Wake of the 2007–2008 Postelection Violence

I examine the promotion patterns of DOs after the occurrence or absence of postelection violence in their jurisdictions. I do so cautiously, however, because the data has clear limitations: it is difficult to determine the precise location of violence; it is hard to evaluate variation in the intensity of violence; and violence was carried out by multiple actors and did not only depend on the political loyalties of the area's DO. But despite these limitations, the data and the following analyses still help evaluate whether

---

36 Interview with MP, March 27, 2012, Nairobi.
37 Interview with then DC, July 15, 2017, Nairobi.

there is a relationship between bureaucratic behavior during the violence and subsequent promotion patterns.[38]

I examine the incidence of postelection violence by coding the locations of arson attacks, which were one of the main forms of violence during this period (Anderson and Lochery 2008; Waki Report; Kasara 2016). While there were numerous reports of multiple forms of violence, complete and systematic data is only available for fire events. I determine the occurrence of arson in a jurisdiction using data from NASA's Moderate Resolution Imaging Spectroradiometer (MODIS) Thermal Anomalies Fire data. The data was processed to eliminate nonfire observations from the dataset.[39]

I code the arson events based on the timing and location of the violence.[40] Specifically, I code violence in Nakuru between January 24, 2008 and February 28, 2008 as incumbent-instigated, and violence that occurred outside Nakuru or in Nakuru before January 24, 2008 as opposition-instigated.[41] I merge the arson attack dataset with datasets on 1) DO posting patterns in the run-up to the 2007 election and 2) DOs' career progression.

Simply regressing DO promotions after 2007 on the incidence and direction of violence may lead to bias precisely because Kikuyu DOs were posted to Kikuyu-majority areas in Rift Valley and were less likely to be posted to office positions, as I showed in Table 8.2, and were more likely to advance, as shown in Table 8.4. I therefore create a matched dataset at the officer level using coarsened exact matching. I match whether there was incumbent-instigated violence in a DO's administrative division on three variables: whether the DO is a Kikuyu, whether the DO was posted to a district headquarters, and whether the DO's division was in a Kikuyu-majority division in Rift Valley. These variables all had a significant effect on posting assignments in Table 8.2 or Table 8.4. The difference in means between the treated and control observations for both of the matched covariates decreases to 0. I created a second matched dataset in which

---

[38] Further, many of the limitations in the data make it harder to find a statistical relationship between bureaucratic behavior during the violence and subsequent promotion patterns should such a relationship exist.

[39] See Hassan and O'Mealia (2018) and Giglio, Descloitres, Justice, and Kaufman (2003).

[40] I exclude Nairobi and Mombasa from the analysis. Administrative jurisdictions in these districts are substantially smaller than jurisdictions in other parts of the country, making it difficult to accurately determine where a fire took place.

[41] This classification is admittedly crude, but the MODIS dataset does not provide information about what, or who, caused a fire. My codings are consistent with reports of violence from the Waki Report and other secondary sources.

the treated variable is the incidence of opposition-instigated violence in a jurisdiction. The balance of this second matched dataset is also substantially better than the original data.

I use these datasets to regress promotions on the incidence of violence in a DO's jurisdiction, as seen in Table 8.5. The dependent variable in Columns 1–3 is the number of job groups that a DO advanced from 2007–2012. The dependent variable in Column 4 is a binary indicator for whether a DO was still employed in 2012, and thus serves as a proxy for whether a bureaucrat was fired before 2012. The independent variable for Columns 1 and 2 is whether a division experienced incumbent-instigated violence; the dependent variable for Columns 3 and 4 is whether a division saw opposition-instigated violence. Column 1 reports the results of a regression on the unmatched data. Column 2 reports the results using the matched data in which the treated variable is a jurisdiction's incidence of incumbent-instigated violence. Columns 3 and 4 use the matched data in which the treated variable is a jurisdiction's incidence of opposition-instigated violence. All of the regressions use OLS.

Table 8.5 lends support to the premise that administrators were promoted (or fired) based on the incidence and direction of violence in their jurisdiction. Column 1, which uses the unmatched data, does not yield significant results for the main independent variable ($p = 0.15$). But Column 2, which uses the matched data, finds that bureaucrats who served in a jurisdiction in which incumbent-instigated violence occurred were more likely to be promoted after the violence abated. The null results from Column 3 indicate that bureaucrats in jurisdictions with opposition-instigated violence did not have substantially different promotion patterns than their peers. But Column 4 suggests that bureaucrats in jurisdictions that experienced opposition-instigated violence were less likely to still be serving in the civil service by 2012.

Though the results in Table 8.5 should be interpreted with caution, they are in line with my theory. The government promoted bureaucrats based on visible signs of loyalty. By privileging those who misused their authority for the government's politicized benefit, and by punishing those who misused their authority to help the opposition, the Provincial Administration reinforced individual bureaucrats' neopatrimonial bonds with the executive. The formal reforms that Kibaki oversaw helped increase the rational-legal norms within the Provincial Administration, but these reforms were undermined by strong, informal, neopatrimonial norms that persisted under the country's more autocratic leaders (Helmke and Levitsky 2004).

TABLE 8.5 *Promotion Trends after the Postelection Violence*

	1 Promotions Unmatched	2 Promotions Matched Data (Incumbent-Instigated)	3 Promotions Matched Data (Opposition-Instigated)	4 Firings
Incumbent-Instigated Violence	0.34 (0.24)	0.49* (0.26)		0.05*** (0.02)
Opposition-Instigated Violence			−0.03 (0.09)	0.00 (0.02)
Kikuyu DO	0.12* (0.07)	0.22 (0.14)	0.08 (0.08)	0.00 (0.02)
Aligned Division, Rift Valley	−0.21 (0.17)	−0.45** (0.21)	−0.31* (0.19)	0.06 (0.04)
HQs	−0.10* (0.06)	−0.14** (0.07)	−0.14** (0.07)	0.05*** (0.01)
Woman	0.10 (0.07)	0.10 (0.08)	0.13 (0.08)	−0.05*** (0.02)
Tenure Length	0.30*** (0.03)	0.28*** (0.04)	0.29*** (0.04)	−0.20*** (0.01)
Intercept	−1.16*** (0.26)	−1.00*** (0.29)	−1.09*** (0.27)	1.53*** (0.05)
Num. obs.	639	538	604	604

$***p < 0.01, **p < 0.05, *p < 0.1$. The table reports the results from OLS regressions in which the dependent variable in Columns 1–3 is the number of job groups that a DO progressed from 2007–2012, and the dependent variable in Column 4 is whether a DO was still employed by 2012.

8.7 SUMMARY

This chapter examined the management of the Provincial Administration under President Kibaki. As under Moi's electoral regime, the greatest popular threat that Kibaki faced was reelection. Kibaki officially won reelection, thanks in part to the actions of the Provincial Administration that both co-opted Kibaki's co-ethnic Kikuyus and coerced the opposition, especially in unaligned areas. I find that the center strategically posted and shuffled bureaucrats to increase compliance where it mattered most. I also examined promotion patterns to analyze whether certain bureaucrats were favored for promotion. In line with my theory, Kibaki's co-ethnic Kikuyu administrators were more likely to advance – as were administrators of jurisdictions that experienced pro-government violence after the 2007 election. Taken together, this chapter illustrates the politicized management of bureaucrats in the Provincial Administration and the favoritism that helped reinforce bureaucrats' politicized behavior.

9

Conclusion

The state is a powerful tool that a leader can use to guard against both elite and popular threats. By incorporating elites into the state and allowing them and their followers to benefit from the state, the leader reduces his rivals' drive to challenge him. Separately, the state can prevent popular threats: bureaucrats can vary the implementation of their mandate to either co-opt residents in their jurisdiction to maintain their popular support or coerce residents and prevent their mobilization against the leader.

These two uses of the state – to prevent elite or popular threats – are seemingly at odds with each other, however. Incorporating rival elites requires diversifying the state, because elites demand state positions for their followers. But bureaucratic compliance with politicized orders that protect the leader from popular threats is thought to be highest among the leader's in-group and lowest among bureaucrats loyal to rival elites.

I develop a theory about the strategic management of bureaucrats in contexts of weak monitoring to solve *both* elite and popular threats. My argument proceeds in two steps. First, and since elite threats are often more dangerous for regime stability, I argue that leaders who incorporate elites will diversify hiring into the state. The leader attempts to mitigate the resulting principal-agent problem and induce compliance from some out-group members through patronage, but most leaders do not have sufficient funds to buy all out-group members.[1] Second, and given the inability to pack the state with loyal bureaucrats (whether through in-group status or patronage), a leader will post and shuffle bureaucrats

---

[1] And many leaders are reticent to allow all bureaucrats to predate at high levels.

across jurisdictions based on the relationships between himself, an individual bureaucrat, and the area in which the bureaucrat serves, as well as the relative importance of different areas within the context of the country's regime type.

The theory yields multiple predictions that the book examines systematically. First, the ethnic composition of the state will reflect patterns of elite incorporation.[2] Second, since not all bureaucrats are equally loyal, the center will assign the bureaucrats who are perceived to be the most loyal to the most strategically valuable areas. In autocratic regimes, these are misaligned areas, in which popular threats are liable to originate, and aligned areas, which constitute the leader's base of popular support and legitimacy. In many electoral regimes, aligned and unaligned areas are considered the most strategically valuable. Aligned areas give the leader high levels of support, and some support in unaligned (swing) areas is often needed to win an election. The center will keep bureaucrats perceived as disloyal away from strategically valuable areas.

Third, the leader will also alter each bureaucrat's level of local embeddedness, depending on whether he intends to co-opt or coerce a particular area. Co-optation is facilitated by posting in-group bureaucrats and lengthening their tenure. The strong social bonds that in-group and long-serving bureaucrats develop with locals compels the official to improve the livelihoods of residents even absent monitoring from the center. To ensure compliance with orders to coerce, the leader posts out-group bureaucrats for shorter tenures, since lower levels of embeddedness prevent the formation of social bonds that might encourage an official to disobey such orders.

I present evidence from the Kenyan case to support my theory. I study the country's most important bureaucracy, the Provincial Administration, using a variety of data sources including the quantitative analysis of some 15,000 officer postings. I find that this bureaucracy has never been packed by a president's co-ethnics, including during the country's autocratic years when presidents exercised strong executive control over the state. And each president was only able to develop financial bonds with a small minority of administrators. Yet I show that each of Kenya's first three leaders relied heavily on this bureaucracy to help him stay in office. Each president maximized compliance where it mattered most by strategically managing bureaucrats throughout the country. The results follow the pre-

---

[2] The following hypotheses assume an unpacked state.

dictions of the theory, across both autocratic and electoral regimes and for presidents who had different bases of support and opposition, which suggests the theory's applicability across a variety of contexts.

In an extension in Chapter 8, I also examine promotions in contexts where monitoring compliance is possible. Bureaucrats whose jurisdictions experienced (highly-visible) political violence during Kenya's 2007–2008 postelection violence were more likely to be promoted after the violence abated. A leader benefits from promoting bureaucrats who (mis)used their authority on his behalf; those promoted to higher ranks have shown their loyalty, and their advancement serves as a signal to others that loyalty is rewarded.

In the rest of this concluding chapter I apply the theory to other contexts, showing its applicability to cases that are similar to Kenya as well as to those outside the scope conditions. I then discuss avenues for future research and the broader policy implications of the project.

9.1 MOVING PAST THE SCOPE CONDITIONS: APPLYING THE THEORY TO OTHER CASES

The argument developed and tested in the previous chapters applies to other countries that have a salient identity cleavage and weak parties. The scope condition pertaining to identity gives the main actors in the theory – the leader, a bureaucrat, and residents in the area in which a bureaucrat is posted – strong and credible signals about the preferences of the other actors. The scope condition pertaining to party strength weakens the center's ability to monitor bureaucrats and limits the leader's credibility in following through with promises to co-opt groups outside his own.[3]

In joint work with Brett Carter, I show the striking similarly in the management of Kenya's PCs and DCs to the management of prefects in the Republic of Congo – Brazzaville, a country where the ruling party is weak outside its base of support and a salient identity cleavage based on region (Carter and Hassan Forthcoming).[4] President Dennis Sassou

---

[3] The theory's third scope condition pertains to the leader's ability to direct management of the bureaucracy. It is strict – I do not expect bureaucratic management in countries in which a leader (or trusted advisor) does not have control over the bureaucratic corps to be able to strategically manage bureaucrats. Though I recognize that this condition runs on a continuum (the higher a leader's level of control over the bureaucracy, the greater his ability to strategically manage bureaucrats to meet his political goals), I do not examine cases that fall completely outside this scope condition.

[4] Also see Carter (n.d.).

Nguesso has stayed in power, in part, due to the actions of his prefects. These bureaucrats are formally expected to implement national-level policies within their respective administrative regions, but informally, they vary their mandate and co-opt or coerce based on the alignment of local residents. In the Republic of Congo – Brazzaville, as in Kenya, there is a lack of packing despite Sassou-Nguesso's strong executive power. His identity in-group are those from his home region of Cuvette, but only 35 percent of prefects since 1997 have hailed from this region.

Further, the level of bureaucratic embeddedness varies by region. Cuvette and other aligned regions could expect nearly 80 percent of their prefects to be natives from the region.[5] However, misaligned regions were assigned nonnative prefects more than 50 percent of the time. We attribute this variation in management strategies to the likelihood of a popular threat emerging in different parts of the country. Popular threats are unlikely in aligned areas due to a self-reinforcing cycle of state co-optation and continued local support, while they are a real possibility in misaligned areas, where prefects must always be ready to coerce locals.

Evidence of bureaucratic management from other cases suggests that my theory can also be adapted to countries that fall outside the scope conditions. In Sections 9.1.1 and 9.1.2, I provide an overview of research on the management of the executive bureaucracy in contemporary Russia and China. Given their size, international importance, and the role of the state in keeping each regime afloat, applying the theory to these two cases is a valuable test of its external validity. Both cases also fall (partly) outside of both scope conditions, suggesting the theory's ability to travel, with minor adjustments. And both countries are also (nominally) federal. Applying the theory to different levels of government shows how a principal, at any tier of government, is liable to strategically manage agents in response to political threats in a similar fashion to national executives as suggested by the theory.

9.1.1 Management of Officials in Russia

Russia does not neatly fit either of the theory's first two scope conditions. It is home to more than 160 different ethnic group, but identity cleavages

---

5 The dataset covers 1997–2010. See Carter and Hassan (Forthcoming).

are much less salient there than in the Kenyan case in large part because nearly 80 percent of the population is ethnically Russian. That said, ethnicity is salient for the country's ethnic minority groups and in jurisdictions in which they comprise a significant portion of the population. The ruling hegemonic United Russia party dominates multiparty elections at the national and regional levels (Reuter 2017).

The management of regional governors and vice governors in Russia follows many of the predictions of the theory. Governors were appointed by the Kremlin from 2005–2012 and elected during other periods. Russian governors have functions similar to those of bureaucrats within Kenya's Provincial Administration, including the maintenance of law and order and oversight of policy implementation. Vice governors are in charge of specific policy domains within a given region (e.g., Vice Governor for Education) and are appointed by governors with little interference from Moscow (Buckley and Reuter 2019).

The application of the theory is clearest to see in the handful of regions with a large non-ethnic Russian population, many of which were classified as "republics" under the Soviet Union in recognition of their ethnic differences. After the end of the Cold War, many former republics became among the most hostile to – or, to put it in terms of the theory, misaligned with – Moscow. Some even launched separatist movements. The Kremlin has responded with high levels of coercion, especially in the North Caucasus (Taylor 2011; Toft and Zhukov 2015). In line with the theory's predictions about how the Kremlin should manage governors to coerce misaligned regions, governors in regions that were more than 30 percent non-ethnic Russian had shorter tenures than their counterparts in regions with a higher percentage of ethnic Russians (Reisinger and Moraski 2013). Holding other factors constant, a 1-percent increase in the percentage of a region that is non-Russian is correlated with a 0.4-percent increase in the likelihood that a governor will not be reappointed (Reisinger and Moraski 2013).

We see managerial practices in line with the theory even in regions where ethnicity is less salient and the most important political goals are winning elections rather than stopping insurgencies. Governors and vice governors play a critical role in elections because they are expected to act as political field agents who monitor the opposition and build clientelistic machines. The unofficial role of executive bureaucrats in Russia, winning elections, is inconsistent with one of their primary (official) roles – increasing economic development:

even the most capable subnational official will find it hard to combine building a political machine and pursuing economic development. This is because the combination of corruption, prebendalism, and patronage spending needed to build a political machine that can deliver the vote is also likely to have deleterious effects on the economy. (Reuter and Robertson, 2012, 1025)

Research on vice governors, who are appointed by the governor, demonstrates the conditions under which principals privilege co-optation through economic development versus coercion through the creation of a political machine, and extends the theory to regional leaders within a federation. The theory would expect a regional governor to manage vice governors in an attempt to temper political threats to himself. Buckley and Reuter (2019) examine reappointment rates of vice governors whose official portfolios were related to regional economic development. They compare "competitive authoritarian" regions (i.e., those in which the opposition has a good chance of winning seats) to autocratic regions (i.e., those that United Russia dominates). They find that vice governors are less likely to be reappointed in competitive authoritarian regions due to the risks of embeddedness.

Interestingly, despite the similarity to my empirical results from Kenya, research on Russian officials emphasizes a slightly different mechanism: embeddedness is lowered in competitive areas to reduce a vice governor's ability to become a political elite who can challenge the leader. Vice governors with an economic portfolio and access to financial resources are the most likely to cultivate their own political followings and create their own political machines. The risk is that the vice governor could take her followers to a political opponent of the governor. However, this logic suggests that reappointment rates for vice governors are higher in areas where United Russia is dominant. In these regions, governors, who are appointed by the Kremlin and are thus part of United Russia, do not have to worry about the increasing clout of vice governors.

The research on Russian officials also suggests that principals take into account visible displays of loyalty and competence when making reappointment decisions, similar to the findings related to promotions in the wake of Kenya's 2007–2008 postelection violence. Governors were more likely to be reappointed if they produced electoral gains for United Russia (Reuter and Robertson 2012). This finding is replicated at the local level: mayors from 2001–2012 who helped improve the performance of United Russia at higher levels of political office were more likely to keep their position (Reuter et al. 2016). These findings suggest that leaders use important political moments as both performance metrics and loyalty tests. Governors who displayed a willingness and ability to help the center were rewarded, in part to encourage future governors to use their authority on behalf of the center.

Comparing the Russian case with that of Kenya allows us to refine certain aspects of the theory. To begin, the Russian case reiterates the important theoretic distinction between autocratic and electoral regimes. A principal manages bureaucrats differently based on the type of threat the population poses to him. While I show this point over time, there is evidence of it across sub-national federal regions in Russia based on the level of electoral competition. Further, Russia's federal system suggests how governors balance competing pressures. Governors want to be reappointed by Moscow, and thus have a strong incentive to manage their regions well and appoint competent vice governors. But the most able vice governors may prove too politically risky precisely because they can manage an economic portfolio well. Similarly, this point reiterates the logic of why aligned areas do better economically. Since these areas do not constitute a political risk, leaders have the luxury of managing them in an attempt to best increase economic development.

9.1.2 Management of Officials in China

China falls outside of the scope conditions of the theory as well, and yet much of the logic laid out in Chapter 2 demonstrates parallels to the empirical realities of its approach to cadre management. As in Russia, China is both largely homogenous and home to many different ethnic groups: it officially recognizes fifty-five ethnic minorities, but is more than 90 percent Han Chinese. Identity cleavages are salient in areas dominated by minority populations, but are peripheral for much of the country. The Chinese Communist Party (CCP) is strong; much of the country exhibits a high degree of party saturation (Koss 2018).

Hiring and promotion decisions work in much the same way they do in Kenya if we replace "ethnicity" with "faction." In the Kenyan case, I describe how citizens often rely on co-ethnic political elites to help get an initial state job and later earn a promotion. In China, a bureaucrat's factional ties affect her management. CCP political elites often cultivate factional ties with bureaucrats who, for instance, attended the same education institutions or worked together.[6] A political elite will lobby on

---

[6] Lieberthal and Oksenberg (1988) as seen in Shih et al. (2012). In some instances, factional ties are identity based (e.g., those between individuals from the same province or town).

behalf of bureaucrats in her faction to raise her own personal standing and guard against threats from rival elites. In return, the supporting bureaucrat owes deference to the elite and expects to benefit if her faction leader is promoted (Nathan 1973; Shih, Adolph, and Liu 2012). This reliance on factions to fill state positions suggests that no General Secretary is willing to pack the state with only his own factional ties. Instead, each leader has allowed other CCP elites to influence hiring, likely in an attempt to alleviate potential elite threats. At the same time, bureaucrats benefit from seeing their faction leader come to power: those with factional ties to a particular General Secretary were more likely to see a change in their rank percentile during the years in which their factional leader was in power (Shih et al. 2012).

The strategic posting of bureaucrats was a main focus of this book's empirical chapters, but there is little quantitative work on the potential strategic management of Chinese bureaucrats.[7] However, research on posting patterns finds that the center can manage bureaucrats to temper popular threats through upward promotions. Party leaders in China have attempted to temper popular unrest through an unprecedented campaign of economic development since the late 1970s. The goal has been to reduce the underlying discontent among the population, despite limited political freedoms, by increasing their standard of living. In line with this goal, principals in China have explicitly linked bureaucrats' performance reviews to economic indicators of their jurisdiction.[8] Economically vibrant coastal regions are thus likely to be the most strategically important for Beijing, since improvements in performance in economic hubs will have an outsized impact on national growth. Indeed, several studies have found that these areas are more likely to be governed by bureaucrats who have shown their ability to improve growth.[9] This finding is in line with the logic in Chapter 2 once we consider the center's economic goals as political.

---

7 The conventional wisdom on cadre advancement in China, as I discuss below, is that cadres who deliver good economic growth are promoted. Yet Shih et al. (2012, 166) note that, "no qualitative or quantitative work addresses the potential selection bias that would arise if politically connected officials could influence the location of their next appointments to claim credit for preexisting growth trends."

8 Unsurprisingly, the focus on official economic growth indicators has led to bureaucrats to manipulate these statistics (Wallace 2016).

9 See, for instance, Lia and Zhou (2005); Landry (2008); Landry, Lu, and Duan (2015), and Jia, Kudamatsu, and Seim (2015).

Separately, research on bureaucratic embeddedness follows some, but not all, of the theory's predictions. The Chinese state, since the Qing Dynasty, has weighed the benefits and pitfalls of embeddedness. For much of the work on cadre management in China, the largest drawback of embeddedness is not necessarily the bureaucrat's willingness to coerce, as I describe in Kenya, or the possibility that the bureaucrat becomes an agent of a local political elite, as in the Russian case. Instead, the Chinese regime fears that a locally embedded bureaucrat will become too corrupt. Lowering embeddedness in this way comes at the expense of local development, which is in line with my theory:

> In its drive to rejuvenate the cadre corps and combat corruption, the Party's informal response is to accelerate turnover among mayors. This tactic seems to have taken precedence over the need to allow officials who perform to remain in place long enough to make a measurable impact in most places. (Landry 2008, 114)

I find that Kenyan leaders were willing to allow local embeddedness in some areas to reap its benefits even at the risk of some officer predation. Yet in China, the drive to limit corruption is so strong that there is a hard rule of term limits; many bureaucrats are rotated before they finish their term (Landry 2008), and a strong "law of avoidance" prevents rotated officials from serving in their home jurisdiction. One potential reason for this variation in attitudes towards embeddedness is party strength. In China, where the party and state are often seen as one, the negative behavior of a state official reflects on the entire party. If citizens perceive the state and party as fused, then predation by bureaucrats is liable to decrease popular support for the party. Further, given the implicit social contract in China, which promises higher economic growth at the expense of political freedoms, the center may be more reluctant to engage in corruption in order to uphold their end of the bargain.

9.2 AVENUES FOR FUTURE RESEARCH

This book's in-depth account of the strategic management of the Kenyan state suggests new avenues for future research on bureaucracy, regime survival, and citizen interactions with the state. I elaborate on two such avenues – the conditions under which bureaucracies (de)politicize, and the effect of bureaucratic management on service delivery.

9.2.1 Depoliticizing the State?

An implicit assumption throughout this book is that the state is politicized. Politicized states are necessarily high in "despotic power," or what the state can do "without routine, institutionalized negotiation with civil society groups" (Mann 1984, 54): a leader strategically posts and shuffles bureaucrats to meet political goals instead of broad policy concerns. But politicization also requires compliance from bureaucrats who themselves have some expectation of advancement due to neopatrimonial ties. A leader only sees value in strategically managing bureaucrats if bureaucrats believe that acting outside the Weberian rational-legal ideal advances their careers. Yet not all states are equally politicized. And perhaps more importantly for policy, the level of politicization within a state can change over time.

One variable that the empirical emphasis on Kenya suggests may change a state's degree of politicization is a country's overall level of democratic consolidation. To be sure, the relationship between democratic consolidation and the depoliticization of the state has received considerable attention in the literature.[10] Prominent work suggests that states will become more rational-legal as democracies consolidate. For instance, former Soviet satellite states that allowed robust party competition after the collapse of the Soviet Union were less likely to politicize the bureaucracy (Grzymała-Busse 2007). At the same time, others find that the politicization of the state continues under electoral competition. Electoral regimes may find it difficult to pass administrative reforms (Geddes 1994), and politicians have weak incentives to enforce the reforms that do get passed (Cruz and Keefer 2015). This is in part because politicians benefit from bypassing meritocratic recruitment and placing their supporters in important positions (Sigman 2017).

Interviews from my field research provide suggestive evidence that competitive elections are reducing bureaucrats' willingness to act as agents of the central government through several different mechanisms. Foremost among them, the potential for real turnover at the top has made many bureaucrats unwilling to carry out politicized directives, whether explicitly stated or implicitly expected, because they do not want to be perceived as an agent of the potentially outgoing president and thus risk their future bureaucratic career. Other administrators discussed the active role of civil society in reporting bureaucrats who misuse their position

---

[10] See Brierley (Forthcoming) for a review of this debate.

for politics in the current era; technological advances have given citizens parallel systems with which to report bureaucrats and publicize deviations from formal duties, so many bureaucrats perceive the costs of using their authority on behalf of a politician as now too high.[11] One administrator I interviewed linked these changes explicitly to electoral competition more generally – since 1992, presidents have been "forced to now propose these [administrative] reforms for the sake of saving the institution. Because there was a lot of pressure from civil society, from the NGOs, the foreign countries with their presence here for changing Kenya. It was the multiparty move."[12] Another discussed the institutionalization of the agency in the 2010 constitution (which also renamed it the National Administration) and subsequently through legislation: "See, the new constitution has been able to anchor the National Administration in law. Unlike in the past when it existed under the president's pleasure, now it's law. So we are more secure and less politicized. Our very existence is secured by law."[13]

Other administrators felt lower levels of politicization in the Kenyan state, but questioned whether their agency could truly be free of political interference. One bureaucrat claimed that agency elites recognized the increased domestic and international scrutiny of the Provincial Administration. In response, the agency has attempted to depoliticize many of its everyday actions (or at least better hide them). The administrator continued, saying that many within the agency thought of themselves as the president's reserve forces: "[the] machinery is still there with our resolve. We are a snake in the grass. We know our boss [meaning the president] and can be mobilized ... If he so wishes."[14] In prior work, I described how this agency stressed its unique role in providing security to maintain a strong relationship with the president despite formal measures intended to weaken that bond and depoliticize it.[15] Still others explained that the public will always think of the Provincial Administration as politicized because it implements policy that has been legislated by a political party: "[the Provincial Administration] has always been politicized because it implements the agenda of the government of the day. Whether we like it or not, all governments are political. So if you are spreading the agenda of the

---

[11] Interview with then DO, July 17, 2017, Machakos, Kenya.
[12] Interview with then DC, June 30, 2017, Nairobi, Kenya.
[13] Interview with then DC, June 9, 2018, Nairobi, Kenya.
[14] Interview with then DC, August 2, 2017, Nairobi.
[15] Hassan (2015).

government of the day how can you not claim to be not be political when you are promoting the interests of a political government?"[16] Since the Provincial Administration lacks the autonomy to design its own policies, it will likely continue to be perceived as the arm of the president at the grassroots.

These interviews also suggested other potential explanations of changes in the level of politicization of the Provincial Administration, and states more generally. For instance, they mentioned that the bureaucratic culture does not change automatically after formal, legalistic changes to administrative codes are enacted. But they also suggested that formal codes do play a role. This discussion also encourages us to think about how levels of politicization are reproduced within organizations, whether by new recruits who came into the profession with strong prior beliefs or by experienced officials who attempt to stymie changes to how the agency operates. These lines of inquiry are especially important as they promise to guide future policy. To the extent that rational-legal norms are good for economic growth,[17] it is imperative that we understand how to design new administrative changes.

9.2.2 Bureaucrats, Service Delivery, and Organizational Change

The issues discussed in this book have implications for improving service delivery, especially in the developing world. Aid to sub-Saharan Africa from the Organisation for Economic Cooperation and Development alone topped $54 billion in 2016, and yet development outcomes there have remained lackluster. Development agencies have blamed these poor outcomes on the weak capacity of recipient countries. In response, the development community has sought to introduce strategies to improve bureaucratic accountability in aid recipients. Many of these strategies involve decreasing bureaucratic autonomy through improved monitoring and contracting on outcomes.[18] These strategies recognize the principal-agent problem inherent in bureaucracy and try to offset the negative effects of delegation. Yet they have had lackluster success in the developing world; recent research has begun to suggest why. Monitoring in

---

[16] Interview with then DC, June 8, 2018, Nairobi.
[17] See Evans and Rauch (1999) for the link between rational-legal norms and growth, as well as Ang (2017) for a refutation of this logic.
[18] Many of these practices stem from ideas about New Public Management. See Hood (1995).

itself is politicized, and therefore can lead to unwanted or unintended outcomes.[19] And performance contracts are difficult to get right and are often incomplete because the work of field bureaucrats in many developing countries is so unpredictable (Honig 2018).

The book's findings instead suggest that countries can improve bureaucratic performance by empowering bureaucrats to recognize the ways in which their work benefits the local community they serve. Bureaucrats who feel socially connected will be more willing to go beyond the formal mandate of their office and to perform at high levels even if their superiors in the chain of command are not monitoring their actions. Taken together, this discussion suggests that governments should recognize the difficulties inherent in working through bureaucrats, and try to accentuate the positive aspects of delegation instead of reducing the negatives. Recent research is moving in this direction. For instance, Ang (2016) shows how China escaped the poverty trap by relying on local bureaucrats to innovate solutions that built and preserved markets. Relying on embedded bureaucrats had its downfalls: they were able to predate, other bureaucrats generated solutions that were specific to a locality, and policy varied across areas. But the center was able to crowdsource different solutions and determine which ones to implement on a larger scale. Others have shown that bureaucrats whose mission aligns with those of the organization are more effective at their job (e.g., Besley and Ghatak 2005).

These discussions leave several questions unanswered regarding other environmental and personal variables that affect important governance outcomes, such as local team dynamics. This book has highlighted the importance of the social bonds between a bureaucrat and local residents in the jurisdiction in which she serves. Just as important, however, is the relationship that bureaucrats develop with other bureaucrats in the jurisdiction. Trained bureaucrats in the Provincial Administration and officials in other executive bureaucracies are rotated across stations. These bureaucrats are expected to coordinate and oversee policies implemented by other bureaucrats.[20] An administrator's ability to perform well thus depends on her relationship with the bureaucrats she oversees and her overall "fit" with the local bureaucratic culture. Further, bureaucracies with rotating agents may allow us to examine organizational change.

---

[19] For instance, see Gulzar and Pasquale (2017), Raffler (2019), and Brierley (Forthcoming).
[20] This can include both bureaucrats who rotate from relevant service ministries and stationary bureaucrats who operate in the same jurisdiction for their entire careers.

As bureaucrats rotate across stations with different relational contracts, we can observe how bureaucratic culture changes in response – either as a function of administrators who are rotated in and have an outsized impact on the locality, or because administrators take up practices from a locality and spread them to their next station. Examining these questions, and others that this book has brought to light, demands that we take bureaucrats seriously.

Bibliography

Adar, Korwa, and Isaac Munyae. 2001. "Human Rights Abuse in Kenya under Daniel Arap Moi, 1978–2001." *African Studies Quarterly* 5(1):1–17. https://asq.africa.ufl.edu/adar_munyae_winter01/.

Adida, Claire, Nathan Combes, Adeline Lo, and Alex Verink. 2016. "The Spousal Bump: Do Cross-Ethnic Marriages Increase Political Support in Multiethnic Democracies?" *Comparative Political Studies* 49(5):635–661.

Africa Watch. 1993. *Divide and Rule: State-Sponsored Ethnic Violence in Kenya.* New York: Human Rights Watch.

Aghion, Philippe, and Jean Tirole. 1997. "Formal and Real Authority in Organizations." *Journal of Political Economy* 105(1):1–29.

Ajulu, Rok. 1998. "Kenya's Democracy Experiment: The 1997 Elections." *Review of African Political Economy* 25(76):275–285.

Ajulu, Rok. 2002. "Politicised Ethnicity, Competitive Politics and Conflict in Kenya: A Historical Perspective." *African Studies* 61:251–268.

Akivaga, Symonds Kichamu, Wanyama Kulundu-Bitonye, and Martin W. Opi. 1985. *Local Authorities in Kenya.* Nairobi: Heinemann Educational Books.

Akiwumi, Hon. Mr. Justice A. M. 1999. *Report of the Judicial Commission Appointed to Inquire into Tribal Clashes in Kenya.* Nairobi: Government of Kenya.

Albertus, Michael. 2015. *Autocracy and Redistribution: The Politics of Land Reform.* Cambridge: Cambridge University Press.

Albertus, Michael, Sofia Fenner, and Daniel Slater. 2018. *Coercive Distribution.* (Cambridge: Cambridge University Press).

Albertus, Michael, and Victor Menaldo. 2012. "Coercive Capacity and the Prospects for Democratization." *Comparative Politics* 44(2):151–169.

Albertus, Michael, and Victor Menaldo. 2018. *Authoritarianism and the Elite Origins of Democracy.* Cambridge: Cambridge University Press.

Anderson, David. 2005a. *Histories of the Hanged: The Dirty War in Kenya and the End of Empire.* New York: W. W. Norton and Company.

Anderson, David. 2005b. "'Yours in the Struggle for Majimbo.' Nationalism and the Party Politics of Decolonization in Kenya, 1955–64." *Journal of Contemporary History* 40(3):547–564.

Anderson, David. 2014. "Remembering Wagalla: State Violence in Northern Kenya, 1962–1991." *Journal of Eastern African Studies* 8(4):658–676.

Anderson, David, and Emma Lochery. 2008. "Violence and Exodus in Kenya's Rift Valley: Predictable and Preventable?" *Journal of Eastern African Studies* 2(2):328–343.

Ang, Yuen Yuen. 2016. *How China Escaped the Poverty Trap*. Ithaca, NY: Cornell University Press.

Ang, Yuen Yuen. 2017. "Beyond Weber: Conceptualizing an Alternative Ideal Type of Bureaucracy in Developing Contexts." *Regulation and Governance* 11(3):282–298.

Arriola, Leonardo R. 2009. "Patronage and Political Stability in Africa." *Comparative Political Studies* 42(10):1339–1362.

Arriola, Leonardo R. 2012. *Multiethnic Coalitions in Africa: Business Financing of Opposition Election Campaigns*. New York: Cambridge University Press.

Arriola, Leonardo R. 2013. "Protesting and Policing in a Multiethnic Authoritarian State: Evidence from Ethiopia." *Comparative Politics* 45(2):147–168.

Baker, Bruce. 1998. "The Class of 1990: How Have the Autocratic Leaders of sub-Saharan Africa Fared under Democratisation?" *Third World Quarterly* 19(1):115–127.

Balcells, Laia, and Christopher M. Sullivan. 2018. "New Findings from Conflict Archives: An Introduction and Methodological Framework" *Journal of Peace Research* 55(2):137–146.

Ballard-Rosa, Cameron. 2016. "Hungry for Change: Urban Bias and Autocratic Sovereign Default." *International Organization* 70(2):313–346.

Barkan, Joel D. 1993. "Kenya: Lessons from a Flawed Election." *Journal of Democracy* 4(3):85–99.

Barkan, Joel D. 2008. "Legislatures on the Rise?" *Journal of Democracy* 19(2):124–137.

Barkey, K. 1994. *Bandits and Bureaucrats: The Ottoman Route to State Centralization*. New York: Columbia University Press.

Bates, Robert H. 1981. *Markets and States in Tropical Africa: The Political Bases of Agricultural Policies*. Berkeley: University of California Press.

Bates, Robert H. 1989. *Beyond the Miracle of the Market: The Political Economy of Agrarian Development in Kenya*. Cambridge University Press.

Bayart, Jean-Francois. 1993. *The State in Africa: The Politics of the Belly*. London: Longman.

Bellin, Eva. 2004. "The Robustness of Authoritarianism in the Middle East: Exceptionalism in Comparative Perspective." *Comparative Politics* 36(2):139–157.

Bellin, Eva. 2012. "The Robustness of Authoritarianism Reconsidered: Lessons of the Arab Spring." *Comparative Politics* 44(2):127–149.

Berman, Bruce. 1992. *Control and Crisis in Colonial Kenya: The Dialectic of Domination*. Nairobi: East African Publishers.

Berman, Bruce, and John Lonsdale. 1992. *Unhappy Valley: Conflict in Kenya & Africa*. Athens, OH: Ohio University Press.

Besley, Timothy. 2006. *Principled Agents? The Political Economy of Good Government*. Oxford: Oxford University Press.

Besley, Timothy, and Maitreesh Ghatak. 2005. "Competition and Incentives with Motivated Agents." *American Economic Review* 95(3):616–636.

Besley, Timothy, and Torsten Persson. 2009. "The Origins of State Capacity: Property Rights, Taxation, and Politics." *American Economic Review* 99(4):1218–1244.

Bethke, Felix S. 2012. "The Consequences of Divide-and-Rule Politics in Africa South of the Sahara." *Proceedings of the 12th Jan Tinbergen European Peace Science Conference* 18(3):1–13.

Bhavnani, Rikhil R., and Alexander Lee. 2018. "Local Embeddedness and Bureaucratic Performance: Evidence from India." *The Journal of Politics* 80(1): 71–87.

Blacker, John. 2007. "The Demography of Mau Mau: Fertility and Mortality in Kenya in the 1950s: A Demographer's Viewpoint." *African Affairs* 106: 205–207.

Blaydes, Lisa. 2011. *Elections and Distributive Politics in Mubarak's Egypt*. Cambridge University Press.

Blaydes, Lisa. 2018. *State of Repression: Iraq under Saddam Hussein*. Cambridge University Press.

Bleck, Jamie, and Nicolas van de Walle. 2018. *Electoral Politics in Africa since 1990: Continuity in Change*. Cambridge University Press.

Bogaards, Matthijs. 2009. "How to Classify Hybrid Regimes? Defective Democracy and Electoral Authoritarianism." *Democratization* 16(2):399–423.

Boix, Carles. 2003. *Democracy and Redistribution*. Cambridge University Press.

Boix, Carles, Michael Miller, and Sebastian Rosato. 2013. "A Complete Data Set of Political Regimes, 1800–2007." *Comparative Political Studies* 46(12):1523–1554.

Boix, Carles, and Milan Svolik. 2013. "The Foundations of Limited Authoritarian Government: Institutions, Commitment, and Power-Sharing in Dictatorships." *The Journal of Politics* 75(2):300–316.

Boone, Catherine. 2003. *Political Topographies of the African State*. New York: Cambridge University Press.

Boone, Catherine. 2011. "Politically Allocated Land Rights and the Geography of Electoral Violence: The Case of Kenya in the 1990s." *Comparative Political Studies* 44(10):1311–1342.

Boone, Catherine. 2012. "Land Conflict and Distributive Politics in Kenya." *African Studies Review* 55(1):75–103.

Boone, Catherine. 2014. *Property and Political Order in Africa: Land Rights and the Structure of Politics*. New York: Cambridge University Press.

Boone, Catherine, and Michael Wahman. 2015. "Rural Bias in African Electoral Systems: Legacies of Unequal Representation in African Democracies." *Electoral Studies* 40: 335–346.

Branch, Daniel. 2009. *Defeating Mau Mau, Creating Kenya*. Cambridge University Press.

Branch, Daniel. 2011. *Kenya: Between Hope and Despair, 1963–2011.* New Haven: Yale University Press.

Branch, Daniel, and Nic Cheeseman. 2006. "The Politics of Control in Kenya: Understanding the Bureaucratic-Executive State, 1952–78." *Review of African Political Economy* 33(107):11–21.

Brass, Jennifer. 2016. *Allies or Adversaries: NGOs and the State in Africa.* Cambridge University Press.

Bratton, Michael, and Mwangi S. Kimenyi. 2008. "Voting in Kenya: Putting Ethnicity in Perspective." *Journal of Eastern African Studies* 2(2):272–289.

Bratton, Michael, and Nicholas van de Walle. 1992. "Popular Protest and Political Reform in Africa." *Comparative Politics* 24(4):419–442.

Bratton, Michael, and Nicholas van de Walle. 1994. "Neopatrimonial Regimes and Political Transitions in Africa." *World Politics* 46(4):453–489.

Bratton, Michael, and Nicholas van de Walle. 1997. *Democratic Experiments in Africa: Regime Transitions in Comparative Perspective.* New York: Cambridge University Press.

Brierley, Sarah. Forthcoming. "Patronage, Meritocracy and Political Party Machines." Working paper, Washington University in St. Louis.

Brierley, Sarah. Forthcoming. "Unprincipled Principals: Co-opted Bureaucrats and Corruption in Local Governments in Ghana." Working paper, Washington University in St. Louis.

Briggs, Ryan C. 2014. "Aiding and Abetting: Project Aid and Ethnic Politics in Kenya." *World Development* 64:194–205.

Brown, David. 1994. *The State and Ethnic Politics in Southeast Asia.* New York: Routledge.

Brown, Stephen. 2006. "Theorising Kenya's Protracted Transition to Democracy." *Journal of Contemporary African Studies* 22(3):325–342.

Brownlee, Jason. 2002. "... And Yet They Persist: Explaining Survival and Transition in Neopatrimonial Regimes." *Studies in Comparative International Development* 37(3):35–63.

Brownlee, Jason. 2007. *Authoritarianism in an Age of Democratization.* Cambridge University Press.

Buckley, Noah, and Ora John Reuter. 2019. "Performance Incentives under Autocracy: Evidence from Russia's Regions." *Comparative Politics* 51(2):239–266.

Burbidge, Dominic. 2019. *An Experiment in Devolution: National Unity and the Deconstruction of the Kenyan State.* Nairobi: Strathmore University Press.

Burgess, Robin, Remi Jedwab, Edward Miguel, and Ameet Morjaria. 2015. "The Value of Democracy: Evidence from Road Building in Kenya." *American Economic Review* 105(6):1817–1851.

Cammett, Melanie, and Sukriti Issar. 2010. "Bricks and Mortar Clientelism: Sectarianism and the Logics of Welfare Allocation in Lebanon." *World Politics* 62(3):381–421.

Carey, Sabine C. 2006. "The Dynamic Relationship between Protest and Repression." *Political Research Quarterly* 59(1):1–11.

Carter, Brett L. n.d. *Building a Dictatorship: Denis Sassou Nguesso, the Republic of Congo, and Africa's Third Wave of Democracy.* Unpublished manuscript, University of Southern California.

Carter, Brett L. and Mai Hassan. Forthcoming. "The Political Geography of the Local Security Apparatus." *The Journal of Politics.* University of Southern California and the University of Michigan.

Chabal, Patrick and Jean-Pascal Daloz. 1999. *Africa Works: Disorder as Political Instrument.* Bloomington: Indiana University Press.

Cheeseman, Nic. 2010. "African Elections as Vehicles for Change." *Journal of Democracy* 21(4):139–153.

Cheibub, Jose Antonio, Jennifer Gandhi, and James Raymond Vreeland. 2010. "Democracy and Dictatorship Revisited." *Public Choice* 143(1–2):67–101.

Clapham, Christopher. 1985. *Third World Politics: An Introduction.* Madison: University of Wisconsin Press.

Cottrell, Jill, and Yash Ghai. 2007. "Constitution making and democratization in Kenya (2000–2005)." *Democratisation* 14(1):1–25.

Cruz, Cesi, and Philip Keefer. 2015. "Political Parties, Clientelism, and Bureaucratic Reform." *Comparative Political Studies* 48(14):1942–1973.

Currie, Kate, and Larry Ray. 1986. "The Pambana of August 1 - Kenya's Abortive Coup." *The Political Quarterly* 57(1):47–59.

Davenport, Christian. 2007. "State Repression and Political Order." *Annual Review of Political Science* 10:1–23.

Davenport, Christian, and David A. Armstrong. 2004. "Democracy and the Violation of Human Rights: A Statistical Analysis from 1976 to 1996." *American Journal of Political Science* 48(3):538–554.

Davenport, Christian (ed.) 2000. *Paths to State Repression: Human Rights Violations and Contentious Politics.* Lanham, MD: Rowman and Littlefield.

Davey, Ken J. 1971. "Local Bureaucracies and Politicians in East Africa." *Public Administration* 10(4):268–279.

Debs, Alexandre. 2007. On dictatorships. PhD thesis, Massachusetts Institute of Technology.

Decalo, S. 2012. *Africa: The Lost Decades.* Gainesville: Florida Academic Press.

Decalo, Samuel. 1990. *Coups and Army Rule in Africa: Motivations and Constraints.* New Haven: Yale University Press.

De Juan, Alexander, Fabian Krautwald, and Jan H. Pierskalla. 2017. "Constructing the State: Macro Strategies, Micro Incentives, and the Creation of Police Forces in Colonial Namibia." *Politics and Society* 45(2):269–299.

Deng, Yanhua, and Kevin J. O'Brien. 2013. "Relational repression in China: Using social ties to demobilize protesters." *The China Quarterly* 215: 533–552.

Diamond, Jared M. 1998. *Guns, Germs, and Steel: A Short History of Everybody for the Last 13,000 Years.* New York: Vintage.

Diaz-Cayeros, Alberto, Federico Estévez and Beatrice Magaloni. 2016. *The Political Logic of Poverty Relief: Electoral Strategies and Social Policy in Mexico.* Cambridge University Press.

Dyzenhaus, Alex. 2018. "Property Rights and Electoral Coalitions in Kenya." Unpublished paper, Cornell University.

Eaton, Sarah, and Genia Kostka. 2014. "Authoritarian Environmentalism Undermined? Local Leaders' Time Horizons and Environmental Policy Implementation." *The China Quarterly* 218:359.

El-Battahani, Atta El-Hassan, and Hassan Ali Gadkarim. 2017. Governance and Fiscal Federalism in Sudan, 1989–2015: Exploring Political and Intergovernmental Fiscal Relations in an Unstable Polity. Bergen: Chr. Michelsen Institute. Technical Report.

Elischer, Sebastian. 2013. *Political Parties in Africa*. Cambridge University Press.

Elkins, Caroline. 2005. *Britain's Gulag: The Brutal End of Empire in Kenya*. London: Jonathan Cape.

Enloe, Cynthia. 1973. *Ethnic Conflict and Political Development*. Boston: Little, Brown and Company.

Epstein, David, and Sharyn O'Halloran. 1994. "Administrative Procedures, Information, and Agency Discretion." *American Journal of Political Science* 38(3):697–722.

Evans, Peter B. 1995. *Embedded Autonomy: States and Industrial Transformation*. Princeton University Press.

Evans, Peter, and James E. Rauch. 1999. "Bureaucracy and Growth: A Cross-National Analysis of the Effects of "Weberian" State Structures on Economic Growth." *American Sociological Review* 64(5):748–765.

Falk, Armin, and Michael Kosfeld. 2006. "The Hidden Costs of Control." *American Economic Review* 96(5):1611–1630.

Fearon, James. 2003. "Ethnic and Cultural Diversity by Country" *Journal of Economic Growth* 8(2):195–222.

Fearon, James D., and David D. Laitin. 2003. "Ethnicity, Insurgency, and Civil War." *American Political Science Review* 97(1):75–90.

Ferlie, Ewan, Louise Fitzgerald, and Andrew Pettigrew. 1996. *The New Public Management in Action*. New York: Oxford University Press.

Ferree, Karen. 2010. "The Social Origins of Electoral Volatility in Africa." *British Journal of Political Science* 40(4):759–779.

Ferree, Karen E., Clark C. Gibson, and James D. Long. 2014. "Voting Behavior and Electoral Irregularities in Kenya's 2013 Election." *Journal of Eastern African Studies* 8(1):153–172.

Fesler, James. 1965. "Approaches to the Understanding of Decentralization." *The Journal of Politics* 27(3):536–566.

Fox, Roddy. 1996. "Bleak Future for Multi-Party Elections in Kenya." *The Journal of Modern African Studies* 34(4):597–607.

Franck, Raphael, and Ilia Rainer. 2012. "Does the Leader's Ethnicity Matter? Ethnic Favoritism, Education, and Health in Sub-Saharan Africa." *American Political Science Review* 106(2):294–325.

Francois, Patrick, Ilia Rainer, and Francesco Trebbi. 2015. "How Is Power Shared in Africa?" *Econometrica* 83(2):465–503.

Frantz, Erica, and Andrea Kendall-Taylor. 2014. "A Dictator's Toolkit: Understanding How Co-optation Affects Repression in Autocracies." *Journal of Peace Research* 51(3):332–346.

Frey, Bruno. 1993. "Shirking or Work Morale?: The Impact of Regulating." *European Economic Review* 37(8):1523–1532.

Gailmard, Sean, and John Patty. 2012. "Formal Models of Bureaucracy." *Annual Review of Political Science* 15:353–377.

Gandhi, Jennifer. 2008. *Political Institutions under Dictatorship*. Cambridge University Press.

Gandhi, Jennifer, and Adam Przeworski. 2007. "Authoritarian Institutions and the Survival of Autocrats." *Comparative Political Studies* 40(11):1279–1301.

Gandhi, Jennifer, and Ellen Lust-Okar. 2009. "Elections under Authoritarianism." *Annual Review of Political Science* 12: 403–422.

Gandhi, Jennifer, and Grant Buckles. 2017. "Opposition Unity and Cooptation in Hybrid Regimes." Working paper, Emory University.

Geddes, Barbara. 1994. *Politician's Dilemma: Building State Capacity in Latin America*. Berkeley: University of California Press.

Geddes, Barbara. 1999. "What Do We Know about Democratization after Twenty Years?" *Annual Review of Political Science* 2(1):115–144.

Gehlbach, Scott, Konstantin Sonin, and Milan Svolik. 2016. "Formal Models of Nondemocratic Politics." *Annual Review of Political Science* 19: 565–584.

Gertzel, Cherry. 1970. *The Politics of Independent Kenya, 1963-8*. Nairobi: East African Publishing House.

Gibbons, Robert, and Rebecca Henderson. 2012. "Relational Contracts and Organizational Capabilities." *Organizational Science* 23(5):1350–1364.

Gibson, Clark C., and James D. Long. 2009. "The Presidential and Parliamentary Elections in Kenya, December 2007." *Electoral Studies* 28(3):497–502.

Giglio, Louis, Jacques Descloitres, Christopher O. Justice, and Yoram J. Kaufman. 2003. "An Enhanced Contextual Fire Detection Algorithm for MODIS." *Remote Sensing of Environment* 87(2–3):273–282.

Ginsburg, Tom, and Tamir Moustafa, eds. 2008. *Rule by Law: The Politics of Courts in Authoritarian Regimes*. Cambridge University Press.

Greene, Kenneth F. 2009. *Why Dominant Parties Lose: Mexico's Democratization in Comparative Perspective*. Cambridge University Press.

Greitens, Sheena Chestnut. 2016. *Dictators & Their Secret Police: Coercive Institutions & State Violence Under Authoritarianism*. New York: Cambridge University Press.

Grossman, Guy, and Janet Lewis. 2014. "Administrative Unit Proliferation." *American Political Science Review* 108(1): 196–207.

Grzymała-Busse, Anna. 2002. *Redeeming the Communist Past: The Regeneration of Communist Successor Parties*. Cambridge University Press.

Grzymała-Busse, Anna. 2007. *Rebuilding Leviathan: Party Competition and State Exploitation in Post-Communist Democracies*. Cambridge University Press.

Gulzar, Saad, and Benjamin J. Pasquale. 2017. "Politicians, Bureaucrats, and Development: Evidence from India." *American Political Science Review* 111(1):162–183.

Hafner-Burton, Emilie M., Susan D. Hyde, and Ryan S. Jablonski. 2014. "When Do Governments Resort to Election Violence?" *British Journal of Political Science* 44(01):149–179.

Hanson, Margaret. 2018. "Managing the Predatory State: Civil Courts and Authoritarian Stability." Working paper, Arizona State University.

Harbeson, John W. 1971. "Land Reforms and Politics in Kenya, 1954–70." *Journal of Modern African Studies* 9(2):231–251.

Harkness, Kristen A. 2016. "The Ethnic Army and the State: Explaining Coup Traps and the Difficulties of Democratization in Africa." *The Journal of Conflict Resolution* 60(4):587–616.

Harkness, Kristen A. 2018. *When Soldiers Rebel: Ethnic Armies and Political Instability in Africa*. Cambridge University Press.

Harms, Robert W. 1974. "Abir: The Rise and Fall of a Rubber Empire." Master's thesis, University of Wisconsin - Madison.

Harris, J. Andrew, and Daniel Posner. 2019. "(Under What Conditions) Do Politicians Reward Their Supporters? Evidence From Kenya's Constituencies Development Fund." *American Political Science Review* 113:123–139.

Harris, Kirk A. 2016. "Kenya's Constituency Development Fund and the Politics of Resource Allocation." Working paper, Susquehanna University.

Hashim, Ahmed. 2003. "Saddam Husayn and Civil-Military Relations in Iraq: The Quest for Legitimacy and Power." *Middle East Journal* 57(1):9–41.

Hassan, Mai. 2015. "Continuity Despite Change: Kenya's New Constitution and Executive Power." *Democratization* 22(4):587–609.

Hassan, Mai. 2016. "A State of Change: District Creation in Kenya after the Return of Multi-Party Elections." *Political Research Quarterly* 69(3): 510–521.

Hassan, Mai. 2017. "The Strategic Shuffle: Ethnic Geography, the Internal Security Apparatus, and Elections in Kenya." *American Journal of Political Science* 61(2):382–295.

Hassan, Mai, and Ryan Sheely. 2017. "Executive-Legislative Relations, Party Defections, and Lower-Level Administrative Unit Proliferation: Evidence from Kenya." *Comparative Political Studies* 50(12):1595–1631.

Hassan, Mai, and Thomas O'Mealia. 2018. "Uneven Accountability in the Wake of Political Violence: Evidence from Kenya's Ashes and Archives." *Journal of Peace Research* 55(2):161–174.

Helmke, Gretchen, and Frances Rosenbluth. 2009. "Regimes and the Rule of Law: Judicial Independence in Comparative Perspective." *Annual Review of Political Science* 12:345–366.

Helmke, Gretchen, and Steven Levitsky. 2004. "Informal Institutions and Comparative Politics: A Research Agenda." *Perspectives on Politics* 2(4):725–740.

Herbst, Jeffrey. 1990. "The Structural Adjustment of Politics in Africa." *World Development* 18(7):949–958.

Herbst, Jeffrey I. 2000. *States and Power in Africa: Comparative Lessons in Authority and Control*. Princeton University Press.

Hodler, R., and P.A. Raschky. 2014. "Regional Favoritism." *Quarterly Journal of Economics* 129(2):995–1033.

Holland, Alisha C. 2017. *Forbearance as Redistribution: The Politics of Informal Welfare in Latin America*. Cambridge University Press.

Honig, Dan. 2018. *Navigation by Judgment: Why and When Top Down Management of Foreign Aid Doesn't Work*. New York: Oxford University Press.

Hood, Christopher. 1995. "The 'New Public Management' in the 1980s: Variations on a Theme." *Accounting, Organizations and Society* 20(2–3):93–109.

Hope, Kempe Ronald. 2012. "Managing the Public Sector in Kenya: Reform and Transformation for Improved Performance." *Journal of Public Administration and Governance* 2(4):128–143.

Hornsby, Charles. 2011. *Kenya: A History since Independence*. London: I.B. Tauris.

Horowitz, Donald. 1985. *Ethnic Groups in Conflict*. Berkeley: University of California Press.

Horowitz, Jeremy. 2012. "Campaigns and Ethnic Polarization in Kenya." PhD thesis, University of California, San Diego.

Horowitz, Jeremy. 2016. "The Ethnic Logic of Campaign Strategy in Diverse Societies: Theory and Evidence from Kenya." *Comparative Political Studies* 49(3):324–356.

Howard, Marc Morjè, and Philip G. Roessler. 2006. "Liberalizing Electoral Outcomes in Competitive Authoritarian Regimes." *American Journal of Political Science* 50(2):365–381.

Huang, Yasheng. 2002. "Managing Chinese Bureaucrats: An Institutional Economics Perspective." *Political Studies* 50(1):61–79.

Huber, John D., and Cecilia Martinez-Gallardo. 2008. "Replacing Cabinet Ministers: Patterns of Ministerial Stability in Parliamentary Democracies." *American Political Science Review* 102(2):169–180.

Huber, John D., and Charles R. Shipan. 2002. *Deliberate Discretion?: The Institutional Foundations of Bureaucratic Autonomy*. Cambridge University Press.

Human Rights Watch. 2008. *Ballots to Bullets: Organized Political Violence and Kenya's Crisis of Governance*. New York: Human Rights Watch 20(1).

Huntington, Samuel P. 1968. *Political Order in Changing Societies*. New Haven: Yale University Press.

Hyden, Goran. 1984. "Administration and Public Policy." In Barkan, Joel D. ed., *Politics and Public Policy in Kenya and Tanzania*. Nairobi: Heinemann, pp. 103–124.

Jablonski, Ryan S. 2014. "How Aid Targets Votes: The Impact of Electoral Incentives on Foreign Aid Distribution." *World Politics* 66(2):293–330.

Jackson, Robert H., and Carl Gustav Rosberg. 1982. *Personal Rule in Black Africa*. Berkeley: University of California Press.

Jacob, Herbert. 1963. *German Administration since Bismarck: Central Authority versus Local Autonomy*. New Haven: Yale University Press.

Jia, Ruixue, Masayuki, Kudamatsu, and David Seim. 2015. "Political Selection in China: The Complementary Role of Connections and Performance." *Journal of the European Economic Association* 13(4):631–668.

Josse-Durand, Chloé. 2018. "The Political Role of 'Cultural Entrepreneurs' in Kenya: Claiming Recognition through the Memorialisation of Koitalel Samoei and Nandi Heritage." *African Studies* 77(2):257–273.

Kagwanja, Peter Mwangi. 2001. "Politics of Marionettes: Extra-Legal Violence and the 1997 Elections in Kenya." In Rutten, Marcel, Alamin Mazrui, and François Grignon, eds., *Out for the Count: The 1997 Elections and Prospects for Democracy in Kenya*. Kampala: Fountain Publishers, pp. 72–100.

Kalyvas, Stathis N. 2006. *The Logic of Violence in Civil War.* New York: Cambridge University Press.

Kanogo, Tabatha. 1987. *Squatters and the Roots of Mau Mau, 1905-63.* Athens, OH: Ohio University Press.

Kanyinga, Karuti. 1995. "The Politics of Development Space in Kenya." In Therkildsen, Ole, and Joseph Semboja, eds., *Service Provision under Stress in East Africa: The State, NGOs, and People's Organizations in Kenya, Tanzania, and Uganda.* London: James Currey, pp. 70–86.

Kanyinga, Karuti. 1998. "Contestation Over Political Space: The State and the Demobilization of Opposition Politics in Kenya." In Olukoshi, Adebayo O., ed., *The Politics of Opposition in Contemporary Africa.* Stockholm: Elanders Gotab, pp. 39–90.

Kanyinga, Karuti. 2000a. "Mix and Match Party and Persons." In Rutten, Marcel, Alamin Mazrui, and François Grignon, eds., *Out for the Count: The 1997 Elections and Prospects for Democracy in Kenya.* Kampala: Fountain Publishers, pp. 365–381.

Kanyinga, Karuti. 2000b. *Redistribution from Above: The Politics of Land Rights and Squatting in Coastal Kenya.* Research Report No. 115. Motala, Sweden: Motala Grafiska. http://nai.diva-portal.org/smash/get/diva2:271584/FULLTEXT01

Kanyinga, Karuti. 2009. "The Legacy of the White Highlands: Land Rights, Ethnicity and the Post-2007 Election Violence in Kenya." *Journal of Contemporary African Studies* 27(3):325–344.

Kasara, Kimuli. 2006. "Ethnic Beachheads and Vote Buying: The Creation of New Administrative Districts in Kenya, 1963-2001." Working paper, Columbia University.

Kasara, Kimuli. 2007. "Tax Me If You Can: Ethnic Geography, Democracy, and the Taxation of Agriculture in Africa." *American Political Science Review* 101:159–172.

Kasara, Kimuli. 2016. "Electoral Geography and Conflict: Examining the Redistricting through Violence in Kenya." Working paper, Columbia University.

Kaufman, Herbert. 1960. *The Forest Ranger.* Washington, DC: Resources for the Future.

Kenya Truth, Justice and Reconciliation Commission. 2013. *Report of the Truth, Justice and Reconciliation Commission.* Nairobi: Truth, Justice and Reconciliation Commission. Technical report.

Kershaw, Greet. 1997. *Mau Mau from Below.* London: James Currey Publishers.

Kimenyi, Mwangi S., and Njuguna S. Ndung'u. 2005. "Sporadic Ethnic Violence: Why Has Kenya Not Experienced a Full-Blown Civil War?" In Collier, Paul, and Nicholas Sambanis, eds., *Understanding Civil War: Evidence and Analysis* (vol. 1, pp. 123–157). Washington, DC: World Bank Publications.

Kimenyi, Mwangi S., and Roxana Gutierrez Romero. 2008. "Identity, Grievances, and Economic Determinants of Voting in the 2007 Kenyan Elections." Economics Working paper, University of Connecticut and University of Oxford.

Kimenyi, Mwangi S., and William F. Shughart. 2010. "The Political Economy of Constitutional Choice: A Study of the 2005 Kenyan Constitutional Referendum." *Constitutional Political Economy* 21(1):1–27.

King, Gary, Jennifer Pan, and Margaret E. Roberts. 2013. "How Censorship in China Allows Government Criticism but Silences Collective Expression." *American Political Science Review* 107(2):326–343.

Kirk-Greene, A. H. M. 1980. "The Thin White Line: The Size of the British Colonial Service in Africa." *African Affairs* 79(314):25–44.

Klaus, Kathleen. 2016. "Land Security and Civilian Victimization during Electoral Violence: Evidence from Kenya." Paper presented at the Annual Meeting of the American Political Science Association.

Klaus, Kathleen. 2020. *Political Violence in Kenya: Land, Elections, and Claim-Making*. Cambridge University Press.

Klopp, Jacqueline. 2001. "Electoral Despotism in Kenya: Land, Patronage and Resistance in the Multi-Party Context." PhD thesis, McGill University.

Klopp, Jacqueline M. 2002. "Can Moral Ethnicity Trump Political Tribalism? The Struggle for Land and Nation in Kenya." *African Studies* 61(2):269–294.

Koss, Daniel. 2018. *Where the Party Rules: The Rank and File of China's Communist State*. Cambridge University Press.

Kramon, Eric, and Daniel N. Posner. 2011. "Kenya's New Constitution." *Journal of Democracy* 22(2):89–103.

Kramon, Eric, and Daniel N. Posner. 2016. "Ethnic Favoritism in Primary Education in Kenya." *Quarterly Journal of Political Science* 11(1):1–58.

Kroeger, Alex. 2018. "Dominant Party Rule, Elections, and Cabinet Instability in African Autocracies." *British Journal of Political Science*. DOI: https://doi.org/10.1017/S0007123417000497

Kunt, Metin. 1968. *The Sultan's Servants: The Transformation of Ottoman Provincial Government, 1550–1650*. New York: Columbia University Press.

Landry, Pierre F. 2008. *Decentralized Authoritarianism in China*. Cambridge University Press.

Landry, Pierre F., Xiaobo Lu, and Haiyan Duan. 2015. "Does Performance Matter? Evaluating Political Selection along the Chinese Administrative Ladder." *Comparative Political Studies* 51:1074–1105.

Lazarev, Valery. 2005. "Economics of One-Party State: Promotion Incentives and Support for the Soviet Regime." *Comparative Economic Studies* 47(2): 346–363.

LeBas, Adrienne. 2011. *From Protest to Parties: Party-Building and Democratization in Africa*. New York: Oxford University Press.

Leonard, David K. 1991. *African Successes: Four Public Managers of Kenyan Rural Development*. Berkeley: University of California Press.

Lessing, Benjamin. 2017. *Making Peace in Drug Wars: Crackdowns and Cartels in Latin America*. Cambridge University Press.

Levitsky, Steven, and Lucan A. Way. 2010. *Competitive Authoritarianism: Hybrid Regimes after the Cold War*. New York: Cambridge University Press.

Lewis, Ioan M. 1963. "The Problem of the Northern Frontier District of Kenya." *Race* 5(1):48–60.

Lewis, Janet. 2017. "How Does Ethnic Rebellion Start?" *Comparative Political Studies* 50(10):1420–1450.

Leys, Colin. 1975. *Underdevelopment in Kenya*. Nairobi: East African Publishers.

Lia, Hongbin, and Li-An Zhou. 2005. "Political Turnover and Economic Performance: The Incentive Role of Personnel Control in China." *Journal of Public Economics* 89:1743–1762.

Lichbach, Mark Irving. 1998. *The Rebel's Dilemma*. Ann Arbor: University of Michigan Press.

Lieberthal, Kenneth, and Michel Oksenberg. 1988. *Policy Making in China: Leaders, Structures, and Processes*. Princeton University Press.

Lipsky, Michael. 1980. *Street-Level Bureaucracy: Dilemmas of the Individual in Public Services*. New York: Russell Sage Foundation.

Lowes, Sara, and Eduardo Montero. 2016. "Concessions, Violence, and Indirect Rule: Evidence from the Congo Free State." Working paper, Harvard University.

Lust-Okar, Ellen. 2006. "Elections under Authoritarianism: Preliminary Lessons fron Jordan." *Democratization* 13(3):456–471.

Lyall, Jason. 2010. "Are Coethnics More Effective Counterinsurgents? Evidence from the Second Chechen War." *American Political Science Review* 104(1): 1–20.

Lynch, Gabrielle. 2006a. "The Fruits of Perception: 'Ethnic Politics' and the Case of Kenya's Constitutional Referendum." *African Studies* 65(2):233–270.

Lynch, Gabrielle. 2006b. "Negotiating Ethnicity: Identity Politics in Contemporary Kenya." *Review of African Political Economy* 33(107):49–65.

Lynch, Gabrielle. 2011a. *I Say to You: Ethnic Politics and the Kalenjin in Kenya*. University of Chicago Press.

Lynch, Gabrielle. 2011b. "The Wars of Who Belongs Where: The Unstable Politics of Autochthony on Kenya's Mt Elgon." *Ethnopolitics* 10(3–4):391–410.

Lynch, Gabrielle, and Gordon Crawford. 2011. "Democratization in Africa 1990–2010: An Assessment." *Democratization* 18(2):275–310.

Magaloni, Beatriz. 2006. *Voting for Autocracy: Hegemonic Party Survival and Its Demise in Mexico*. Cambridge University Press.

Magaloni, Beatriz. 2008. "Credible Power-Sharing and the Longevity of Authoritarian Rule." *Comparative Political Studies* 41(4–5):715–741.

Magaloni, Beatriz, and Ruth Kricheli. 2010. "Political Order and One-Party Rule." *Annual Review of Political Science* 13:123–143.

Makara, Michael. 2013. "Coup-Proofing, Military Defection, and the Arab Spring." *Democracy and Security* 9(4):334–359.

Malesky, Edmund, and Paul Schuler. 2010. "Nodding or Needling: Analyzing Delegate Responsiveness in an Authoritarian Parliament." *American Political Science Review* 104(3):482–502.

Mamdani, Mahmood. 1996. *Citizen and Subject: Contemporary Africa and the Legacy of Late Colonialism*. Princeton University Press.

Manion, Melanie. 2015. *Information for Autocrats: Representation in Chinese Local Congresses*. Cambridge University Press.

Mann, Michael. 1984. "The Autonomous Power of the State: Its Origins, Mechanisms and Results." *European Journal of Sociology/Archives Européennes de Sociologie* 25(2):185–213.

Marinov, Nikolay, and Hein Goemans. 2014. "Coups and Democracy." *British Journal of Political Science* 44:799–825.

Mboya, Tom. 1970. *The Challenge of Nationhood: A Collection of Speeches and Writings*. Nairobi: Heinemann International Inc.

Mburu, Nene. 2005. *Bandits on the Border: The Last Frontier in the Search for Somali Unity*. Trenton, NJ: The Red Sea Press, Inc.

McCarthy, John D., and Mayer N. Zald. 1977. "Resource Mobilization and Social Movements: A Partial Theory." *American Journal of Sociology* 82(6): 1212–1241.

McCulloch, Neil, and Edmund Malesky. 2014. "What Determines the Quality of Subnational Economic Governance? Comparing Indonesia and Vietnam." In Hill, Hal, ed., *Regional Dynamics in a Decentralized Indonesia*. Singapore: Institute of Southeast Asian Studies, pp. 208–230.

McLauchlin, Theodore. 2010. "Loyalty Strategies and Military Defection in Rebellion." *Comparative Politics* 42(3):333–350.

Meier, Kenneth John, and Lloyd G. Nigro. 1976. "Representative Bureaucracy and Policy Preferences: A Study in the Attitudes of Federal Executives." *Public Administration Review* 36(4):458–469.

Meng, Anne. 2019. "Accessing the State: Executive Constraints and Credible Commitment in Dictatorship." *Journal of Theoretical Politics* 31(4): 568–599.

Meng, Anne. 2018. "Leadership Succession in Modern Autocracies." Working paper, University of Virginia.

Migdal, Joel S. 1988. *Strong Societies and Weak States*. Princeton University Press.

Miyazaki, Ichisada. 1976. *China's Examination Hell: The Civil Service Examinations of Imperial China*. New Haven: Yale University Press.

Morjaria, Ameet. 2018. "Democracy and the Environment: Evidence from Kenya." Working paper, Northwestern University.

Morse, Yonatan L. 2012. "The Era of Electoral Authoritarianism." *World Politics* 64(1):161–198.

Mueller, Susanne. 1984. "Government and Opposition in Kenya, 1966–9." *The Journal of Modern African Studies* 22(3):399–427.

Munck, Gerardo L. 2006. "How to Craft Intermediate Regime Categories." In Schedler, Andreas, ed., *Electoral Authoritarianism: The Dynamics of Unfree Competition*. Boulder, CO: Lynne Rienner Publishers, pp. 27–40.

Murunga, Godwin R., and Shadrack W. Nasong'o. 2006. "Bent on Self-Destruction: The Kibaki Regime in Kenya." *Journal of Contemporary African Studies* 24(1):1–28.

Nathan, Andrew J. 1973. "A Factionalism Model for CCP Politics." *The China Quarterly* 53:34–66.

Nathan, Andrew J. 2003. "Authoritarian Resilience." *Journal of Democracy* 14(1):6–17.

Nathan, Noah. 2019. *Electoral Politics and Africa's Urban Transition.* Cambridge University Press.

Ndegwa, Stephen N. 1996. *The Two Faces of Civil Society: NGOs and Politics in Africa.* West Hartford, CT: Kumarian Press.

Ndegwa, Stephen N. 1997. "Citizenship and Ethnicity: An Examination of Two Transition Moments in Kenyan Politics." *American Political Science Review* 91(3):599–616.

Ndung'u, Paul. 2004. *Report of the Commission of Inquiry into the Illegal/Irregular Allocation of Public Land.* Nairobi: Government of Kenya.

Nepstad, Sharon Erickson. 2013. "Mutiny and Nonviolence in the Arab Spring: Exploring Military Defections and Loyalty in Egypt, Bahrain, and Syria." *Journal of Peace Research* 50(3):337–349.

Ng'ethe, Njuguna. 1991. *In Search of NGOs: Towards a Funding Strategy to Create NGO Research Capacity in Eastern and Southern Africa.* Nairobi: Institute for Development Studies, University of Nairobi.

Ng'ethe, Njuguna, and Joel D Barkan. 1998. "Kenya Tries Again." *Journal of Democracy* 9(2):32–48.

Nielsen, Richard. 2013. "Rewarding Human Rights? Selective Aid Sanctions against Repressive States." *International Studies Quarterly* 57:791–803.

Njonjo, Apollo L. 1977. *The Africanisation of the 'White Highlands': A Study in Agrarian Class Struggles in Kenya, 1950–1974.* Princeton University Press.

Obong'o, Sylvester Odhiambo. 2009. "Implementation of Performance Contracting in Kenya." *International Public Management Review* 10:66–84.

O'Dwyer, Conor. 2006. *Runaway State-Building: Patronage Politics and Democratic Development.* Baltimore, MD: Johns Hopkins University Press.

Okoth-Ogendo, H. W. O. 1972. "The Politics of Constitutional Change in Kenya since Independence, 1963-69." *African Affairs* 71(282):9–34.

Okoth-Ogendo, H. W. O. 1991. *Tenants of the Crown: Evolution of Agrarian Law and Institutions in Kenya.* Nairobi: African Centre for Technology Studies Press.

Olken, Benjamin A., and Rohini Pande. 2012. "Corruption in Developing Countries." *Annual Review of Economics* 4:479–509.

Ombongi, Kenneth. 2000. "Gusii Politics: An Analysis for the 1997 Elections." In Rutten, Marcel, Alamin Mazrui, and François Grignon, eds., *Out for the Count: The 1997 Elections and Prospects for Democracy in Kenya.* Kampala: Fountain Publishers, pp. 471–494.

Onoma, Ato Kwamena. 2010. *The Politics of Property Rights Institutions in Africa.* Cambridge University Press.

Opalo, K. Ochieng'. 2019. *Legislative Development in Africa: Politics and Postcolonial Legacies.* Cambridge University Press.

Opalo, Kennedy. 2014. "The Long Road to Institutionalization: The Kenyan Parliament and the 2013 Elections." *Journal of Eastern African Studies* 8(1):63–77.

Osborne, Myles. 2015. *Ethnicity and Empire in Kenya: Loyalty and Martial Race among the Kamba, c. 1800 to Present.* Cambridge University Press.

Oyugi, W. Ouma, ed. 1994. *Politics and Administration in East Africa.* Nairobi: English Press.

Padro i Miquel, G. T. 2007. "The Control of Politicians in Divided Societies: The Politics of Fear." *The Review of Economic Studies* 74(4):1259–1274.

Parsons, T. 2012. "Being Kikuyu in Meru: Challenging the Tribal Geography of Colonial Kenya." *Journal of African History* 53:65–86.

Parsons, Timothy. 2003. *The 1964 Army Mutinies and the Making of Modern East Africa*. Santa Barbara, CA: Greenwood Publishing Group.

Parsons, Timothy. 2011. "Local Responses to the Ethnic Geography of Colonialism in the Gusii Highlands of British-Ruled Kenya." *Ethnohistory* 58(3):491–523.

Pepinsky, Thomas B., Jan H. Pierskalla, and Audrey Sacks. 2017. "Bureaucracy and service delivery." *Annual Review of Political Science* 20:249–268.

Pierskalla, Jan, and Audrey Sacks. 2016. "Personnel Politics: Elections, Clientelistic Competition and Teacher Hiring in Indonesia." *British Journal of Political Science*. DOI: https://doi.org/10.1017/S0007123418000601

Pierskalla, Jan H., Alexander De Juan, and Max Montgomery. 2017. "The Territorial Expansion of the Colonial State: Evidence from German East Africa 1890–1909." *British Journal of Political Science* 49(2):711–737.

Pitcher, Anne, Mary H. Moran, and Michael Johnston. 2009. "Rethinking Patrimonialism and Neopatrimonialism in Africa." *African Studies Review* 52(1):125–156.

Policzer, Pablo. 2009. *The Rise and Fall of Repression in Chile*. Notre Dame, IN: University of Notre Dame Press.

Popkin, Samuel. 1979. *The Rational Peasant: The Political Economy of Rural Society in Vietnam*. Berkeley: University of California Press.

Popova, Maria. 2010. "Political Competition as an Obstacle to Judicial Independence: Evidence From Russia and Ukraine." *Comparative Political Studies* 43(10):1202–1229.

Posner, Daniel. 2005. *Institutions and Ethnic Politics in Africa*. Cambridge University Press.

Prendergast, Canice. 2007. "The Motivation and Bias of Bureaucrats." *American Economic Review* 97(1):180–196.

Quinlivan, James T. 1999. "Coup-Proofing: Its Practice and Consequences in the Middle East." *International Security* 24(2):131–165.

Raffler, Pia. 2019. "Does Political Oversight of the Bureaucracy Increase Accountability? Field Experimental Evidence from an Electoral Autocracy." Working paper, Yale University.

Rasul, Imran, and Daniel Rogger. 2018. "Management of Bureaucrats and Public Service Delivery: Evidence from the Nigerian Civil Service." *The Economic Journal* 128(608):413–446.

Rasul, Imran, Daniel Rogger, and Martin J. Williams. 2018. "Management and Bureaucratic Effectiveness: Evidence from the Ghanaian Civil Service (English)." Policy Research working paper; no. WPS 8595. Washington, D.C. : World Bank Group. http://documents.worldbank.org/curated/en/335361537384686708/Management-and-Bureaucratic-Effectiveness-Evidence-from-the-Ghanaian-Civil-Service

Reisinger, William M., and Byron J. Moraski. 2013. "Deference or Governance? A Survival Analysis of Russia's Governors under Presidential Control." In Reisinger, William M., ed., *Russia's Regions and Comparative Subnational Politics*. London: Routledge, pp. 40–52.

Reuter, Ora John. 2017. *The Origins of Dominant Parties: Building Authoritarian Institutions in Post-Soviet Russia*. Cambridge University Press.

Reuter, Ora John, and Graeme Robertson. 2012. "Subnational Appointments in Authoritarian Regimes: Evidence from Russian Gubernatorial Appointments." *Journal of Politics* 74(4):1023–1037.

Reuter, Ora John, Noah Buckley, Alexandra Shubenkova, and Guzel Garifullina. 2016. "Local Elections in Authoritarian Regimes: An Elite-Based Theory with Evidence from Russian Mayoral Elections." *Comparative Political Studies* 49(5):662–697.

Riedl, Rachel Beatty. 2014. *Authoritarian Origins of Democratic Party Systems in Africa*. Cambridge University Press.

Riedl, Rachel Beatty, and J. Tyler Dickovick. 2013. "Party Systems and Decentralization in Africa." *Studies in Comparative International Development* 49(3):321–342.

Robertson, Graeme. 2010. *The Politics of Protest in Hybrid Regimes: Managing Dissent in Post-Communist Russia*. Cambridge University Press.

Robinson, James A., and Ragnar Torvik. 2009. "The Real Swing Voter's Curse." *American Economic Review* 99(2):310–315.

Roessler, Philip G. 2017. *Ethnic Politics and State Power in Africa: The Logic of the Coup-Civil War Trap*. New York: Cambridge University Press.

Rozenas, Arturas, and Yuri Zhukov. 2019. "Mass Repression and Political Loyalty: Evidence from Stalin's 'Terror by Hunger'." *American Political Science Review* 113(2):569–583.

Saha, S. 2014. "Iran's Situations: Military Violence Protests, & Group Dynamics." PhD thesis, Harvard University.

Salehyan, Idean, Cullen S. Hendrix, Jesse Hamner, Christina Case, Christopher Linebarger, Emily Stull, and Jennifer Williams. 2012. "Social Conflict in Africa: A New Database." *International Interactions* 38(4):503–511.

Sambanis, Nicholas. 2004. "What Is Civil War? Conceptual and Empirical Complexities of an Operational Definition." *Journal of Conflict Resolution* 48(6):814–858.

Sassoon, Joseph. 2011. *Saddam Hussein's Ba'th Party: Inside an Authoritarian Regime*. New York: Cambridge University Press.

Savage, Donald C., and J. Forbes Munro. 1966. "Carrier Corps Recruitment in the British East Africa Protectorate 1914–1918." *The Journal of African History* 7(2):313–342.

Schatzberg, M. G. 1988. *The Dialectics of Oppression in Zaire*. Bloomington, IN: Indiana University Press.

Schedler, Andreas. 2002. "The Menu of Manipulation." *Journal of Democracy* 13(2):36–50.

Schmitter, Philippe C., and Terry Lynn Karl. 1990. "What Democracy Is … and Is Not." *Journal of Democracy* 2(3):75–88.

Scott, James C. 1998. *Seeing Like a State: How Certain Schemes to Improve the Human Condition Have Failed*. New Haven: Yale University Press.

Shen-Bayh, Fiona. 2018. "Strategies of Repression: Judicial and Extrajudicial Methods of Autocratic Survival." *World Politics* 70(3):321–357.

Shih, Victor, Christopher Adolph, and Mingxing Liu. 2012. "Getting Ahead in the Communist Party: Explaining the Advancement of Central Committee Members in China." *American Political Science Review* 106(1):166–187.

Shikuku, Joseph Martin. n.d. *The People's Watchman: The Life of Martin Shikuku*. Edited by Derek R. Peterson. Unpublished manuscript.

Sigman, Rachel. 2017. "Which Jobs for Which Boys? Patronage for Political Finance." Working paper, Naval Postgraduate School.

Singh, Naunihal. 2014. *Seizing Power: The Strategic Logic of Military Coups*. Baltimore, MD: Johns Hopkins University Press.

Skocpol, Theda. 1985. "Bringing the State Back In: Strategies of Analysis in Current Research." In Evans, Peter B., Dietrich Rueschmeyer, and Theda Skocpol, eds., *Bringing the State Back In*. New York: Cambridge University Press, pp. 3–38.

Slater, Dan. 2003. "Iron Cage in an Iron Fist: Authoritarian Institutions and the Personalization of Power in Malaysia." *Comparative Politics* 36(1):81–101.

Slater, Dan. 2010. *Ordering Power: Contentious Politics and Authoritarian Leviathans in Southeast Asia*. Cambridge University Press.

Slater, Dan, and Sofia Fenner. 2011. "State Power and Staying Power: Infrastructural Mechanisms and Authoritarian Durability." *Journal of International Affairs* 65(1):15–29.

Smith, Benjamin. 2006. "The Wrong Kind of Crisis: Why Oil Booms and Busts Rarely Lead to Authoritarian Breakdown." *Studies in Comparative International Development* 40(4):55–76.

Smith, Brian Clive. ed. 1967. *Field Administration: An Aspect of Decentralisation*. London: Routledge & K. Paul.

Svolik, Milan W. 2012. *The Politics of Authoritarian Rule*. Cambridge University Press.

Tajfel, Henri, and John C. Turner. 1979. "An Integrative Theory of Intergroup Conflict." In Worchel, Stephen, and William G. Austin, eds., *The Social Psychology of Intergroup Relations*. Monterey, CA: Brooks/Cole, pp. 33–47.

Tamarkin, M. 1978. "The Roots of Political Stability in Kenya." *African Affairs* 77(308):297–320.

Tarrow, Sidney G. 2011. *Power in Movement: Social Movements and Contentious Politics*. Cambridge University Press.

Taylor, Brian D. 2011. *State Building in Putin's Russia*. Cambridge University Press.

Thomson, Henry. 2018. "Grievance Attribution, Mobilization and Mass Opposition to Authoritarian Regimes: Evidence from June 1953 in the GDR." *Comparative Political Studies* 51(12):1594–1627.

Thomson, Henry. 2019. *Food and Power: Regime Type, Agricultural Policy, and Political Stability.* Cambridge University Press.

Thomson, Henry, Halvard Buhaug, Elisabeth Rosvold, and Henrik Urdal. 2019, January 29. "Elections, Democracy and Urban Political Mobilization in the Developing World." Tempe, AZ: ASU Center for the Study of Economic Liberty Research Paper No. 18-5. Available at SSRN: https://ssrn.com/abstract=3054750 or http://dx.doi.org/10.2139/ssrn.3054750

Throup, David. 1987. *Economic and Social Origins of Mau Mau: 1947–1953.* Oxford University Press.

Throup, David. 1993. "Elections and Political Legitimacy in Kenya." *Africa: Journal of the International African Institute* 63(3):371–396.

Throup, David, and Charles Hornsby. 1998. *Multi-Party Politics in Kenya: The Kenyatta and Moi States and the Triumph of the System in the 1992 Election.* Athens, OH: Ohio University Press.

Tilly, Charles. 1985. "War Making and State Making as Organized Crime." In Besteman, Catherine, ed., *Violence: A Reader.* London: Palgrave Macmillan UK, pp. 35–60.

Toft, Monica Duffy, and Yuri M. Zhukov. 2015. "Islamists and Nationalists: Rebel Motivation and Counterinsurgency in Russia's North Caucasus." *American Political Science Review* 109(2):222–238.

Tordoff, William, and Robert V. Molteno. 1974. *Politics in Zambia.* Manchester University Press.

Truex, Rory. 2016. *Making Autocracy Work: Representation and Responsiveness in Modern China.* Cambridge University Press.

Tsai, Lily. 2007a. *Accountability without Democracy: Solidary Groups and Public Goods Provision in Rural China.* Cambridge University Press.

Tsai, Lily. 2007b. "Solidary Groups, Informal Accountability, and Local Public Goods Provision in Rural China." *American Political Science Review* 101(2):355–372.

van de Walle, Nicolas. 2001. *African Economies and the Politics of Permanent Crisis, 1979–1999.* Cambridge University Press.

van de Walle, Nicolas. 2003. "Presidentialism and Clientelism in Africa's Emerging Party Systems." *Journal of Modern African Studies* 41(2):297–321.

van de Walle, Nicolas. 2006. "Tipping Games: When do Opposition Parties Coalesce?" In Schedler, Andreas, ed., *Electoral Authoritarianism: The Dynamics of Unfree Competition.* Boulder, CO: Lynne Rienner Publishers, pp. 77–92.

van de Walle, Nicolas. 2007. "Meet the New Boss, Same as the Old Boss? The Evolution of Political Clientelism in Africa." In Kitschelt, Herbert, and Steven I. Wilkinson, eds., *Patrons, Clients, and Policies: Patterns of Democratic Accountability and Political Competition.* Cambridge University Press, pp. 50–67.

Vanden Eynde, Oliver, Patrick M. Kuhn, and Alexander Moradi. 2018. "Trickle-Down Ethnic Politics: Drunk and Absent in the Kenya Police Force (1957–1970)." *American Economic Journal: Economic Policy* 10(3):388–417.

Wallace, Jeremy. 2014. *Cities and Stability: Urbanization, Redistribution, and Regime Survival in China.* Oxford University Press.

Wallace, Jeremy. 2016. "Juking the Stats? Authoritarian Information Problems in China." *British Journal of Political Science* 46(1):11–29.

Wasserman, Gary. 1973. "The Independence Bargain: Kenya Europeans and the Land Issue 1960–1962." *Journal of Commonwealth and Comparative Politics* 11(2):99–120.

Weber, Max. 1958. *From Max Weber: Essays in Sociology*. Oxford University Press.

Weeks, Jessica L. 2012. "Strongmen and Straw Men: Authoritarian Regimes and the Initiation of International Conflict." *American Political Science Review* 16(2):326–347.

Weis, Toni. 2008. "The Results of the 2007 Kenyan General Election." *Journal of Eastern African Studies* 2(2):1–41.

Weitzer, Ronald. 1990. *Transforming Settler States: Communal Conflict and Internal Security in Northern Ireland and Zimbabwe*. Berkeley: University of California Press.

Widner, Jennifer A. 1992. *The Rise of a Party-State in Kenya: From "Harambee" to "Nyayo!"*. Berkeley: University of California Press.

Wilkinson, Steven. 2015. *Army and Nation: The Military and Indian Democracy Since Independence*. Cambridge, MA: Harvard University Press.

Williams, Martin J. 2019. "Beyond State Capacity: Bureaucratic Performance, Policy Implementation, and Reform." Working paper, Oxford University.

Wilson, James. 1989. *Bureaucracy: What Government Agencies Do and Why They Do It*. New York: Basic Books.

Wilson, Matthew Charles. 2015. "Castling the King: Institutional Sequencing and Regime Change." PhD thesis, Pennsylvania State University.

Wimmer, Andreas, Lars-Erik Cederman, and Bran Min. 2009. "Ethnic Politics and Armed Conflict: A Configurational Analysis of a New Global Data Set." *American Sociological Review* 74: 316–337.

Woldense, Josef. 2018. "The Ruler's Game of Musical Chairs: Shuffling during the Reign of Ethiopia's Last Emperor." *Social Networks* 52:154–166.

Woo, Ae sil, and Courtenay Conrad. 2019. "The Differential Effects of 'Democratic' Institutions on Dissent in Dictatorships." *Journal of Politics* 81(2):456–470.

Wright, Joseph. 2008. "Do Authoritarian Institutions Constrain? How Legislatures Affect Economic Growth and Investment." *American Journal of Political Science* 52(2):322–343.

Wright, Joseph, Erica Frantz, and Barbara Geddes. 2015. "Oil and Autocratic Regime Survival." *British Journal of Political Science* 45:287–306.

Xu, Guo. 2018. "The Costs of Patronage: Evidence from the British Empire." *American Economic Review* 108(11):3170–3198.

Xu, Guo, Marianne Bertrand, and Robin Burgess. 2018. "Social Proximity and Bureaucrat Performance: Evidence from India." NBER Working Paper 25389. Cambridge, MA: National Bureau of Economic Research.

Young, C., and T.E. Turner. 1985. *The Rise and Decline of the Zairian State*. Madison: University of Wisconsin Press.

Zakaria, Fareed. 1997. "The Rise of Illiberal Democracy." *Foreign Affairs* 76(6):22–43.

Zeng, Qingjie. 2015. "The Perils of Centralization: Cadre Rotation, Campaign Mobilization, and Anticorruption in China." Working paper, University of Michigan.

Zhukov, Yuri, and Roya Talibova. 2018. "Stalin's Terror and the Long-Term Political Effects of Mass Repression." *Journal of Peace Research* 55(2): 267–283.

Ziblatt, Daniel. 2009. "Shaping Democratic Practice and the Causes of Electoral Fraud: The Case of Nineteenth-Century Germany." *American Political Science Review* 103(1):1–21.

Zolberg, Aristide. 1966. *Creating Political Order: The Party-States of West Africa.* University of Chicago Press.

Index

John D. Huber and Charles R. Shipan, *Deliberate Discretion? The Institutional Foundations of Bureaucratic Autonomy*

Ellen Immergut, *Health Politics: Interests and Institutions in Western Europe*

Torben Iversen, *Capitalism, Democracy, and Welfare*

Torben Iversen, *Contested Economic Institutions*

Torben Iversen, Jonas Pontussen, and David Soskice, eds., *Unions, Employers, and Central Banks: Macroeconomic Coordination and Institutional Change in Social Market Economics*

Thomas Janoski and Alexander M. Hicks, eds., *The Comparative Political Economy of the Welfare State*

Joseph Jupille, *Procedural Politics: Issues, Influence, and Institutional Choice in the European Union*

Karen Jusko, *Who Speaks for the Poor? Electoral Geography, Party Entry, and Representation*

Stathis Kalyvas, *The Logic of Violence in Civil War*

Stephen B. Kaplan, *Globalization and Austerity Politics in Latin America*

David C. Kang, *Crony Capitalism: Corruption and Capitalism in South Korea and the Philippines*

Junko Kato, *Regressive Taxation and the Welfare State*

Orit Kedar, *Voting for Policy, Not Parties: How Voters Compensate for Power Sharing*

Robert O. Keohane and Helen B. Milner, eds., *Internationalization and Domestic Politics*

Herbert Kitschelt, *The Transformation of European Social Democracy*

Herbert Kitschelt, Kirk A. Hawkins, Juan Pablo Luna, Guillermo Rosas, and Elizabeth J. Zechmeister, *Latin American Party Systems*

Herbert Kitschelt, Peter Lange, Gary Marks, and John D. Stephens, eds., *Continuity and Change in Contemporary Capitalism*

Herbert Kitschelt, Zdenka Mansfeldova, Radek Markowski, and Gabor Toka, *Post-Communist Party Systems*

David Knoke, Franz Urban Pappi, Jeffrey Broadbent, and Yutaka Tsujinaka, eds., *Comparing Policy Networks*

Ken Kollman, *Perils of Centralization: Lessons from Church, State, and Corporation*

Allan Kornberg and Harold D. Clarke, *Citizens and Community: Political Support in a Representative Democracy*

Amie Kreppel, *The European Parliament and the Supranational Party System*

David D. Laitin, *Language Repertoires and State Construction in Africa*

Fabrice E. Lehoucq and Ivan Molina, *Stuffing the Ballot Box: Fraud, Electoral Reform, and Democratization in Costa Rica*

Benjamin Lessing *Making Peace in Drug Wars: Crackdowns and Cartels in Latin America*

Mark Irving Lichbach and Alan S. Zuckerman, eds., *Comparative Politics: Rationality, Culture, and Structure, 2nd edition*

Evan Lieberman, *Race and Regionalism in the Politics of Taxation in Brazil and South Africa*

Richard M. Locke, *The Promise and Limits of Private Power: Promoting Labor Standards in a Global Economy*

Julia Lynch, *Age in the Welfare State: The Origins of Social Spending on Pensioner's Workers and Children*

Printed in Great Britain
by Amazon